MW00641991

Deeper
than
African
Soil

KINGSBURY AWARD WINNER

FAITH EIDSE

Deeper than African Soil
by Faith Eidse

Cover photo of Faith Eidse in the Lutembo River
colorized by cousin Jim Peters. (Hope Wiebe 1969 photo)

Library of Congress Control Number: 2023933290
International Standard Book Number: 978-1-60126-847-1

𝔐𝔞𝔰𝔱𝔥𝔬𝔣 𝔓𝔯𝔢𝔰𝔰
219 Mill Road | Morgantown, PA 19543-9516
www.Masthof.com

TABLE *of* CONTENTS

6°°

2|24

For my "little brother" Paul Zook
and all the global nomads.

———————

*"I'm not going to tell the story
the way it happened.
I'm going to tell it
the way I remember it."* [1]
PAM HOUSTON

———————

[1] Some names have been changed, some events compressed and some dialogue recreated.

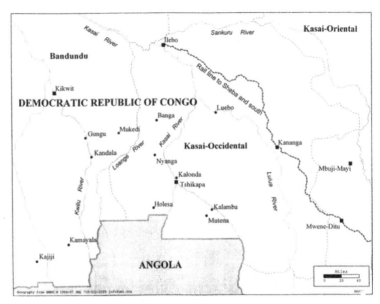

Kamayala in the Southern Democratic Republic of Congo (GMMS © 1994-1997) was my first home. I was raised among worlds—Congo, Canada and the U.S.—with sisters Hope, Charity and Grace by Canadian Mennonites—a theologian-linguist ("father of truth-telling") and tropical medicine nurse ("Congo's Mother Teresa").

"I have a responsibility to all the sources that I am,
to all past and future ancestors, to all the places I've touched down…
to all voices, all women, all of my tribes, all people, all earth,
and beyond that to all beginnings and endings."
JOY HARJO

"Writing is a debt of honor."
ANNE LAMOTT

Dad, me, Hope, Mom and Charity at Kamayala on Dec. 23, 1956, two months after Charity was born—the greatest of us all at 10 lbs.—and before we left for Mom's health. I love how Dad is holding my writing hand as though passing on his story-telling gift. (Peter Falk photo)

"A place belongs forever
to whoever claims it hardest,
remembers it most obsessively,
wrenches it from itself,
shapes it, renders it, loves it..."
JOAN DIDION

Palm Avenue, Kamayala, where we carried water and kicked raffia balls. The church, built by Dad and men of Kamayala, is still the center of the community. (Ron Goertzen photo)

1

BAREFOOT WITH JIGGERS

Congo had a way of drawing you in, coaxing you from letter-writing and spelling lessons. A way of begging you to enter, barefoot, short-sleeved, long hair loose, lifting on currents dense with sour manioc, smoked caterpillars, ripe mangoes. Especially if you were eight and you had a yen for velvet sand under bare feet—nevermind the jiggers—tiny black insects that dug under your toenails.

You couldn't resist the thud of a raffia ball on the dappled dirt avenue, the call of children poking goal sticks into dirt, dividing into teams and positions—goalie, forward, defense—charging one another for the raffia-woven ball.

"*Ni yami!*" (Me too!) I'd bang out the kitchen screen door. *Tata* Michel kneading dough at the counter, flour dusting his bib apron, called "*Sapato!*" (Shoes!) But I just waved and ran out. The road was smooth underfoot, and trash-free. Every scrap of paper had been crunched inside that ball, giving it extra bounce.

It didn't matter that my feet were clean and recently de-jiggered because soon they'd be black and itchy again. I charged Musasa for the ball, kicked it, and then we'd be chasing flying ants instead because the ball had knocked the winged creatures out of their holes in the grass. We'd crunch their acidic tartness and spit out the wings. An antlion pit might open like some ravenous funnel with larvae at the bottom sucking ant bits and we'd be feeding antlions instead.

Marie in her faded dress and cheek-bulging smile came swinging a water pail from the orphanage across the street calling, "*Ufudielo.*" (Faith.) My name in Chokwe. She was big sister Hope's *ndoyi*. (Namesake, best friend.) Round and muscled from fieldwork and water-carrying, she'd laugh and imitate me. I'd kick the ball to her along the palm-lined avenue where only one or two trucks passed each year. It was like a party when anyone showed up from somewhere else—a merchant who'd lost his way or a public health nurse giving polio vaccines. We passed around fresh jam cookies and the visitor would tell us all about the world beyond.

Marie kicked the ball back and I bounced it off my knee, launching it straight up, stretching my arms as it fell, my eyes on the ball until—*moto!*—I hit it with my head, surprising even myself. I jigged my ash hair and shouted, "*Soukous!*" I didn't know where the word came from or its literal translation, didn't know it was the tinny descant music exported from Congo and woven into Cuban jazz, or the other way around. I said *soukous* because it was the word for "fooled you," "shake" or "move!" It stood for feeling good, being cool and trusting the beat.

I heard expressions every day that I didn't know the proper meaning of, many not in the local Chokwe, so I just spewed what I heard in Lunda or Phende, or the trade languages, Lingala and Kituba. My dad, the linguist, said that Congo had 500 languages and dialects and when I asked what an expression meant, orphan Musasa might fool me. He might tell me I said, "get out" when I'd said, "go to hell." How was I to know? So I lived dangerously and laughed at eyebrows raised my way.

Because I was the missionary kid, Faith Eidse, and could maybe get away with it.

"Eidse, like 'beware the Ides of March.'" Dad's eyes twinkled, mischievous and magnified behind thick, dark-rimmed glasses. He brushed back thick dark hair from his high forehead. He had whole worlds of language, stories and parables, and we loved hearing them soft and low in flickering lamplight.

Our prim 1963 prayer card stuck to fridges from Canada to the U.S. while we spread our wings and explored Congo (l to r, Helen, Charity, Hope, me, Ben, Grace).

I didn't notice the jiggers until they laid a nest that grew the size of an orange seed and sting-itched like a match burn. First I'd scratch with the heel of my other foot, then I'd scratch with my fingers practically tearing off the toenail. Evenings I sat around chiffon lantern light with my three sisters, dipped sewing needles in kerosene and we did surgery on our own toes.

Since the whole family was gathered with heads bowed over our feet, Mom and Dad noticed it was a good time to make *schluss*, low German for closing prayer. Our English-only cousins in Canada called it "slush" like something squishy you walked through in spring. Which is how it felt sometimes, since I had to get all soft and mushy and ask my sisters to forgive me for things I did, like sneak out on big sister Hope when we were doing dishes. Or leave little sister Charity behind with baby Grace while we ran to the river. I had to ask forgiveness for things I called them like, "Bossy" or "Temper, temper."

It was important not to fall asleep with unconfessed sin in case I died with black spots like jiggers on my soul. I didn't want the sun to go down on my wrath because I might wake up in heaven and be judged that way. Or, worse, the other place. So I said a blanket prayer, one that covered anything I had forgotten and prepared me to die—that night. "Now I lay me down to sleep, I pray the Lord my soul to keep; if I should die before I wake, I pray the Lord my soul to take. Forgive all my sins and bless my grandmas, aunts, uncles and cousins in Canada. Amen." I crooked my arm around my pink plush pajama doll, Polly, a gift from our parents for traveling.

Hope preferred the high German prayers we'd learned from our grandmas. "*Lieber Heiland mach mich fromm das ich in den Himmel komm.*" (Dear Savior make me good so I can come to heaven.) Her voice was often the last I heard falling asleep. Decades later, those were often the last words her patients heard on the COVID ward at Steinbach Resthaven.

All this made me relieved to wake in the morning and see that the day had a solid feel to it. I might finish a letter to cousins in Canada describing our warm sunny sands, playing soccer with or-

In summer 1963, a hunter came with a bird and snake. I wanted to touch its fangs, wrap it around my neck. But the hunter said no. Our tribe didn't eat snakes so he put it under a bush and left with his bird. When we checked later, the snake had slithered away (Ben Eidse photo)

phans and eating flying ants. That was all compared to their blizzards, sledding and skating on frozen ponds.

On Sunday morning the church bell rang a warning at quarter to ten, which meant it was time to put on my head scarf and find my Bible. We also brought our hymnbooks because the books were counted along with the people every Sunday morning. It wasn't just that the missionaries couldn't provide books for everyone—ours was a poor mission that couldn't afford to give them away—but also that not everyone could read. So we brought our hymnbooks and raised them high. First the counter counted the men, women, and children. Then he (was it always a "he"?) counted the Bibles and hymnbooks.

Dad had translated his favorite hymns from English or German so that we from *putu* (far-off land) could carry the tune and read the Chokwe words. But the most sweetly sorrowful hymn of all, I didn't remember hearing in Canada where everyone wore shoes. It reminded me of the many *mangenene* (cracked heels), I'd seen oozing garnet blood. "Amid the trials that I meet, amid the thorns that pierce my feet, one thought remains supremely sweet, thou thinkest Lord of me. *Kuwakungnyonga, chichi kwivwa woma nawa, kuwakungunyonga.*"

In church, the village mothers broke fresh splinters off the wooden pews and poked at their children's feet and nails while the service rolled on. Jiggers liked burrowing into the soft inner flesh of cracked heels and even under fingernails if we dug in the dirt.

Just like in Mennonite churches back in Manitoba, men and women sat separately. The song leader and pump organ stood in front of the men and boys. This allowed the women to feel invisible, so they could groom their children, something they didn't have time for otherwise. Dressed in their colorful wax print wraparounds and head scarves, they cradled curly heads on their laps and searched for bugs or stroked sand from their childrens' tucked up legs and feet.

The singing at church got especially lively if the women's choir, or the high school students, got up to swing and sway, weave elaborate harmonies and tap layered rhythms with spoons on Fanta bottles. No drums in those days. Drums had been banned because of dancing since 1930 when the first missionaries walked into Kamayala. They were sisters, Mary and Bertha Miller, one who still lived here. Short, round "Aunt" Bertha—not our real aunt—but someone who loved telling us stories and teaching us choruses.

"Ghosts," the Chokwe had called them, and took them to see the chief. They called Bertha Mama *Tambula* (walk) for walking 300 miles inland to live with them. On their way, the sisters had paid for a *kepoy* (carried hammock) through a "cannibal village," she told us, where "headhunters" spiked skulls on posts and people chanted, "one is fat and one is thin." Poor Aunt Bertha was the fat one.

She was still walking but with a limp from arthritic hips. She had cared for dozens of orphans who had become her family. Her older, taller sister, a nurse, had run the clinic and leprosarium. I didn't remember her from our first term when I was just a toddler.

"Before your Dad came to build churches, schools, clinics and houses," Aunt Bertha liked to say, "we met under mango trees for worship and classes."

Mary had died and was buried eight miles away by road—five by shortcut trails—at the state post in Kahemba, the first white woman "laid to rest" here. In 1946, another young nurse Theresa Chaponniere (mother of my future schoolmates), joined the medical work and noticed that Kamayala was getting no government aid, though the Belgian hospital at Kahemba was. She went to the capital and petitioned that all medical work serving lepers receive the same subsidies.

In the chief's hut on that long-ago day, the sisters found three mounds of dirt.

"What are these mounds?" The Miller sisters spoke Kituba, a trade language.

The chief may have worn his gleaming neck medal for the meeting. "They stand for father, son and messenger."

The sisters marveled. "Where did you learn that?"

"From our ancestors. They said someone would come with a message from God."

The women must have sat up that night, lost in the quivering flame of a village fire, wondering at how much these people already knew about God.

The spoon-on-bottle rhythms were handed down without drums. You could beat on anything if necessary—tin cans, glass bottles, pot lids, church benches. *Dum-ba-da-dum-ba-da-dum*. The starting beat was bass, the next was tenor, then came the bells and rattles. And after that the moving and shaking. *Soukous*!

One Sunday, *Tata* Michel with his full lips, distinguished goatee and button-down shirt, was the counter. With his practiced confident tone he tallied tens on one hand and ones on the other, like an abacus. After he'd counted all the men, women, children, Bibles and hymnbooks, he called up three leggy boys from the village. They swaggered up the center aisle to the platform.

"Should these boys be praised?" *Tata* Michel asked.

I recognized them as boys my age who hung around our house after school. They learned from us like we did from them by watching, teasing, imitating.

"Yes," called some people in the audience.

"No," said others.

"Have these boys worked hard? Have they found good things to do?"

"Yes," chorused some, especially the younger ones, the boys' friends.

Tata Michel raised his voice and rocked up on his toes. "These boys have taught the missionary parrot to take God's name in vain. They must stay away from the mission house."

It was true, our parrot, Kusu, had the gall to fluff his gray and white feathers, blink his white-rimmed eyes, open his curved beak and croak, "*Nzambi!*" (God!) At the worst possible moments.

Like when the Belgian priest from Kahemba came putt-putting on his motorcycle, his white robes flapping, to play chess with Dad and show the people that Protestants and Catholics got along after Vatican II.

"*Tufi na nge!*" (Shit on you!) Kusu squawked.

And the priest turned red as his beard.

The boys looked down at their bare feet. *Tata* Michel gripped the nearest by the arm and turned him over his knee. His big hand came down on the boy's ragged shorts, one, two, three times.

Hope shared a hang-dog look with me. We had enjoyed kidding with them and now they'd been ordered away.

The boys shuffled back to their seats, tears streaking their dusty cheeks.

I swallowed hard and looked at Mom beside me, who sat with a straight face. Dad's expression behind thick glasses was impossible to read, especially from across the aisle. Aunt Bertha sat in the front row clutching her Bible and hymnbook, a silent witness to it all.

The public spanking seemed heavy-handed, as though the boys had to walk an endless hallway lined with accusing eyes.

I'd had my own spankings and, at age four, my mouth washed out with bar soap for saying "shit." I knew how it felt. Low down, awful, endless, the sting going on long after the spanking. The soap was cloying and bitter all the way through dinner while I lowered my eyes and swung my feet defiantly under the table. Spankings didn't always work to keep you soft and pliant. Sometimes they made you blurt insults like "NincomPOOP!" Even though you knew you could burn in hell for it.

Was it possible that you would somehow be punished for every daring thing you did or said? And if you weren't, would you find it necessary to punish yourself? Ration your food, prick yourself with needles, force yourself to swim against river current ten times fast?

After church, I asked Dad if the spanking was too mean. He said it was okay. *Tata* Michel was doing what he thought was necessary. Sometimes I felt my family and the mission were too strict.

Soon a girl my age, Jeannette Buller—Jette—a missionary kid from Mukedi, would come to live with us in a home school exchange. She would take grade three by correspondence with me before Christmas, and I'd take grade three with her family after. Perhaps she could loosen us up. Jette's family might laugh at a missionary parrot squawking *Nzambi* at the worst moments. Maybe living with her in the new year, 1964, would be more fun. I'd maybe wear shorts like Jette—even though she was Mennonite.

But already *Jeunesse* (youth revolutionaries), were roaming Congo, gathering in the forests, angry that the struggle after independence had taken so much—their first elected president Patrice Lumumba, their hopes for jobs and wealth. Lumumba's Minister of Education, Mulele Pierre, had returned from China to the Phende area near Jette's mission, Mukedi. It was 300 kilometers (180 miles) northwest of us and just 15 kilometers (9 miles) from Mulele's village.

His revolution anthem was sung by Phende students around Kamayala and became even more popular after thirty *Jeunesse* were caught near the Kwilu River in September 1963 with guerilla warfare manuals. The army responded in colonial style, setting fire to thatched roofs, stealing goats and chickens. There was no question anymore who was more popular in our region. The president offered half a million Congo francs for Mulele, but no one betrayed him.

Most Congolese got primary educations under the Belgians but that was all. The mission's secondary schools were filled to capacity. The people wanted more education, more of their own wealth, their money from palm oil production.

That dry season, the *Jeunesse* attacked government schools, administration buildings and bridges, all in Kwilu province. The secondary students at Kamayala said the revolution was especially strong at Mukedi because Mulele lived so nearby.

I begged my parents to let me go anyway. Everything would be all right wouldn't it? Like a raffia ball caught in a gust, I had an untethered, wild faith.

2

WHITE SHADOWS

Our neighbor on the mission, Aunt Bertha, invited us for dinner soon after we arrived. We walked a block down Palm Avenue past a lush garden and the girls' fence (school dorm). The stately palms and garden, Mom and Dad said, were planted by students of Victor Buck, brother-in-law of Nobel author Pearl S. Buck. Mrs. Buck had said that the purpose of a novelist was not to make art but to speak to the people. Mr. Buck had come to the Belgian Congo in 1919 to do just that, a preacher who also taught agriculture. After

Rev. Victor Buck, Bertha Miller and Erma Birky in 1950s Kamayala. (Family photo)

11

China Inland Mission (CIM) missionaries were killed or fled the 1900 Boxer revolution, and Congo Inland Mission was formed, Mr. Buck and his workers planted everything. Mangoes, avocadoes, bananas, oranges, pineapple, coffee, mulberry, even apples and strawberries, which sometimes fruited on this high plateau. Hope remembered pedaling her trike to visit him and his wife when she was just three.

As a family, we entered Aunt Bertha's tin-roofed, cement block and quarried stone house. Dad lingered a moment admiring the decorative river stones. It was one of the permanent houses he had built with the Kamayala men during his first term. Aunt Bertha had added comfy sofa cushions, matching pillows, rugs and doilies.

This was opposite our house with its stark furnishings and cleared counters where Dad put away pens, papers and his transistor radio obsessively instead of displaying what we had and others didn't. With revolution in the air, he was concerned that we not show off our privilege like some white people did. Instead we invited people in for meetings and meals, let our friends play with our dolls and gave them clothing and books. In this way we learned not to throw out used envelopes. Teachers or pastors taking notes swooped on discarded envelopes and opened them into full sheets of unused paper.

We were ushered around Aunt Bertha's dark wood table laid with lace tablecloth, huge porcelain plates and bowls, several spoons, forks and a knife each—even the kids. She called her cook with a Swiss cowbell that was painted in dainty edelweiss. The kitchen door swung open and *Tata* Mataya entered in a white bib apron. A slender, sinewy man, he walked softly with a large soup tureen in knotted hands. I had never seen such servant-like behavior. It was as though we were royalty, princesses in a castle.

Tata Mataya went first to Aunt Bertha and silently served her bowl. Then he moved around the table, dipping and pouring, careful not to spill a drop. I barely breathed as he served me salty beef broth with bits of onion and potato. I felt both queenly and mortified. He was our friend's father who knew Chokwe, local stories and customs—and yet he was serving me.

After filling our bowls, he stood behind Aunt Bertha, hands folded in front of him, transparent as the sheers at the window. I tried to catch his eye, to let him know I saw, but he stepped forward and filled my water glass instead. The rest of the meal I barely ate or drank.

————————————

Our cook, *Tata* Michel, did not serve our dinner. He whistled intricate melodies while he baked bread and controlled a cash box for buying produce or meat at our door. He was our advisor learning a valuable trade as chef, Mom said. He filled the pantry with banana bunches or bartered for chickens, chopped off their heads on a wooden stump and waited while they ran headless around the yard, spewing blood.

Around the house, *Tata* Michel issued orders and we obeyed. With Michel running the house, and we girls washing floors and dishes, Mom could go to work as a nurse again, something she had not done with four girls under ten in the U.S. and Canada. She dressed in white, auburn head high, and assigned us schoolwork or chores before she left for the clinic, tuberculosis ward or leprosarium. To help Mom learn frontier medicine, like performing emergency c-sections on a tabletop, Aunt Bertha connected Mom with Mother Superior *Soeur Marie-José* and the other nursing nuns at the Kahemba Hospital. We loved their twinkly eyes, Belgian cookies and special attention as though we were a secret girls' club.

While Mom diagnosed patients, handed out drugs and prayed over curly heads, Dad traveled to surrounding villages with local pastors, recorded interviews and learned more about their language, customs and proverbs. People feared sickness from curses and wore

Bertha Miller (back, third from left) hosted the nursing sisters from Kahemba Hospital, us Eidses and Vangie Claassen (seated) in a kind of single girls' club. (Ben Eidse photo)

carved charms stuffed with leaves for protection. Mom and Dad, pastors, teachers and nurses taught lessons about germs, washing often, praying for protection and not harming others.

If I finished my lessons early, *Tata* Michel invited me into the kitchen, "*Tweya kosa yenga, Ufudielo.*" (Come wash dishes, Faith.) I felt central and significant washing dishes in his kitchen. It was a dark narrow room, painted enamel green, but its windows opened onto the road where men and women passed and stopped to tell stories. Hunters gathered, handmade guns on their shoulder to tell about the buck that got away. *Tata* Michel interrupted for details. Describe its horns, hoof mark, tail.

Women paused, hoes in hand, firewood on their heads, to tease and flirt with Michel. His ebony face softened and creased when he smiled, but he was not easily persuaded. Your story had to be convincing. If not, he'd challenge you. "Uh, uh, uh," he'd say to certain boasting hunters or sweet-talking women. "Nooo, not so. I'm not like the other fools."

The dip and flow, rising action, climax and resolution taught me stories by their sound, sense and rhythm. And by the details *Tata* Michel wheedled. One story always called up another and, in this way, I learned the craft, its proofs and reproofs, like sacrament or ritual. A good story made a good day, even when the antelope got away.

Every day at the door hungry children gathered and sometimes I could not resist feeding them. Once I raided the pantry for a hoarded box of tea biscuits. We picnicked on the front porch in full view of the village and children streamed to our door. I broke the remaining cookies in halves and then quarters, but the supply ran out. One bird-thin girl cried when she got nothing, and I could not face her tears.

How closely we lived to one another. My actions could make other children suffer. All around me I could see that while I rode, my friends walked. While I ate, their stomachs rumbled. While I slept in a soft bed, they slept on a grass mat, dirt floor around a smoky kitchen fire.

If we played with Dad's wood-carved, raffia-haired Chokwe *mukishi* (masks), the children stampeded from our door. Dad taught us not to disrespect them. *Mukishi* were spirits of the departed who came back during dry season to chase children and women from circumcision camps. We had to let the children see us spit in the masks before putting them on or they'd fear the departed spirits had entered us.

To narrow distances with our friends, my sisters and I hunted flying ants, grasshoppers and tender fiddlehead ferns that sprang from the old burn after grass fire season.

We joined our friends clapping under shady palms, hands like fern fronds twisting. We repeated rhymes so old, even the village girls no longer knew their origin, knew only this—*ndoyi* (namesake-girlfriend-sister)—a promise to ease the work of womanhood until we died.

We joined them in pounding soaked and dried manioc chunks. We dropped and heaved pestles thick as our thighs into oaken mortars. We hit a rhythm and grunted in counterpoint—*unh-huh-unh*—until all that leaped back was flour fine as talcum. Firewood cut from the forest was laid on live embers and blown into flame, pans of river water were coaxed to a rolling boil, taken from the fire logs and flour mixed in with large wooden spoons for *chindu* (manioc mush) thick as rubber balls. We sat around supper fires and pulled off pieces, dipped them into peppery greens or caterpillar gravy, until we wiped the dishes clean.

Under the radiant silver of a platter moon, Marie started up the airplane propeller game, *"Avion, ndeke, avion."* It was a spinning circle romp so lively that even the village children left their home fires and crossed the school grounds to join us. Marie positioned us—big, small, big, small—small kids sitting, hands reaching to be lifted up by big kids, small legs straight out like propeller blades, heels anchored in the center. We big kids lifted and walked, then sped up, turning the propeller circle by hanging onto their little hands—sister, *Vumbi* (Grace) on one side of me, and her *ndoyi*, Pauline, on the other. We lifted and turned until the blade spun, heels anchored, hands pulling. Sometimes the circle got going so fast that the spinning human blades could believe in flight, which was why the big kids begged for their turns, too. Even Hope, Charity and I tried it, skirts tucked between our legs, pulling ourselves up, spiraling higher with each round until the circle collapsed and we landed in a heap. We shivered in the cool dirt and crept closer to the fluid supper fire.

Children gathered sticks, blew cooking embers to flame and begged Marie for *yishima* (stories). There is a rule against story-telling during the day, not just because there's so much work to do, but because the only time stories are told during the day is at a death. Then, to keep watchful against evil spirits, stories are spun around the clock.

There's something comforting about a fire like a lullaby at the end of a day. You give yourself to its leap and tremor, empty your spent thoughts, your aching muscles to its fluid rhythm. Marie waved the smoke from her face. What images rose before she settled on a story to tell? Her mother lying still, not responding to her cry? Her mother's brother driving her with a switch to Mama Tambula's orphanage so that she arrived welted and bleeding? Her uncle returning five years later, after she started school, saying, "She's old enough to work my fields"?

Mama Tambula refused to let Marie go. It was the same with a seven-year-old slave girl, Kamena, brought to her orphanage in the 1950s. When slavers returned for her—after she'd married Pastor Wayindama and had several children—the missionaries obtained her freedom. Her next daughters she named after Charity and me— *Zango* and *Ufudielo—ndoyi*.

Marie pulled square-headed Ilunga close and Charity wrapped one arm around Grace and another around Pauline. Hope and I each found a toddler to hold. Some had six toes, others had parents quarantined in the leprosarium a mile away. Ilunga was so weak during his first months at the orphanage that he could not lift his head or roll over. This molded his head flat on three sides. Marie became his arms and legs, holding him against her body to feed him, carrying him on her back to the fields, until his head rounded out and he started to crawl and walk by age three.

Marie knew stories about our mother Naweji, a glittering snake who made all things and gave birth to the first man and woman. She carried her children on her back. Or our father Njaji, thunder, who marches across his big house in the sky. His night fire—the moon— big and bright like tonight, watched over his children, the stars.

"Tell, tell," we begged.

Marie squinted into the flame. "Hungry hunters in the forest came upon a house made of human bones with a honey pot inside."

"Don't eat!" listeners cried. "It's a trap!"

"The hunters met *Chingandangali*, a monster big as palm trees with pointy teeth." Branches rattled overhead.

I shivered, clutched my sleepy toddler tighter and moved closer to the fire.

"A young woman has a child but no one to watch him when she goes to her fields. She's far from her family since marrying and going to her husband's village. So she wraps her child in a cloth around her back and goes to her field near the river. She nurses and lays him under a tree. When the child cries, the mother goes but finds the baby in the arms of an antelope.

"The antelope says, '*Hola*, be quiet. I'm a child guardian. I won't hurt you. The trouble will come in the future.'"

Marie glanced around the fire circle. "Is the antelope a sorcerer's antelope or God's antelope? Should the woman trust it or not? Maybe the antelope is really the woman's mother who comes from the spirit world to help?

"The woman tells her husband and he polishes his gun. The next day, again, the child cries and the mother turns to see the child in the arms of the antelope. 'I won't hurt you. The trouble will come in the future.'

"The hunter raises his gun. 'The antelope is threatening us.'"

"He'll shoot!" the listeners cry.

"The hunter shoots and the antelope and child vanish. The hunter, his wife and the villagers wail and mourn."

"Bring back her child," the listeners say.

"The mother goes to the river to cry and hears her mother singing in the bush. 'There where the man shoots at me, take your bullets out of the tree.' The woman runs to the tree and finds her baby still sick from the shooting and needing healing. We've heard the warnings. Fear the future and the unknown, beware the death of babies, clear yourself of wrongdoing, respect departed spirits" (Fretz, p. 168).

Around the dying fire, a child scoops up dried grass and throws it on the coals where it writhes and bursts into momentary flame. We cradle our toddlers and carry them to bed, snuggling them tight in their blankets.

3

RIVER RUN

Wherever you have friends that's your county
and wherever you receive love that's your home.

— TIBETAN PROVERB

M arie came swinging her water pail and I ran in to get *Yaya*
(big sister). Hope was my boss, conscience, guide and best
buddy. I climbed into my high-neck tank suit, pulled on my dress
and fetched my shiny, hard-shelled water gourd from the kitchen.
I would never again go empty-handed—not since we were scolded by the orphan mamas Luisa and Luta on our first day back in
Congo.

Like pebbles out of slingshots, we had pelted headlong into
the jungle valley where clear springs bubbled through fine sand—the
best water in the universe. So how could we stoop and drink just for
ourselves? No, we would take containers, fill them and carry them
home for everyone.

I banged out the screen door with my gourd and head pad,
Hope right behind me with a five-gallon pail, Charity behind her
with an empty NIDO milk tin and curly-haired Grace trailing us
with her sock octopus Oscar.

Mom had just returned from the clinic and was surrounded by people—all kinds, all sizes. She sank to the porch windowsill, leaned over heat-swollen feet and reached for Grace, smiling. The lesson she taught—and lived daily—was, "JOY: Jesus first, Others second, Yourself last." Girls probably wouldn't have much joy without it. Even in Africa, girls did all the carrying, pounding, mixing, serving. The only way to feel happy about that was to think of others as more important than yourself. The sooner you could do that, the happier you would be.

It was *ola yakuwhima* (rest hour). Time for Grace and Mom to nap. Dad said that *ola,* Portuguese for "hour," was a foreign concept of time division imported to Chokwe culture by 1480s slave traders or merchants criss-crossing Africa. Kamayala was on an ancient trade route and even Livingstone had plunged through here with his Lozi and Kololo explorers on his way to Tanzania. Their stories of brutal slave treks helped end slavery. We hadn't yet heard that Livingstone had opened the continent to explorers, railroads and theft by colo-

Praise singers Antoine and Pierre with their guide Ngituka. (Ben Eidse photo)

nists. We were only just learning to look at ourselves and ask what harm we were doing.

Among those gathered on our porch were the famous praise-singing twins, Antoine and Pierre, from the state post. Disabled from birth, the slight men had been carried piggy-back from Kahemba, escorted by their guide, Ngituka. They crawled on twisted legs or slid on their backsides. Their eyes were milked over, their sight gone. Yet they were sensory geniuses—great at guessing who approached them—a game everyone loved to play with them.

They swayed their heads and sang Chokwe praises to Mama *"Ayize."* The Chokwe said our name with an emphasis that sounded like "they are the ones." These are the people prophesied to come live here, learn our language and discover with us a message from God.

The singers accompanied their praise songs on traditional instruments—Antoine by tapping and sliding a wooden peg along his walking stick, Pierre by plucking bamboo strings of a harp gourd—*plink-a-plink.* "She's rain on our peanut fields, chicken in our cooking pots. She sits with the sick and outcast, she gives with both hands." They ended with a rapid vibration of the last note, *plinkplinkplink pliiink.*

Charity eased through the crowd and sat beside Mom on the porch sill. I felt outdone and slid around the other side, slipping my hand inside Mom's big freckled one. Engulfed. I was probably like any other kid who had a nurse for a mother. I wished I'd get seriously ill—tuberculosis or leprosy—so I could earn her full attention.

"Listen," Mom said, "after their song they will ask for three things. The first two I can refuse. The last one I have to give them."

"Mama," said one twin in Chokwe, "we need chickens."

"Do you see chickens?" Mom grinned, gesturing at the open lawn.

"Mama," said the other, "we need sweets."

"Sorry, we have no sweets."

"Mama." The first rose up on folded knees. "New shorts please." His shredded shorts, showed dusty buttocks. His twin rose to show a matching pair. Laughter rained down on the praise-singers and they settled back on their haunches, grinning up at us.

Mom and Grace went to rummage among the used-clothing bundles packed in church basements from Lancaster to Vancouver, which was why we knew Nebraska was No. 1 and Toronto had the Maple Leafs. Just read the billboard tee-shirts running around Africa. Our friends said Kamayala was "the best dressed" in our region.

"We're going to the river now!" Hope skipped down the road with us close behind.

"*Yako kabema!*" (Go well!) Mom's words buoyed us as we skipped down the road.

The path to the river was wide and gullied from erosion, and our shadows bounced from one side to the other, sometimes clearing gulches as big as ourselves. We slipped on the bare, steep path and grabbed at wire grass to keep from sliding into the rifts. Rainy season had turned dry savanna into lush hillside and washed rugged new stream beds into old paths. This one was the historic road to fresh limestone springs, original baptism pools, the purest drinking water in the universe.

Tea-cup sized orchids sprang from the rain-wet earth that had been scorched by controlled burns—new life arching out of ash. They were deep purple, fading to mauve at their fluted edges, a yellow swish along one petal, like a teaspoon left in the cup. Mom had said orchids were rare, specially imported to Canada, worth at least $2 each. We were surrounded by wealth.

"*'Fudielo* is going to Mukedi after Christmas," *Yaya* told Marie in Chokwe.

"Truly?"

"*Ewa!*" Yes! I said. *Ufudielo*, or *'Fudielo*, meant "believe" and I liked it, because around Kamayala I was not the only girl with that name. Here were other "*'Fudielos,*" and each could call me *ndoyi*.

We'd share a special handshake and I'd go inside and find a small gift—a dress I'd outgrown or a crisp new Sunday School paper with colored pictures.

"I'm going to Mukedi if the *Jeunesse* don't come first." I tripped and caught myself on sharp wiregrass. Dad kept reminding me of the "unrest." Some Baphende students had tried to burn our car by dipping dried grass in the gas tank, which was almost empty, and lighting it on fire under the rear engine. But it only burned for a few minutes, drying the rubber beneath. Later, while driving near Mukoso, the dried rubber sparked and smoked. We all got out and threw sand on it.

Still my stomach leaped a little at the thought of leaving home, being on my own in a new family, one without the controls of my own. Jette's family was from the States, which seemed like the center of the universe. Even our national holidays seemed to declare that she was freer than I. She celebrated Independence, we celebrated Dominion Day. The U.S. had gone to war, Canada had just negotiated an agreement.

"But what if Mulele comes?" There was a tightness in Hope's voice that sounded like a mix of excitement and fear.

Marie smiled her big, cheek-bulging smile, and sang, "*O Mulele, oooh-oh, O Mulele O.*" It was the revolution chorus, a catchy tune with verses about freedom, wealth and change.

"What will we do?" *Zango* (Charity) meant love, want or need.

"We'll flee to the jungle." Marie was always upbeat, a can-do person.

"What will we eat?" I feared it would not be my favorite fried potatoes and fresh tomatoes.

"Queen termites, ferns, sand at the bottom of the river—."

"Yum!" Hope cut in. "I love fat, juicy termites running down my chin."

"We can bring canned food." I couldn't help myself.

"You are such a picky eater." Charity knew me too well.

"Am not." I hated when Charity called me picky eater. She would have something to apologize for tonight. But I knew she was right. My biggest fault in fitting in here was the way I skimped on *chindu* and *matamba* (manioc mush and greens). You were supposed to take big helpings and belch your praise to the cook.

"Anyway, you're going to Mukedi." Was there a hint of jealousy in Charity's voice? Jette was right between us in age, playful enough for Charity, bookish enough for me.

"If the *Jeunesse* come first, I'll flee to the jungle with you." I tried to take away the sting, wanting to be at the center of action but not wanting to be resented for being there.

The valley floor opened before us and we hurtled down the last steep grade in a reckless, breezy descent. The air filled with the sweet green scent of rainy season, the woodsy smell of the river jungle. The path opened onto a fringed moss carpet and trampled grass that stretched to a treed, vine-bowered river.

Our swimming spot and water-drumming log on the spring-fed Kamayala River. (Grace Eidse photo)

"*Pwo!*" Girls!, we called announcing our gender.

"*Lunga!*" Boys!, came a tenor reply from the preferred up-stream swim hole. That meant the girls would have to swim down-stream again, dodging soap suds and urine-warmed water. The boy who spoke was wrapped in a strip of cloth, laying out his washed school uniform—white shirt, blue shorts. His skin shone like dark chocolate in the noonday sun. When he glanced up, caught in my sights, he tensed for a moment, and adjusted his cloth. It was Rafael, our pastor's son.

"*Moyo.*" (Hello.) I felt my intrusion. His wide, alert eyes re-minded me of a gazelle startled in high grass.

Rafael relaxed and called an insult to Marie. "*'Fudielo* is fast. She makes you look like a turtle.*"

"*Zungo!*" (Noise!) Marie tsked.

I skipped along the downstream path, past scattered water buckets and laundry baskets, unbuttoning my dress as I went. By the time I reached the smooth diving log, I had peeled and tossed it. I dodged several village women rubbing clothes with bar soap and beating them on river rocks, Mama Beya likely among them. A cheerful, round-faced friend of Mom's, she was known for her bril-liant hunting, gathering and gardening skills.

"*Moyowenu.*" (Hi to you all.) I clapped out the syllables, a po-liteness if you couldn't shake everyones' hands.

I grabbed a hanging vine and launched myself over the chilly, spring-fed river. At the top of my swing I dropped, entering with a muffled crash and explosion of soft bubbles. The water was cool, lush, engulfing. I glided along the sandy bottom, yellow through tannin-stained water and piled in waves, striped by overhanging branches. The hollow-crashing rhythms of distant water drums reached me. I surfaced to watch the Kamayala women answer the call.

They wrung their laundry and lined up thigh-high along a submerged log to drum a response to village women several kilome-ters away. They beat the river like a drum with cupped hand booms and flat forearms cymbals, their dark-tipped breasts flying in rhythmic arcs. Point and counterpoint—bass, soprano and tenor—they churned the river into a frothing boil. The drums down river sped up and the drummers crescendoed together. The women listened and crescendoed again. Finally, grinning, their arms shimmering with exertion, they helped each other out of the water and grunted loads of wet laundry and water buckets onto each other's heads. They straightened beneath the neck-crushing weight, bearing it with their whole backs, thighs and legs, swaying uphill, talking and laughing with lilting voices.

We lingered in the river and Hope swam to the drumming log, balanced on it and cupped her hands, forearms flat to the water. "Make the water yeasty." She beat her cupped hands, swirled her arms, concentrating on the rhythm. "Make the water white." She slapped her hands and arms against the surface, speeding up, stirring up a boil. "Make the-water-yeasty-water-white."

Her motions were more rhythmic and contained than those of the village women, her body encased in a tank suit, and I could see how white people were this continent's living cartoons. I caught Marie's grin and circled an index finger around my ear. Marie circled a finger back, learning our culture the same way we learned hers. Then she dove in, raising her bare rump high as she aimed her head straight down. Charity shot a secret smile at me and dove after Marie, imitating her rump shot. Marie came up with a mouthful of bottom river sand, opening it for me to see.

"*Kudia?*" (Food?) I thought she was going to eat it.

Marie spat it out and answered in Chokwe. "Only if your belly's empty."

"Whew!" Hope called from the drumming log. "That's a workout. You need strong muscles for that."

"Let's see." I waded to the log. My arms were freckled sticks, my body boyish, but I tried her rhythm and rhyme a few times hard, until my arms ached. Muscles helped when you had to carry a two-gallon gourd uphill, and I wanted to be strong. It was a yearning that would propel me into basketball and soccer at school, running out the open prairie in Congo, Canada, and as the first woman on the men's cross-country team at Eastern Mennonite University in Virginia.

In a river alcove, we dipped pure water from natural springs, bubbling miniature geysers from limestone cavities through white sand. It was water so clear and sweet that government officials from the capital city 500 miles away would one day fly to this village in southwestern Congo—just to bottle it. Those who dipped from this spring entered with clean feet. They didn't scatter laundry suds or soap bubbles here.

While Hope and Marie found fern fronds to lay on top of their full water pails, Charity and I re-twisted our head pads. We shook out our square cloths and wound them first into a twisted rope, then into a tight platter. If we forgot our cloths, we could wind wire-grass the same way.

Then Hope helped Marie, and I helped Hope lift their five-gallon pails to their heads. Since my gourd was only two gallons and Charity's tin only one, we could lift ours by ourselves. I knew the size of my container would win me no prize, but that was part of our sister pact. We could let Hope do the heavy lifting so people noticed. "Those sisters work hard." We could follow in her shadow and not worry about our smaller efforts.

We caught up with Hope and Marie, swaying with the slosh in their gourds, following the water a mile uphill. Halfway up, I realized the gourd and I were setting a new record. We were one, united. We had not jolted or slipped, and I had not touched it since setting it on my pad, not even to steady it.

"*Tala kuno!*" (Look here!) Charity turned, hand on her tin. "No hands yet."

Hope said goodbye to Marie at the orphanage and we turned toward the kitchen porch.

"Hey *Yaya!*" We reached the water barrel in the kitchen porch together. "I got all the way home without touching my gourd once." I reached up to lift it down but the gourd leaped from my hands, crashed to the cement and broke into wooden shards.

Hope gasped, her long hair dried in whisps around her face.

Tata Michel appeared at the door in white apron and neat goatee and uttered his familiar reprimand. "Uh-uh-uh."

I studied his frown. Clearly I didn't know the gourd's worth or how I'd insulted the hands that grew and weathered it.

There was a strange emptiness where the gourd had sat. It had been an extension of me, a part of my free, swaying, growing body. The shards lay there sharp and resolute, the pure water bleeding away.

"It took years to grow that gourd." Hope fetched a rag and wiped up the spill, washing away our tracked-in dirt.

I knew the rest. How the gourd's wholeness was preserved—all the seeds and pulp lifted out bit-by-bit through the neck—before it was dried and wetted gradually in the sun and rain, so it wouldn't crack. And to preserve it as one unified whole.

But did I break my gourd before the revolution? Memory has a way of telescoping time, repositioning events like cautionary symbols. Memory is faulty, story is true.

4

STRANGE MAGIC

We missed our close connections with the orphans when we moved from across the street to the house at the end of the station. But we had to make room for Jette and her pet monkey. There, near the high grass, strange animals crept into our yard. One morning it was a giant, forest hinge-back tortoise, asleep under its round, saw-toothed shell. I wanted to feed it, coax it from its shell, even ride it.

But Dad had other ideas. "Leave it alone, let it sleep. It's probably older than your grandmas."

"Wow, like 100?"

Strange woodland creatures crept into our yard at the end of the station. (Ben Eidse photo)

"Could be." He laughed. "But your grandmas are only 60."

It crawled away on its own when no one was looking.

Another morning, I went to the porch to brush my teeth and found a glistening brown log on our front lawn. No, not a log—a twelve-foot python with a big lump in the middle. I hurried in to call my sisters.

Dad took one look and headed next door to call our school director, Mbuyuyu Pierre. The director arrived with a sharpened machete. "I'm missing a hen. I counted. That snake has eaten my chicken!" He marched right up to the python and chopped it in two right at the lump, then pulled out a bedraggled chicken and carried it home—to put in his own pot.

I looked at Dad, startled. "Is he going to eat that slimy thing?"

Dad shrugged and grinned. "I guess so."

Another day someone brought us a wobbly spotted gazelle, a grassland baby. We filled a spouted honey bottle with milk and it suckled until it could walk and leap around again.

Someone else brought two jackals wrapped in white cloth from Shamwana or nearby Shakenge in Feshi territory, their mother shot by hunters. Their pointy faces, long pointed ears, dainty legs and bushy tails were more like foxes than dogs. But we bought them to be our pets and called them Nakenge and Shakenge. Out back, behind the kitchen, we built them a two-by-three-meter chicken wire cage. We let them out daily to hunt as a pair in the grassland.

Our African grey parrot, Kusu, was moved to a cage outside our bedroom window. There, he mimicked our voices all day long and, like an intercom, passed messages from *Tata* Michel in the kitchen. It worked out beautifully, never interrupting our parents' midday naps.

Dad built us a cement swimming pool and we added a turtle to our zoo. Dozens of frogs and tadpoles moved in all by themselves—to swim with us!

One animal we did not have was a horse. But Dad loved to

play "horsey" with us, down on all fours, carrying us on his back. He'd neigh and buck like the horses on his boyhood farm in Manitoba.

Sometimes a girl from Manitoba, Leola Falk, came to play with us. Her parents taught in Kajiji, 90 kilometers away. Once she came for a sleepover in our VW van. We told her our family jokes, like how we girls were named. Mom, who came from a family of nine chatty girls and two quiet guys, told Dad she rather wanted boys. When the first girl was born, they "hoped" the next would be a boy. When the second daughter was born, they had "faith" the next would be a boy; when the third arrived, they knew they would love her anyway—so, Charity! Also, Mom got so sick afterwards, she was told to leave Congo and not come back and not have anymore babies. It was by "grace" that she had Grace and soon after we returned to Congo

Leola, who only had a brother Marvin, enjoyed being around so many girls. But she looked at us with her large brown eyes as though she felt sorry for us—for such a story. Eventually, we stopped telling it.

That night, we woke up and stepped outside, right into a line of pinching driver ants. We jumped and stamped and swatted them off, more careful from then on where we stepped in the dark.

Another critter we met in the sandy driveway under the mango tree, was chameleons. Silent, focused, they turned their eyes, not their heads. They watched us, or stalked walking stick bugs. They lifted one foot, swayed back and forth and set the foot on a green leaf. We waited breathless while the crystals in their upper skin layer relaxed, opening space in the layer beneath and reflected more blue light, turning the yellow chameleon green.

———————

Jette arrived with her parents, Peter and Gladys Buller, and little brother, Charlie, on a weekend in September 1963. Her big brother, Jim, age 10—same as Hope—was already away at school in the capital. But our Mom and Dad had decided to keep Hope home a year longer so we could go to the mission dorm together when I was in grade four.

Jette's father, tall with a blonde crewcut, took videos of us girls-in-dresses with our village friends walking down Kamayala's beautiful palm-lined avenue from the church and orphanage. He was our "Uncle" Pete, not our blood uncle but our mission family uncle. In this way we claimed them and tried to fill gaps left by relatives back home.

Uncle Pete filmed Mama Tambula with the orphans in their Sunday whites. She swaddled and held two babies at once, her dark hair curled around the nape of her neck. She looked up and smiled naturally through clear spectacles.

On the palm-shaded avenue, we girls jumped rope, Jette and I skimming down the road like whirligigs. Then slender, athletic Hope in a light blue dress skipped with Jette in one rope.

We grouped up as a family for goodbyes, Jette in the middle between Charity and me, fitting right in with her flaxen hair. She waved her parents off smiling, hand held high.

Jette had brought her small rhesus monkey, Willy, a wiry playful pet that jumped from dressers to beds, keeping us entertained. Mom endured the chaos briefly, then interrupted in her charge-nurse voice. "The house is no place for animals. The monkey goes outside in the cage."

"But the jackals are there—" My hair stood on end.

"They'll eat him." Charity's face flushed.

"There's no roof. He'll run away." Hope tried to sound reasonable

Dad joined the discussion. "We'll cover it in chicken wire and put a few large tree branches inside so Willy can stay high up."

Jette and I still worried. Couldn't the coyotes jump and climb?

Kamayala's carpenter came and helped Dad extend the five-by-eight-foot cage straight up eight feet and added a chicken-wire cover. We let the jackals out for their daily run and put Willy inside. He scampered up the branches and around the top of the cage. Then we called the jackals using their high-pitched yipping language, *mo-mi-mow-mow-mow*. They came running and Willy scampered above them. He picked leaves and pieces of bark and threw them at the jackals. The pair chased him around from the ground but Willy kept right on teasing them. They became our very own circus in a cage.

We'd let all the pets out in the morning when we could watch them, and Willy loved bounding among the tangerines and mulberries. He ate them by the cheek-full and rained them to waste on the ground.

Jette divided her time between us sisters, dressing Barbie dolls with Charity and joining me each morning for grammar, arithmetic and reading. Her left hand was withered by the polio vaccine when she was a baby but she pushed herself to use it anyway. We devoured books, thrilled by how our childhood heroes survived adversity—from the plucky *Boxcar Children* to the independent Jo March and four sisters in *Little Women*.

Jette even learned some *Plautdietsch*, low German, so she could speak to two-year-old Grace. Dad wanted our family to be able to speak with our grandmas so we had a family rule to speak only *Plautdietsch* to Grace. One Saturday, Jette found Grace about to bathe the fresh-dressed barbies in a bucket of dirty floor water. *"Dow, dow!"* Do, do! Jette cried instead of *"Dow nich!"* (Do not!) Cheered on in her task, Grace plunged the white-lacey dolls into the dirty water.

That Christmas 1963 our family vacationed at Shakenge. Mom took a break from medical work and jumped rope with us girls. Always inventive, she involved baby Grace by handing her one end of the rope. We three older sisters took turns jumping in and then Hope took the rope and Mom jumped in like a little girl! I laughed and grinned and could not stop. We had become the family I always wanted—the kind that could let go of serious stuff, cut up, act ridiculous and have fun.

But by suppertime I had become flushed, overheated and nauseous. That night, delirious with malaria fever, I saw a harlequin clown sitting high on a tightrope. I chattered on about "that man, sitting on that wire, eating grapes." Mom bent close, following my finger, searching the darkness for my circus tent vision. She left and returned with a small white pill and glass of water and helped me sit up to swallow it. My fever broke that night in the comforting weight of her presence.

She had sat up half the night to treat my malaria and had conquered every other disease that had nearly killed me. I was alive at all because of her.

When I was just six months old, I started running a fever and Mom set me in my walker at Dad's feet while she made lunch, re-

Mom took frequent breaks from medical work to play with us. She involved baby Grace by giving her one end of the jump rope to hold. (Ben Eidse photo)

luctant to leave me alone. A few minutes later Dad looked up from language study and saw me slumped backwards, my eyes rolled back in my head. He called to Mom in the kitchen, "Something's wrong with Faithie."

Mom ran into the living room and realized I was having convulsions. She stuck her finger, wet with potato salad, in my mouth to keep me from swallowing my tongue. Just that week she had lost three village babies to cerebral malaria, a disease carried by mosquitoes.

"Get me a spoon," she said to Dad.

"What kind?" he asked.

Any kind, she wanted to say, but kept her head and said smoothly, "A teaspoon. And call Sister Berta."

Sister Berta Mangold, another nurse on the station, came running in her white, rubber-soled shoes, and set me in a tub of lukewarm water, bathing my head, arms and legs. Still no response. They switched to alcohol, rubbing my arms, torso and legs. Mom went to the door and called a bicyclist to fetch the Belgian doctor from Kahemba five miles away.

Half an hour later the messenger returned on bicycle without the doctor. This was not what Mom had envisioned. She had expected a jeep, a doctor, arriving in double time at her door. Instead the messenger had cycled back like the wind while I continued in crisis. His name is lost to history. He handed her two vials, quinine and anticonvulsive medicine. There were no dosage instructions. Mom filled syringes and injected me in each thigh muscle, not knowing if she were killing or saving me.

Sister Berta took me from Mom's arms. It had been two hours and still there was no response. "It's too late. She's gone." She laid me on the bed and covered me with a sheet.

Mom sat numb beside the tub. Why should her baby live if three Chokwe babies had already died of the same disease? She was meant to weep with the mothers who had buried their babies in African soil.

Dad knelt by the bed and prayed. "Lord, bring her back!" He picked me up, held me to his shoulder and called my name, "Faithie, Faithie." My eyes opened. When Dad told the story he always said, "And those were the most beautiful eyes I'd ever seen."

It took great faith to keep me alive 'til my first birthday, here with Mom, Dad and Hope at Kamayala. (Ben Eidse photo)

5

FLEEING

I was eight, going on nine, when New Year's Day 1964 dawned, a foggy Congo morning in rainy season. What I would be doing, whether I would be going to Jette's or staying home, was like a ghostly shadow on the horizon. I padded through the dark dining room, scanning the savanna for spears poking from long grass or soldiers with guns lying in wait. The ground outside was still clutching a fog blanket. Rainy season humidity flowed through the open screen windows, and women carrying bundles of firewood on their heads hurried by on the sandy, palm-lined road.

At this time of year, the most delicate visitors of all alighted on our lawn under the *fungu* (African plum tree). Snowy white egrets plucked up the purple plums for days on end without a care in the world. Angels of God, the local pastor called them, and forbade anyone to shoot them. An arrow through the heart of one of those birds was a bad omen and spelled calamity for the village—deaths of youngsters and babies.

One student, new to the area, did and was expelled from school. It was a searing punishment that made him feel marked as a murderer for life. He struggled on, enrolled in a new school, faced new challenges as penance and ended up in charge of the entire water system for the capital city.

To us, the pure white birds were a comfort that reminded Dad of the cattle egrets that followed the plow in Manitoba. Had they flown all the way across Atlantic billows to be our December snow? We liked to think so.

I eased back to my cot and opened my Bobbsey Twins mystery. "*'Fudielo, 'Fudielo*," Kusu squawked from his cage outside the bedroom window. He relayed a message from the cook. "*Tweya fela.*" (Come iron.) *Tata* Michel often spoke through the parrot to avoid calling through the house. "Squeak, squeak," the parrot added, filtering nothing. That was the sound of the cast iron already stroking dresses and shirts. My job was ironing the pillow cases and tea towels. I closed my book and passed Charity and Grace buttoning a shirred doll dress onto our cat Orbit. Dad had suggested her name but he also teased us over it. "When I kick her, she flies into orbit!" Still, to us the choice was clear for our bright white and gold kitty. On moonless nights, above the open savanna, we tracked the first glimmering satellites orbiting Earth. Dad, who listened to the BBC broadcast on Everlasting Love Winning Africa (ELWA) out of Monrovia, Liberia, sometimes named them.

"That's Gemini 7." Or, "Vostok 6, first woman in space, Valentina Tereshkova." There was pride in his bass voice, and not just because of the doors it opened for his daughters. "See, you too, could be astronauts. You can do anything." But also because our Dutch Mennonite ancestors—burned at the stake in Holland, silenced for their sweet singing in Poland—had found a temporary home in Russia. Under Catherine the Great, they farmed the Steppes until they were conscripted for the Balkan War of 1875. Rather than fight, they loaded ox carts and trekked back cross-continent to Holland where they caught ships for Canada. Their voyage was sponsored by the Pennsylvania Dutch and landed them on the Red and Rat Rivers in Manitoba.

From our home office, the two-way radio crackled on for the morning broadcast. "Police in Kwilu region are rounding up and beating youths sympathetic to Mulele." Kwilu region was where Jette lived. How close had the *Jeunesse* come? Would they reach Kamayala in the new year?

In the kitchen, I clipped a wooden handle to the iron heating on the stove and stroked it across a pillow case. "Squeak, squeak,"

Kusu squawked, fluffing its feathers and preening its wings. The *Jeunesse* could ruin my plans to live with Jette in a few weeks. If the bush pilots saw villages burning, I might as well forget it. Better I stayed home.

I folded the last tea towel, still scorch-stained from the last time I'd been daydreaming while ironing, put the iron back on the stove, and unclipped the handle. At the counter, *Tata* Michel was leavening dough for bread. The sweet hay aroma of the heating savanna drifted through the back screen door. It mixed with the sharp scent of jackal dung from the pen out back.

"'*Fulielo,*" *Kusu* called in a nasal version of Hope's voice.

"What?" I asked.

"What? What? What?" *Kusu* echoed. The parrot often repeated words in several registers, as though tuning a stringed instrument.

"Come 'ere." *Kusu* imitated Hope's voice exactly.

I found Hope in the bedroom, already dressed and with her long hair braided. "We've got to plan."

She closed her Bible and thunked it under her cot. The solid thud of it reminded me I hadn't yet had my morning devotions. Until I did, I would feel some essential thing missing, as though I hadn't dressed or brushed my teeth.

"Plan what?" I pulled my Bible from under the bed.

"Hey Faith, let's play paper dolls!" Charity held up the envelope with Citronella, Jacqueline and all their dresses. "Please? You can make the ball gowns." Only in paper doll land were we permitted to dress in strapless gowns and go to balls. Even our "Barbie" doll was a Vogue "Jill" doll, less shapely, more ordinary. *Shaped like a real woman,* Mom always said.

"Wait a minute. Hope's planning something." I loved how Charity's cheeks flushed when I put her off. "Besides I have to have devotions first." I ducked a little, hearing how annoying that sounded.

"Oh you're always so holier-than-thou." Charity tossed her short hair out of her crystal blue eyes.

"Stop it," Hope cut in, adjusting her rhinestone cat eyeglasses. "Faith don't bait her."

"Yeah, don't abate me." Charity lifted her pert chin.

"Okay I won't." I closed my Bible and caught Hope's twinkling eyes.

Hope picked up her pillow and pulled off the case.

Curly-haired Grace laughed melodiously from the closet where Orbit dodged her and tried to bite off the doll dress.

"Come on, Charity." Hope pulled off Charity's pillowcase, too. "You can help me."

"Do what?" I didn't like being played against my little sister. Once Hope told us both the same secret hiding place, made us promise not to go near it, and sent us to find each other's hiding place. We searched all afternoon.

"Stuff pillowcases." Hope exhaled softly not wanting to alarm Grace. "For fleeing."

I pulled off my pillowcase, too. Fleeing was a word Mom and Dad used often those days. "Do you think we'll have to flee? Will the Africans?" Mom wanted to take the kids and go, even if just to the capital 'til the trouble passed. Dad wanted to stay with the people and help them escape if necessary.

Hope went on. "We can stuff these with cans of sardines, beans, corned beef. We'll keep them under our beds so we're ready to run."

Hope's plan gave me a sense of control, as though the *Jeunesse* would come to the front door, knock and wait politely while we ran out the back.

We tiptoed past the organ in the living room, past the kerosene fridge in the dining room, through the kitchen where *Tata* Michel was filling the stove with firewood to keep the heat high for ironing and baking. He had a batch of buns already rising on the stove shelf, their malted smell drawing passers-by for a chat on the back porch and an early, pan-fried sample. We closed the pantry door behind us, noses wrinkling at sour millet and smoked fish odors. In the mid-morning heat, we gently lifted cans down into our pillow cases.

Spam was perfect with its key opener attached to the lid. I dropped it in my bag with a solid thud.

Hope held a finger to her lips. "Shh."

My pillowcase was half full when I tested the weight. "This is all I can carry. Here, you take the peaches."

"Shh!" But it was too late.

Tata Michel stood at the door, full lips pursed, hands on his hips. "*Achichika?*" (What is this?)

"It's for running from the *Jeunesse*," Hope said in Chokwe.

"Mmm." *Tata* Michel raised his eyebrows and went back to the kitchen, probably knowing he'd have to come ask for a can of peas before supper.

We crept through the kitchen with sacks over our shoulders like little elves. Serious little elves, because with the weight of the pillowcases came a lost playfulness. No more cutting loose across the yard, pounding down sandy paths like the wind, swinging from vines, entering the river with an explosion of bubbles. There would be no more beating frenzied water drums without a thought for our safety. What had crept in was a quietness, a drawing back from carefree living. Where once all our senses screamed for expression, now we had applied an internal soft pedal. Instead of shouting ourselves hoarse, we turned down the volume and drew inward.

Tata *Michel was like another parent—or sometimes a co-conspirator with us.*

We shoved our pillowcases under our beds and lay quietly on our blankets. How would I carry that weight for kilometers, and how would I sleep on bare, scratchy ground? A moment later *Tata* Michel was at our bedroom door. Did he need my perfect Spam?

Instead he held out the can opener.

I laughed sheepishly and reached for it, sharing a grin with *Tata* Michel, our co-conspirator.

We had to band together. There would be no more rivalry. Like statuettes of perfect sisters, we would look out for each other, and never say anything nasty to each other again. We would forget all our squabbles and behave like small adults.

Hope called Grace over and lifted her up. "I will carry you piggyback and always look out for you." We were no longer ages 2, 7, 8 and 10. We had leaped to 12, 17, 18 and 20 in one morning.

Tata Michel whistled in the kitchen, the ups and downs and trills of a tune ancient as the Kamayala River. At the sink, he washed tin cans, sliced and rolled them into shot. Once, when a greedy chief had transformed into a lion, his footprints changing on the road right behind the church, Michel had joined the hunt. He was a hunter, not a fleer.

––––––––

That night, I heard a familiar trumpeting from the savanna. Were those elephants guarding us? We had never seen elephants except at feasts where we were served big chunks of it, sometimes with a coarse hair sticking out. Decades later, I heard the trumpeting again at a wedding in the Emerald Coast Zoo near Crestview, Florida. It rose, a deep *whoo-ooo* from the lion's cage just as the groom—the lion feeder—spoke his vows. Those had never been elephants circling us but lions all along.

6

WALK THROUGH FIRE

Tires mushing along sandy roads feel different from tires humming along tarmac or concrete. But that's not the only difference between traveling in Africa and traveling in Canada. The other is not knowing what's around the bend.

Mom and Dad thought it risky driving me to Mukedi on Saturday, January 11, 1964, with *Jeunesse* rallying. The worst part, Dad said, was leaving the Lunda-Chokwe people who trusted him and driving into Phende territory. But Jette's father had assured Dad over short-wave radio that the *Jeunesse* had not yet killed or threatened any missionaries.

Their fight, Dad explained, was with a corrupt government that "used the national treasury as a piggy bank" and provided no services to its people. So far, the only buildings they had torched between Kamayala and Mukedi was the state post at Kandala.

The road to Kandala mission (a misspelling of the village, Kandale), where we'd spend the night, and Mukedi the next day, ran along the Kwilu river, crossing open grasslands, dipping into the Kwilu flood plain and crossing the meandering river on ferries or log bridges. The concrete ones had already been targeted by army soldiers or *Jeunesse*. The log bridges, built mostly for foot traffic, were sometimes held together with hemp rope.

Charity, especially, sensed Dad's nerves when risking these wobbly crossings. She grew pale, shut her eyes and prayed wordlessly. Some of our passengers crossed themselves, and she added that too, for good measure. As a former Belgian colony, Congo was more

Catholic than Protestant. Dad would say all cultures have a mix of "magic, miracle and medicine." Charity drew on them all.

Our VW van bumped along the Kwilu like an unscheduled bus service, dropping off and picking up passengers. We'd taken several people from Kamayala and dropped them at a mother's village or uncle's house. The familiar Chokwe banter had switched to basic trade Kituba with undercurrents of Giphende. Dad said that if we carried passengers who spoke the local language, they could help us at any unscheduled roadblock.

Along the road, Hope noticed an albino boy—white skin, fluffy white hair, red-veined eyes—hemmed in by protecting friends. We later learned that albino births were more common—and revered—among the Baphende since they revealed black women could have mothered the white race. Also, albino children were at risk for kidnapping and use in magic ceremonies.

When we entered villages, people ran to the road shouting a hopeful destination. "Kikwit?" Dad called back, "Kandala, Mukedi." And if they were willing to go halfway, they shouted back, "Mukedi." If the van wasn't full, Dad stopped and let them gather some food and clothes, detach clinging children, hand them to waiting aunts or uncles and squeeze onboard.

But the route on this trip was filled with people already on the road, carrying basins full of cooking pots, blankets and smoked legs of goat. The familiar feeling of not being able to do enough filled me when we passed them. Dad slowed so we wouldn't cover them in dust and our passengers waved, sometimes calling out greetings or encouragement.

Overhead the sun blazed and turned the van into an oven. In the distance black smoke rose, dense enough to be a village burning. The van's rectangular wing windows stood open, catching eddies of ash, light and stale as gnats. It was the wrong season for grass fires and it was hard to shake the feeling that something was going wrong in Congo.

Dad slowed for a woman with a huge load, forty kilos at least, and a baby on her back. She scurried into the tall grass when she heard the van with its rear motor only meters behind her. But then she waved her hand in a chopping motion for him to stop, her eyes large, her forehead lined and pouring sweat. We were already filled up but her expression was enough to stop river rapids.

Dad eased up on the gas, pushed in the clutch, shifted into neutral and braked. Mom opened the door and got out to help the woman down with her load and lift it in after her. Charity and I moved over, already soaked in our own sweat and resigned to a pungent ride. We shook hands, Hope said *"Moyo"* from the back seat where she sat with baby Grace and the other passengers. The woman clutched her baby as the car began to roll, fear in her eyes.

"What's burning?" Dad asked.

"Houses." She wiped her face with her cloth wrapper. "More villages."

"Who's doing this?"

"Gendarmes."

Mulele had announced that a people's revolution should not harm the population but government soldiers were putting it down and things were getting out of control. Dad stood on the brake, and we bumped over a trench cut clear across the road.

The baby grew slack-mouthed at his mother's breast, the sky clouded over, not with rain clouds, but with a dry, threatening heat. She clutched her sleeping baby closer—devoted to rescuing him.

Dad had rushed into secession wars alone in 1961 to feed refugees while we tried to stay safe in Canada. But even there, Red River floods rose on Grandma Eidse's farm. Mom was pregnant with baby Grace, Charity was sick with celiac, and Hope and I were told to just dangle our feet off the dock. Still, our dainty, yellow-haired dolls wanted to swim and soon got away from us. Hope jumped in after them, sinking into gluey mud and was pulled by an angry current. I tried to yank her out and slipped in myself, landing on sharp sticks and stones stuck in the mud. Water rose to my neck, tugging, pushing, sweeping our dolls away.

Grandma, age sixty-five and napping, heard our screams. Five-foot-nine, and heavyset, she pounded down the narrow walkway, past the eighty-foot windmill, past the four-hole outhouse. She broke off a thick elm branch, pulled us out and set us shivering on a patch of grass. Then she turned back for our dolls.

"Don't!" we screamed.

Grandma plunged into the current in her thin house dress. She plowed against the rising river, her muscled arms tilling floodwaters, gradually closing the distance to our pitiful dolls—thin-legged, prissy things, with names like Roxanne and Rosie—their stiff hands useless in the current. Grandma scooped them up and swam back grinning like a schoolgirl.

In the van, the baby cried and his mother rocked him tighter. A stand of lush green mango trees lurched into view, marking an approaching village. Mud and thatch huts appeared. Men sat on narrow verandahs and women pounded manioc around charcoal fires. Children ran to the road rolling metal bicycle rims, trailed by dogs, pigs and chickens. Dad motioned the children away; afraid one would slip under his wheels. But the children waved and ran closer, banging on the windows.

The front wheel thudded against something and a piercing squeal rent the air.

"*Mam!*" The woman beside me startled her baby awake and he wailed at the jolt.

"Daddy!" I screamed. "You hit a—"

"Pig," Mom said. She touched Dad's arm. "You better not stop here."

Dad sped up and the children fell back. I craned around to watch the pig drag its back end off the road. "Don't you have to pay for the pig?"

Dad had hit free range goats and chickens before but he'd always stopped and settled up. "Not this time."

A scowling man outside raced alongside and slapped our windshield.

How could people run so fast? "Dad, they want you to stop!"

"I can't stop now." Dad gripped the steering wheel and gunned the engine. "These are fighting men."

Several men had caught up and were keeping pace with the van, shouting at my window. My hand flew to the raw scar beside my eye left over from a schoolyard fight—not in Congo, but in Canada.

Dad shifted into high gear. The men shouted and banged the van with sticks. Dad kept the pedal down and the van leaped through ruts and over tree roots.

Finally the men crashed sticks along the van as they dropped off.

Trees and huts gave way to open savanna again and Dad slowed down. I lowered my hand and caught his eye in the rearview mirror. He had his own scar high on his left cheek from falling off the kitchen steps when he was two and hitting the metal boot scraper. He loved to name his villains "Scarface" in his bedtime stories.

My scar was from a hurled turkey bone that lodged a half-inch from my eye while I clung to the school wall, trying not to get tackled in the boys-kiss-girls game. Feeling punished, strange and numb I stumbled into class and sent kids screaming behind the teacher's desk. "Your bone is coming out!" Warm sticky blood oozed onto my hand and the teacher steered me to the principal's office where the dentist was visiting. The dentist yanked out the bone with tooth pliers, staunched the blood, bandaged the wound and sent me home with an order to get a tetanus shot.

Dad's scar crinkled when he grinned at me in the rearview mirror. He slowed and shifted down as we approached a river crossing. There he stopped to test the log bridge and give everyone a break.

Safely across, and back on the open grassland road again, Mom tucked stray auburn curls into the tight roll at her neck. "Do you think we should leave her in Mukedi at a time like this?"

"Yes, please?" I leaned over the front seat.

"Who knows?" Dad said. "She might be safer there than at Kamayala."

Mom tightened her lips and searched the tall grass and low scrublands. The Kamayala students had said there would be more killing by the *Jeunesse*, but we were all hoping they were wrong.

"You know our verse?" I repeated the family verse Dad had given us. "All things work together for good to them that love God." I realized in the next moment how reckless it sounded at a time like this. Perhaps Dad and I were too close and Dad found it hard to say no to me. He had called me to help change the oil before the trip—hold the flashlight, hand him a wrench. *You're bright and outgoing, you'll easily adjust to school away from home. You should consider going to college.*

Or maybe he thought it best we separate after our father-daughter buying trip to Kikwit. I had snuggled close all the way there, happy to have him to myself, and then stiffened silently all the way home after the warm gushy dream that I'd won my trim, princely Dad for myself—and killed mom to do it. But he had studied psychology and might have guessed. He even forgave me when, decades later, the dreams resurfaced in therapy.

Mom finally turned back from the window and caught Dad's eye. "*Si Dieu veut.*" (God willing.) Dad reached over and squeezed her freckled hand.

At Kandale, we left the main road and drove beneath shady mango trees to Jim and Jenny Bertsche's cement and tin roof house. Tall "Uncle" Jim and short, kind "Aunt" Jenny welcomed us on their porch with hugs. They were our mission family and they wouldn't want us to get back on the road and cross the river by ferry yet that night. They had made us dinner and planned to keep us overnight.

Their six-year-old son Timmy was playing with a new puppy and we kids gathered round to pet the soft squirmy dog. The kitchen smelled of savory chicken and rice and we sat around the dining room table, passed serving bowls and filled our plates. Uncle Jim gazed at us through thick glasses and spoke in a deep, calm voice. "Several Kamayala families, Pastor Wayindama and his Bible school students, told us some students were studying warfare in forest camps. Our pastors were concerned enough that we called in VJ for a meeting."

"VJ" was Vernon J. Sprunger, our mission head in the capital. I took a bite of chicken and ducked my head pretending not to listen to the grown-ups talk.

"He advised everyone to stay calm. 'Show no fear. Fear only makes fools of people.'" Uncle Jim's low calm voice gripped me.

I glanced up slightly but Timmy kept his dark, curly head raised, eyes wide, at talk of village burnings and *Jeunesse* rallies nearby. It was as though the grown-ups could not help themselves anymore. They talked about the revolution in the open with children listening. Or maybe that was the way it was in Tim's family, everything out in the open like that.

Uncle Jim was thorough and detailed, holding nothing back and I felt that we'd be safe no matter what. "Rebels with torches and machetes burned a building at the state post... They're angry over the assassination of Lumumba. They say the West is trying to control us."

Like my dad, Mr. Bertsche was a translator and listened closely to the people. The army chief Mobutu had threatened to send strike forces to Kwilu province if the people did not denounce Mulele. The people refused.

"Troops would not be good." Aunt Jenny's voice was soft and sympathetic and she glanced around the table taking us all in.

I nodded, feeling included, even brave. Besides, we all knew, missionaries had to stay out of politics.

Aunt Jenny gazed at Mom and us girls. "We hope all our children will be safe away at school. There wasn't enough room in the capital so we sent Sandra and Linda to the Presbyterian Central School at Lubondai."

"Yes, I hope so." Mom laid her warm hand on my back.

"How will all this affect the new Bible School?" Dad's forehead creased with concern.

"I don't know." Mr. Bertsche gathered the dishes. "But the students worry too... They understand, the people hardly get any say. Their officials are appointed from Leopoldville. They never got what they were promised after independence...."

We helped clear the table and scratched Tim's puppy behind the ears. Tim set up the checkerboard and we pushed buttons into ambush and capture positions, taking each other by surprise. Tim's mom called him to get ready for bed and we girls rolled up in blankets on the wicker sofas. Tim came out to say goodnight in billowing homemade pajamas and I hid a smile behind my hand. Those pajamas were what I remembered when we next heard from Kandale.

7

MISSING HANDS

Mukedi, where I came to stay with Jette in January 1964, had been built in 1923 along a high ridge overlooking a wooded valley and snaking river. Some of its houses were cavernous, with thick walls of quarried stone, gleaming tin roofs and soaring ceilings. Bordered by bright canna lilies and zinnias, they seemed like decorated fortresses.

Thorny bougainvillea reached fuchsia petals into deep shaded porches and white children ranged the station. Four families and

Jette Buller's family at an interstate rest stop with brothers James and Charles and mom Gladys. (Pete Buller photo)

several single women—a midwife and teacher—worked in the clinic and school and visited each other over potluck.

The things I missed my first days away from home and family were Mom's soft cheek and *Tata* Michel's fresh baked buns. But on days off from directing school, Jette's dad played hide-and-seek, tag or catch with us. He'd grab us kids in strong arms, his chin rough against our smooth ones.

Jette's little brother Charlie was happiest tearing around on his red tricycle, carrying one or two village friends on the running board. Or he let them pedal his trike all they wanted while he ran alongside. He was the sharing-est five year old I'd ever seen.

I felt like a princess moving into Jette's huge bedroom, which she shared with Charlie. Tall, regal Aunt Gladys had assured my parents that I would be safe. "Our Africans won't let us starve."

I wasn't sure the Africans wanted to be owned that way, but they were "our friends" and I also knew the bond of love between us—and the law of the village—you killed your last chicken and shared your last ball of chindu with your neighbors.

From Jette's bedroom, wooden shutters opened onto a fenced backyard that had everything you'd expect in an American playground—merry-go-round, seesaw, swings. Beneath the high pink of having it all was the dark feeling of having too much. How could villagers not be jealous of this?

The grown-ups talked about how Mulele was getting most of his followers from this area. They saw how after fighting hard for independence, others had moved into privileged Belgian government roles, leaving them behind. The Phende tribe had been oppressed, put down, and had only received a few seats in local parliament. They had scratched and pecked like chickens without feed.

The Bullers knew more than we did about *Jeunesse* activities, and they were reluctant to let us leave the yard. But I missed our daily outings with my sisters and *ndoyis* to the river. In a matter of days I had become more separated from Africa than I could imagine. When the Mukedi *mamans* cut across Jette's front yard with their water pails and bowls of laundry, I begged to go along. They were taller and more angular than Chokwe women, but every bit as hardworking. Finally Aunt Gladys agreed to let us follow the women as long as we stayed close to them.

We descended through flowing grasslands, muddy hardwood forests, over worn stumps and exposed roots. The river was cool and brown-stained from forest leaves. When I entered, bare feet on water-worn logs, and plunged into the languid flow, it tasted sweet and woodsy on my tongue. Just like the Kamayala River, it flowed fresh and constant through the valley, a place of permanence and peace. While we swam, the women pounded laundry on rocks, wrang it out and laid it on the grass to dry. They filled gourds and water pails and beckoned us uphill again.

Mulele Pierre had set up a command post just six miles away and was promising change, a caring government, a better life. The name "Mulele" was on every lip, his anthem was sung as though the black Messiah had come.

One day while Pete Buller rode through the village on the open gate of a pick-up truck, the people called, *"Bulele Pierre!"* He was their beloved school director and he waved and grinned at being compared to the popular revolution leader.

For Geography, we went to Charles Sprunger's house where his wife Aunt Geraldine taught us to draw maps and ask questions about how different people lived. She had a one-year-old boy so we helped change diapers and learned some biology, too. Her daughter Kathleen was a cute preschooler with dark, wavy hair, and they were all worried about what had happened to their dad who was supposed to deliver a transmitter to Kandale. No transmitter had yet crackled on the airwaves and we had no way of knowing that he and Loyal Schmidt had been taken hostage, marched 70 kilometers and held before *Jeunesse* tribunals.

I wondered how close the revolution had come when the Bullers' cook came to work one morning, eyes droopy and wearing a cloth wrapper instead of Western trousers. Had he spent the weekend with Mulele in the forest learning guerilla tactics?

In China, we later read, Mulele had learned the need for a million lives lost to bring about political change.

With the African leaders, the grown-ups discussed whether it would be right for missionaries to leave when the Baphende themselves faced so much hardship. During independence, the whites had fled while the Congolese stayed and suffered.

In my dreams I stood alone on the high wall of Jericho. Seventy feet below the ground shook, a fissure opened. A jump would surely kill me. Yet I couldn't stay on the wall because cracks split its base and raced towards me. Rubble flew, rocks skidded, the wall shook and trembled, threatening to bury me alive. I had to jump. I had no choice. I balled my hands and let them dangle again, shuddering with the quaking ground. I shut my eyes and opened them again. Finally I pushed off and left the wall. I plunged through ochre air and knew that death was rushing up to meet me. At the last minute, a gushing wind caught and floated me to the ground. I fell into myself and jerked awake in total darkness.

On Thursday morning, January 23, 1964, before the heavy wooden shutters were opened, the front door shook with urgent knocking. I padded through slatted light to the master bedroom but was afraid to wake Aunt Gladys. She was a hill under a fancy quilt—a tall, regal queen who liked her beauty sleep.

"*Ko-ko-ko*," came a trembling voice at the door.

I raced back into the bedroom. "Jette. Wake up."

Jette sat up, wavy hair frizzed around her. "What? Are the rebels here?"

"Someone's at the door."

People came to the door all the time. Sometimes they were just children who wanted to ride Charlie's tricycle. So, instead of waking her parents, Jette and I tip-toed across the rattan rug to the door.

We opened it a crack and peeked out. A dark, muscled man trembled there in white shirt and dark shorts, eyes wide, sweat pouring from his face. He spoke rapidly in Giphende and handed us a note.

Behind him in the yard, Dr. Nickel, the neighbor, called, "Pete, it's an emergency!"

What had the trembling man seen? People shot with arrows, tied up and cut with machetes, houses doused with gasoline and torched?

Uncle Pete came out of the master bedroom buttoning his shirt, reached over us, took the note and stepped outside. Jette and I were left to our imaginations. We didn't know the note was written by Kilembe's Mother Superior and delivered by the school director after hiding in the forest all night.

"Sirs, please come over and help us. Last night all the priests at the mission were massacred. Terrible! Please come get us to take us, if possible, on to Idiofa" (a Catholic mission 70 miles north).

We could only guess this was it. The *Jeunesse* had arrived. The wait was over.

Outside on the porch, voices were low and urgent. Priests chopped "*kyaa*" with machetes, jeeps and houses burned. The school director had run under flying arrows.

Uncle Pete crossed to the bedroom, bumping into tow-headed Charlie. We crowded around the bedroom door, but Aunt Gladys was already tying on a robe, reaching to shut the door. "Children to the living room."

The Bullers spoke briefly, then Uncle Pete raced past us with the keys to the mission pickup, stopped for Dr. Nickel and bounced off the station. They were speeding into ruins to rescue survivors and we could only pray for safety.

We sat on the rug and took up the game we'd been playing for weeks—planning our escape. We had already decided to take the path that cut through the yard to the river. There were acres of long grass to hide in, and we could swim and drink from the river.

"We can take our blankets." Jette started the take-along list.

"Okay, small blankets." I had learned from Hope to be realistic. "One each but no pillows. They're too big."

"We can take sardines." Jette brightened. "They come with keys to open them."

"Sure okay, we can carry them in our pillowcases." I preferred Spam but I'd eat sardines if necessary.

"I'm going to take my trike!" Charlie pedaled madly around the edge of the rug, ghostly rebels already in hot pursuit.

"How are we supposed to carry it when we leave the path?" I was practiced.

"Put it in a barrel."

"How are we supposed to carry the barrel?" Jette grinned at me.

"Just roll it down the hill."

Jette and I laughed. It was almost as though we could slip into the grass, wait for the rebels to march past, then emerge as if from a camping trip, to take back our beds, clothes and toys. We did not understand the finality of that morning. It would be the last time for months we would be surrounded by familiar things—rugs, sofas, tricycles. The last time for weeks our lives would feel like our own. The last time for years that missionaries would live in the grand colonial houses of Mukedi.

Aunt Gladys came from the bedroom, buttoning her dress, and heading in several directions at once. At the bathroom door, a travel case in hand, Aunt Gladys turned to us on the rug still in our pajamas. "Get dressed, children. Harvey's radioing for evacuation. I'm packing a few things we need. You can each take a change of clothing, a favorite toy and book."

The Harvey Barkmans were a family from our area of Manitoba. They'd look out for us—for me. At the bureau drawer I gazed at several pairs of shorts Jette had given me, sewed by Aunt Gladys. They were my first ever, bright new prints, with tops to match. I wasn't finished wearing them yet, wasn't finished hanging out of mango trees or tipping way back on the swing without worrying about my skirt flying up. I hated to leave them, but if we were fleeing Mukedi, I'd be going back to my family, and they didn't think shorts were proper for girls.

Two weeks were barely enough to figure out who I could be without my folks. I'd discovered, for instance, that I could drink a whole syrupy Fanta soda by myself, a treat my family would have divided six ways with ice and water. I shut the drawer and went to the closet where I chose my best pink Sunday dress off a hanger. I folded it into the zipper skirt of my pajama doll, Polly—the one I'd named for Pollyanna—a story my parents loved about always looking on the bright side. Polly, with her twinkly eyes and plastic smile, was one of three our parents had bought us older sisters in Canada, and the name seemed perfect for facing the unknown. I picked up my Jill doll, the one that wasn't quite a Barbie. She would have to stay behind since I'd already picked Polly.

I added my Bible from the nightstand. These choices would be a kind of sacred protection, a shield against the arrows of the rebels. Part of me understood how the *Jeunesse* believed Mulele turned bullets to water. It was like Dad said, all cultures have a mix of magic, miracle and medicine.

There were few other things to consider. From the bureau drawer, a pair of socks and underwear. That was all. On my nightstand, I left notebooks, pencil crayons, an American geography book and reader. The cover was of a sunny farm, a white house, red barn, brown horse pulling a red apple off a green tree, two blonde children—boy and girl—playing with a black and white dog.

"Jette? Charlie?" Aunt Gladys walked into the room. "Faith? Are you packed? Rebels burned the Catholic mission last night. We don't think they'll come here, but we're leaving just in case."

What if they did come? Would I ever see my parents and family again? What would the fighters do to us? Would they cut us with machetes? Kill us? I didn't ask these questions aloud. The internal soft pedal was down and I felt numb with worry. I sat on the bed and looked over the sill, clutching my overstuffed Polly with her button nose and rosy cheeks. It was possible we wouldn't get away at all. I might not see Hope, Charity, Grace, or Mom and Dad, again. The Bullers would try to get us out, but what if the plane was too small? What if we overloaded, crashed and burned? What if I had to wait for another flight? My own parents weren't here, and if it came to grabbing children, wouldn't any parent take theirs first? Maybe I had separated too easily from my parents, had wanted too much to escape the daily drill at home: clear the table, sweep the floor, comb your hair, stand up straight, brush your teeth. At the moment, that dull, predictable routine seemed the best life ever.

"Pete has gone to get the nuns." Aunt Gladys circled the room, touched a handmade doll, a batik hanging—her creations—crafts she'd made with her sewing classes. For the moment, she was my substitute mother and her solidity reassured me. "Three priests were killed. The planes are on their way now. The youngest mothers and children will go first. Then the rest of the women and children—that's us."

"What about the dads?" Charlie's blue eyes flashed, so like his dad's.

"They'll get out." Aunt Gladys' voice seemed tight and forced. "We'll all get out. Don't worry, honey."

"What about my family?" I barely dared to ask.

Aunt Gladys had grey moons under her eyes. "The pilots say the countryside is on fire. Everyone is leaving."

I shadowed Aunt Gladys who raced around the house, looking through desk drawers, stuffing papers, passports and cash into her handbag. Perhaps I should look away, not follow so closely, try to believe I was not invisible and would not be left behind.

In the kitchen, the cook *Tata* Gregoire washed a tub full of dishes. Aunt Gladys spoke to him in short words, and he answered in shorter ones. Aunt Gladys backed up and stepped on my toes. She threw up her hands. "Outside!" she said. "Children, outside. Go watch for the plane."

Yikes, I had made her send us out into the open—by being too clingy.

The Bullers' house was at the end of the road, the last one on the station ridge, so we were close to the high grass if we had to run. We twirled on the merry-go-round, checked the grass for arrows and clutched our Bibles like shields. We sang Sunday school choruses as though music itself were a weapon. "I stand alone on the word of God..." Louder. Stronger. Faster.

Dizzy. Dizzy with spinning on the merry-go-round, dizzy with fear.

Maybe if we spun fast enough, we'd blur out, turn to vapor and the arrows wouldn't hit us.

We pushed the merry-go-round by turn, our thin legs, tan feet pounding the ground.

Harder, harder.

The rebels were coming.

Faster, faster.

Until our lungs burst.

Jump on the seat, eyes wide, heads back, the blue and white sky spinning, filling with a toy plane that grew larger through the mango canopy.

"Airplane!" Jette shouted and we ran out the gate and down the road.

"Where do you think you're going?" Aunt Gladys stood on the kitchen doorstep.

"The plane—"

Her face was gray and lined. "That is not our plane. That one's for the babies—the Sprungers and Nickels. The next one will be ours. And we're not walking to the airstrip. It's not safe."

My stomach felt like raw eggs slipping on grease. I was one person too many pushing us to wait for the next plane with the *Jeunesse* already here. We gathered around her on the step and followed her inside.

"The pilot, Wes Eisemann, radioed that a band of shirtless men with bows and arrows was headed to the airstrip," she said. "He ordered us to 'Call off the fighting. I don't want to be a pin cushion!'"

I clutched my Bible to my chest. Would we get out alive?

"We have to trust our leaders," Aunt Gladys said. "Chief Nzamba is patrolling the airstrip with his twelve sons. They all have shotguns."

Uncle Pete had returned from the Catholic station with six nuns and a Belgian teacher in the back of the pickup and we went to Dr. Nickel's house to gather around them. Dr. Nickel and Uncle Pete had helped bury the priests in a shallow grave. The doctor had noticed the swollen foot and bloody cast of the priest whose leg he'd set the Sunday before. Both legs had been broken and the priests had been gashed with machetes, some of their hands and fingers missing.

Seven women, six in habits as white as their faces, stood around the Nickels' quarried stone fireplace. The crinkle-eyed Mother Superior in wire-rimmed glasses hovered over a young, shaken teacher. She related in French how the tin roof was pelted with stones and they had huddled in the locked back office of the church. Even while Uncle Pete drove them into Mukedi, they were threatened by men running along the road.

While they waited, a man entered the house and said he was sent to kill them but would spare them if they paid him. Nowhere were they safe. The women huddled and took a collection. After he left, the young teacher, already red-eyed, sobbed again, and the Mother Superior wrapped her arms around her and rocked her like a baby. One nun cradled a newborn whose mother had died at their clinic the night before. "I must take her with me from here," she said in French. The baby was a tiny doll, with loose curls and a soft, hazel face. They waited behind locked doors, drawn curtains.

Uncle Pete left to radio for help from Idiofa, the nearest Catholic mission. The mood had turned against the Europeans, especially the Belgians. Would the Americans be next?

Uncle Pete spoke with Kakesa Samuel, a mission leader, who said the missionaries must leave. Women and children first, then the nuns and men. The fighting was beyond their control.

The buzz of a second plane opened overhead. The pickup bounced up to the back door. "This is your plane!" Uncle Pete grabbed Aunt Gladys' case and hurried us into the truck. "Wes Eisemann buzzed Kandale and their houses and cars are burned. The missionaries—Bertsches, Grabers and Selma—are standing outside the dispensary in their pajamas. Vernon is trying to get U.N. helicopters to rescue them."

Poor Timmy, out shivering in the wet grass. The last time I'd seen him, he was saying goodnight in his pajamas. And what about his puppy? I clutched Polly and clenched my teeth over the rutted road. Tim would later tell us how happy they were for their pajamas and bathrobes and that he even had a burned patch on them.

We jolted onto the airstrip and Uncle Pete braked near a yellow single-prop plane.

Avril Barkman, their preschool son Lowell and Betty Quiring were already huddled under the wing, seven people to be squeezed into three seats.

"Adults first." The pilot placed our few bags in the cargo hold and assigned the women to the three passenger seats and the children one or two to a lap. He scanned the sky and climbed in.

But just then, an army transport plane appeared on approach for landing, soldiers in helmets at the windows.

Several *Jeunesse* with machetes surrounded Mr. Buller shouting, "You called the army. If you let that plane land, we'll kill you!"

The pilot flung open his window, "Get that pickup truck on the airstrip fast!"

"Yay, the army!" Charlie cheered

"Not yay." Mrs. Buller's eyes darkened. "If they land, there'll be all out war."

Harvey Barkman jumped into the truck and raced onto the runway. The plane's lowered wheels barely missed the cab, then lifted and flew away.

"I cut them off when I landed," Mr. Eisemann said. "I didn't think they'd be back."

Decades later, each of us three children—Jette, Charles and myself—recalled seeing the plane nearly demolish the truck in real time and Mr. Eisemann's flight logs indicate we did. However, written reports differ and put midwife Elda Hiebert on the first flight, teacher Betty Quiring on the second and Gordon Fairley as second flight pilot that day.

"I hope Harvey gets out okay." Mrs. Barkman clutched Lowell on her lap. Her daughter Sandra and son Gerald were away at school with Jim Buller. What had they heard?

And what about the nuns? They made up at least two more flights before the fathers could leave—unless the Catholics at Idiofa sent a plane to rescue them.

Mr. Eisemann put on his headphones and radioed for takeoff. He revved the engine, sending dust flying and the fathers back against the high grass—where *Jeunesse* hid with arrows nocked in their bows. Everyone looked at the dads who nodded back with solemn eyes, grim smiles, raised hands.

Mr. Eisemann revved the engine hard again, shuddering us against the brakes as if to shoot us out of a sling, released the brakes and launched us down the runway.

I held myself straight and light, next to Jette, my knuckles white on the seat in front of me. "You'll have to sit very still," Ms. Quiring (or was it Ms. Hiebert?) spoke firmly. "You don't have a seat belt."

The loaded plane lumbered and bumped down the runway. It didn't seem near fast enough to break free. High grass and stunted trees filled the windscreen. A final heave and the runway dropped downhill. We hovered over high grass and scrub brush. At last the plane nosed up, shaving treetops. A hundred feet below, the airstrip fell away and with it the fathers, waving.

Idiofa could not supply a plane and when Eisemann returned from Kikwit to Mukedi, his log says, "Congolese approach plane with bows & arrows. Took off with all haste, circled station until chief drove off rebels."

The Mukedi fathers put the Catholic nuns and teacher on the next two flights and waited hours for their rescue plane. All afternoon they squinted into hazy skies. Chief Nzamba and his twelve sons paced the airstrip with their rifles, holding off the rebels in the tall grass. At any moment their leader could come and issue orders.

Finally the last flight arrived, a welcome thrum overhead. The pilot had been flying for hours, lost over a burning countryside, blown off course by a strong north wind. The fathers shook hands with pastors, leaders and Chief Nzamba, climbed aboard and buckled up. The flight to Kikwit followed the setting sun into tropical night. Behind them at Mukedi, *Jeunesse* with sharpened machetes arrived from the forest, saying, "We got the priests. Where are the Protestants? We have to kill at least one Protestant."

Uncle Pete had raised the shrouds that covered the mutilated priests before laying them in a shallow grave, he wrote later (Buller, p. 7). Some arms ended in clotted stumps, hands and fingers taken. There was only time to throw shovels full of dirt on top and to wonder about the missing digits and hands. Were they cured and eaten as a power source at ceremonies in the forest?

During the nine-month Kwilu uprising no one mentioned to me the Congolese hands King Leopold's agents cut off in the 1890s rubber harvest. As a girl I had no idea how violent colonialism had been. What did the king do with those hands? Did he cure and eat them or wear them as amulets around his neck? No, no—he paid bonuses for them so that eventually Belgian forces went out to harvest hands instead of rubber (Forbath, p. 374). Mulele investigated these raids when he was conscripted into the Belgian forces as punishment for breaking secondary school rules (Kelly, p. 94). In 1964, he tortured Congolese who did not return plunder to him (Hege, p. 209).

In 2010, I reconnected with my ndoyi, Ufudielo *Sylvie Wayindama, and husband Damien Kakhenda. They were four when* Jeunesse *burned their Kandale homes and beat Pastor Wayindama. His student, a rebel leader, would not permit his hand to be cut off. Afterwards the people said, "These people have walked through fire. Listen to their words." (Hope Wiebe photo)*

In the 1970s, Leola's dad searched for and interviewed the children maimed in colonial raids. She helped index names and places mentioned in letters Protestant missionaries wrote in outcry, resulting in the king's removal and Congo given to the Belgium Parliament (Falk).

In Florida, where I now live, we occasionally drive through Sanford founded by U.S. Minister to Belgium Henry Sanford. Here he entertained U.S. presidents and lobbied to participate in Leopold's exploits, which contributed to an estimated 10 million lives lost over 20 years—for a profit of millions. Sanford's commercial steamers, *Florida* and *New York*, were the first to penetrate the upper Congo. He merged with the Belgian export company whose atrocities inspired Joseph Conrad's *Heart of Darkness*. There, Captain Marlow found the fevered Kurtz who muttered, "The horror, the horror."

Teacher Collette Ramm and Charity at Kandale, November 2017, during one of several reconciliation celebrations between community members who participated in destruction and those who felt badly that they could not stop it. (Collette Ramm photo)

Decades later, the burned-out homes of Kandale helped launch a 2017 dream to rebuild by Collette Ramm founder of REVE Kandale, the Congo Mennonite Church, Africa InterMennonite Mission and Hope4Congo, founded by a hostage family's son. (Brad Graber photo)

8

REFUGEE

Wrapped in a deep cottony quiet, I hardly noticed the stutter hum of the mission van ferrying us from the rescue plane. We bumped over the red dirt roads of Kikwit, toward the Mennonite Brethren guest house but I was lost to it all, lost to myself. A tangled jungle screened the Kwilu River flashing past. Mud and thatch huts and market stalls wafted burnt wood scents of roasted peanuts and cassava. Vendors in colorful wrappers blurred past the passenger window.

Jette was still there beside me but we likely no longer had a home in Mukedi behind us, no idea what lay ahead. When and where I would see my family, I did not know. I had no place to cling to or belong, did not know what my life was or would become. I was a cocoon dangling in space by a thread.

"Faith?" Aunt Gladys touched my arm, her tired eyes crinkled a little. "Faith, I have a surprise for you."

I struggled up through layers of gauze. We had entered the guest house compound with its screened porch dining hall and a row of tin-roofed cottages.

"There." Aunt Gladys pointed since I still was not registering everything outside. A girl ran across the deeply shaded lawn. She sprinted towards us with long, familiar strides, her blonde bangs and ponytail flying. It was Hope—expecting me before I appeared—anticipating me before I emerged.

Aunt Gladys flinched but let me climb over her long, cramped legs. I jumped out and Hope caught me in a solid bear hug, strong muscles, silky ponytail in my face. Big sister, family, home.

"You're alive!" She looked into my eyes, searching for any harm I might have faced. "You're safe. We didn't know if you'd make it." For the first time I realized that my absence must have left a hole in the family.

She held me at arm's length, hands on my shoulders. "I can't believe it. I worried that you were dead."

"You did?" I was overwhelmed by her delight at my escape and wholeness. I glanced at the cottage Hope had run from, dark and still in the early afternoon humidity. I was hoping to see Mom, Dad, Charity and two-year-old Grace. I wanted to shout. *You're here, I'm back!*

Hope followed my gaze. "They're asleep. I couldn't lie down. I've been out here, waiting."

For all her energy and mischief, Hope was the searchlight in our churning seas making sure no harm would come to any of us.

"Our family is supposed to go to a U.N. refugee camp in Leopoldville and I didn't want to leave without you. I was hoping you'd get here before we left." She pushed back her bangs and grinned big.

We went to join the family napping in the cool guest house. Mom reached out, and I fell into her arms, moist cheek pressed against her soft one. She hugged and rocked me, Dad reached muscled arms and Charity and Grace rushed to join the family hug.

The massive Congo River surged past the U.N. refugee camp in lower Leopoldville, wide as a lake. From a hill behind barbed wire, our family watched fishermen in dugouts pole past.

The distant shore was a thick, blue-green line. That was Congo, Brazzaville, a nation sympathetic to the *Jeunesse*. It was also a place of escape. If you were hunted in this country, you could pay a boatman, or maybe swim across upriver, and you'd be free. I tried to make out several block shapes on the opposite shore. But they stayed grape-grey and fuzzy.

Mom's eyes glinted hazel in the sun. To her, every moment was a teaching moment. "That's Stanley Pool, named for the explorer who staked out Congo for King Leopold."

Staked out—stake in the heart. We had just fled echoes of that attack. But I did not fully understand that yet. Later the river lake name would revert to Pool Malebu.

Below us, the shallow pool created counterflow eddies along the edges. A plunge in there would wash away days of salty sweat, clinging sand and dust. In camp, we rarely arranged for showers in the soldiers' barracks, and usually sponge-bathed over basins filled from outdoor taps. It was never a total, soaking clean. But it was the way we lived with the blue-helmeted U.N. soldiers from Ghana, Nigeria, South Africa.

At night, the soldiers filled the courtyard under the ficus trees, popped Primus beer caps and clanked bottles. Their talk and laughter embroidered our sleep. Mom said they kept her awake at night but, for me, a sense of buffering safety set in.

Mornings we woke to the endless Congo drifting by, bordered by palms, papyrus, pricker vines and invasive water hyacinth. Its lavender flowers were accented on one petal by a bright yellow eye with deep purple shading—like a peacock's feather—or the teacup orchids growing out of fresh grassland burns at Kamayala. A danger for boats and fish alike, they were a parasite from Europe carelessly released from some settler's garden pool. Tightly rafted, the hyacinth looked like it could carry you away from here. But one trusting step and you'd plunge beneath the fat rubbery leaves and fight against white bulbous roots for air.

You never knew, in a big river like this, whether crocodiles lurked. Some said the noise from the CHANIC ship-building company drove them away. The clang of metal-on-metal rang through the still afternoon, a grating comfort. Others said that not all the bodies in the river were escaping political prisoners. Some were dead prisoners, dumped by the jeep load, their limbs gangrenous, hacked off to prevent escape. We learned later of bloated bodies floating through the basin, hung up on rocks and broken up in the rapids below, until arms, legs, and trunks pounded through the Devil's Cauldron and drifted like so much bait through the shipping lanes, eighty-five miles to the Atlantic. There the river gushed brown-green into the aqua ocean.

I scanned the river as though the surface might reveal some startling truth—a giant eel, crocodile eyes, toothy goliath tiger fish. Instead there were the hyacinth rafts twisting, drifting, using up oxygen, breeding mosquitoes. There was so much moving beneath the surface that I could not fathom, name or talk about. On the outside we carried on as though our family hadn't escaped the scariest moments of our lives, as though we weren't living in grey barracks with no idea what would happen next.

I trudged back uphill to the long, concrete barracks and stretched out on my low army cot, my feet not quite reaching the laundry drying over its edge. The afternoon's oven stewed us—Mom, my sisters, the other refugees.

Hope remembered the Grings family arriving there, too— Ruth (her age), Becky (mine) and Daniel (Charity's). Their aunt Irene Ferrel had been killed by *Jeunesse* at Mangungu with a poison arrow on January 25, 1964, shortly after Mukedi was evacuated. Her nurse colleague, Ruth Hege (author of *We Two Alone: Attack and Rescue in the Congo*) had hidden for a week while MAF pilots flew the Kwilu searching for her and other missionaries hiding from *Jeunesse*. Becky Grings later became my friend and classmate.

I didn't get to see Jette much anymore because they had started a new life in the city. Mukedi was still under *Jeunesse* control, its leaders hiding or captured and working in forest camps for Mulele.

The Bullers had moved to a verandah house on stilts in the Baptist Mission Society compound overlooking the Congo River near Kalina church. They were surrounded by other families in verandah houses on stilts, like the Dirkses and Neufeldts. Uncle Pete worked across the street at LECO, a Christian printing press, and Jette seemed happy when I saw her at church on Sundays and at her birthday sleepover. Their lives upcountry were gone; they had lost everything. Later, a partial set of Aunt Gladys' dishes showed up and Uncle Pete got $40 for his VW Beetle.

Our lives upcountry were on hold, though Kamayala had not yet fallen or been punished like Mukedi had. Our lives in the camp were hemmed-in, our movements limited. Revolutionaries in the East, called *Simbas* (lions), had established headquarters in Rwanda and were operating forest camps in Eastern Congo near Bukavu.

Mornings we rose to a breakfast bell that called us and the U.N. soldiers to a free buffet of halved grapefruit, fresh bread, margarine and jam. It was provided in a sunlit dining room and I was permitted to pile glistening sugar on the sour grapefruit.

At rest hour, our canvas cots sagged with moms dozing beside babies and toddlers, all of us sweating into rancid clothing. Our little sisters whispered about whose doll was visiting or who was talking too loudly.

I reached for Polly and hooked my elbow around her soft form. She'd been with me through everything—the fleeing, the landing here in this compound, the emptiness, the starkness. Everything that had once surrounded me was gone: the geography book, the bedside stand, the bright shorts that would be so much more comfortable than the two dresses I took.

Since I could not talk about these things—could not admit to the shorts I'd worn or mention the books, notebooks and pencil crayons I missed when others had so little—I dwelt on them, making them more than what they were. They appeared in technicolor and I felt their absence.

That is, until I realized they might have become a gift to some needy Phende child. Perhaps a mission leader walked into the old Mukedi home with his children, exploring our bedroom, lifting out the shorts set in my drawer. A little boy put on the shorts, a little girl put on the matching shirt and hugged my Jill doll to her cheek. They took turns pedaling Charlie's trike around outside, the boy pumping his little legs, the girl jumping on, holding his shoulders 'til her turn.

Mom had tried to create a space of our own across from the door. It was less private but caught river breezes. The only other openings were louvers and small windows high in the wall to let out the hot air, which seemed to descend rather than rise. It covered us like deep blankets, making it hard to wake from our afternoon naps. We drifted in and out, sometimes until the supper gong clanged at six o'clock.

The refugee camp was my first time living publicly—undressing, sponge-bathing, washing my only other underwear and dress—in full view of the others. There was a boy in our room, another eight year old, Danny Gerber. He and his little sisters were Jette's cousins, but he seemed nervous around me and having to avert his eyes from the other moms and girls. We weren't easy playmates. Too close at bedtime, mealtime, bath time, we found our own corners in the fenced compound or docked at our cots as though they were private piers in a stagnant pond.

Our little sisters, Charity and Becky—and sometimes our baby sisters, Joanna and Grace—played imaginary house for hours in a well-furnished fantasy land. I settled with Polly on my cot, unzipping her skirt to read my only other possession—the Bible—including all the "begats" (Abraham begat Isaac begat Esau and Jacob). They stretched like the endless days at the U.N. camp but I vowed to read it through from Genesis, every word.

The fathers slept in the barracks next door, and from their room came the rising, falling crackle of a transistor radio. They collected easily in their own group, heads bent over the radio or raising urgent voices outside after dark. What would happen to Congo? Dad said he hoped the *Jeunesse* wouldn't target Kamayala since we had left. If they did cross the Kwilu, Kamayala families would run to the jungle or distant villages. Local pastors and teachers would be killed or captured for the revolution. No one knew which way the movement would swing next. It might even come 300 miles to Leopoldville.

At first I quieted way down, or crept close and listened, believing their talk would solve our problems.

"They're shooting themselves in the foot."

"It was better before independence."

"Congo isn't ready for independence."

Dad straightened and frowned at such tones. "Well, maybe they have to make some mistakes...like we did—we do." After independence, the African leaders had asked to run their own country and Mom and Dad and the mission agreed. They would walk alongside and help if needed.

Dad's ideas captured the attention of U.N. soldiers and they joined in.

"How ready do you 'ave to be for freedom?" a soldier from Ghana spoke up in pidgin-English.

Dad's huge grin creased his face. "Yes exactly. Ghana has been independent since 1957, right? Your president, Kwame Nkrumah, is a good man!"

"Saa!" another Ghanaian soldier agreed. "Nkrumah pleaded to America in 1960 to spare Congo's prime minister Lumumba."

An American father scowled. "Yeah but then Lumumba turned to the Soviet Union for help with the Katanga secession."

"We-ell yes, but," Dad said slowly, evenly, "Lumumba only requested help from the Soviets because the U.S. wouldn't help him."

"Humph," the American father said. "That's because Belgium wanted to control the uranium. And if you ask me—"

No one asked him.

"Who knows?" Dad pushed a dark lock from his forehead. "Maybe this whole revolution could have been avoided."

Things got lively some evenings but, as the days rolled by, the conversations repeated themselves and I moved on. The dads sat on their cots, elbows on knees, and seemed to have gone away, leaving only their bodies behind.

Some mothers protested the separation of families, but Mom said there was little choice in the open rooms. On the porch, she held curly-haired Grace and they played with her sock octopus Oscar. Grace sang, twirled and clapped in several languages on her way to becoming "the human jukebox," as eco-villagers on the Canadian prairie would one day call her. All the moms agreed, she was a charmer.

We lived practically outdoors, the river flowing steadily in its old familiar bed. Fishermen drifted into view around the river bend, floating in their canoes with the center current, dragging their poles, bent slightly at the knees and shoulders. Or they poled up the river's edge in counter eddies, sinews flexing, torsos heaving. They had places to go, things to be. They set woven bamboo traps, collected fish, took them to market. There was a tempo and order to their day. There was meaning in their waking, eating, sleeping. In ours, a dull waiting set in, a numb listening for word that we could return to our lives upcountry. Or, possibly, that we couldn't. The country might change forever and no longer let us stay.

More news arrived via Dad's preferred BBC broadcast from Monrovia, Liberia. On February 13, *Jeunesse* had been repelled outside Kikwit, bombed from the air. Dad and Mr. Gerber couldn't help worrying over mission teachers, pastors and school directors, pressed into service for the revolution. Only later did we learn that it was not the Congo army, but CIA-trained Cuban refugee pilots from Florida flying U.S.-built World War II T-6 training planes. They fired air-to-ground rockets and .30 caliber machine guns

blasting Mulele's estimated 2-3,000 *Jeunesse*. This was despite the
U.S. signing a 1961 U.N. resolution to keep mercenaries out of
Congo (Kelly, p. 97).

––––––––––––

A debate rose in the camp. What was worse, strafing people
from the air or cutting them up with machetes? Some men seemed to
think it was better to kill from a distance. Dad said it was all murder.
Violence was not the answer.

Weeks passed, and gradually Hope and I were permitted to
scout further around the U.N. compound. We left our barracks,
passed the stooped-shouldered fathers and waded along the sandy
road to the metal gate and guardhouse.

My ninth birthday was a week away, and I knew there would
be no cake, candles or presents. Dad said we should deny ourselves
and think of others. I practiced this often, thinking it would be easier
to be someone else, someone whose waking and sleeping wasn't full
of wishes for things she couldn't have. I could be the Ghanaian guard
at the gate in pressed blue uniform, thick, beefy hands holding an
oiled rifle, shiny black lace-up boots crunching on the gravel.

"Hello." He stood sucking a Belge cigarette, breathing smoke
through his nose. Calm inside, quiet.

"Agh, uhm." I pulled back to myself. "Hello." Returning to
my own head was the hard part because when I did, all that I wanted
came rushing back. I wanted a party with children, balloons, games,
an iced layer cake like the ones in my third grade reader. But how
could we expect presents or treats when other people had so little?

Behind the guard, beyond the spiked gate, square Toyotas and
nose-down Fiats whizzed by on Trente Juin Boulevard. Across the
busy street, a row of shops emptied women with bowls of bread and
boxes of nails on their heads. They swayed under their loads and
crossed the bridge downtown to re-sell single buns and nails for a

few francs. The fresh-malt smells of warm baguettes rose above the sulfuric stench of black exhaust. My mouth watered for some special treat to share for my birthday.

A gong sounded dinner, and we circled back to the barracks and dipped our hands in wash basins.

"Time for dinner!" I called to Dad who was underlining a French Bible with a red pen. He rarely got down on his knees to play horsey with us anymore.

He looked up startled. "Oh, dinner already? How's my Daddy's girl?" He placed a hand on my shoulder, still my dear Dad drawing me in, claiming each one of us with a special name.

We followed the line of ragged refugees to the low-ceilinged dining room and sat on plastic chairs at long tables. We filed past the serving window and held our plates to be filled from pots of boiled chicken, potatoes, greens. The U.N. soldiers sat at their own table and ate dense *chindu* and *mwamba* (manioc mush and chicken sauce). Dad glanced their way and grinned, a mischievous twinkle in his eye.

I realized, maybe even before Dad did, that he was about to stir things up.

"Let's get some *chindu*," I whispered, not too loud.

"Naw, we'll eat this." He speared a boiled potato on an aluminum fork and watched it crumble.

"We should tell the cooks not to prepare anything special for us." He looked up at the other families. "We can all eat *fufu*." (That was Lingala for *chindu*.)

Dad had "gone native" four years earlier when he'd lived in Congo without us for half a year. He had grown a beard, strummed guitar and eaten in the village every night. Dad smiled into the silence around the dining table. The refugees shifted in their seats.

One father spoke up. "Sure I like *musa* once in a while."

A mother said, "This may not be the tastiest food but it's good enough for us."

Finally it was decided that Dad should petition the cook to give us a choice—overcooked American or just right African. Dad went to the serving window and called the cook who grinned and spoke to his kitchen workers. "These *mindele* want to eat like us. Bring them *fufu*."

Afterward, our bellies heavy with the starchy mush, Dad joined me on the rise to watch a purpling sky reflected in the flowing river. Fishermen, black against the glinting river, poled home. "Wouldn't it be nice to get a canoe ride?" I asked. Another father joined us, and another, but I stayed, even though I knew they wanted to talk about the revolution.

"An interesting idea." Dad patted my shoulder. "Shouldn't you be getting to bed?"

"You know all kinds of languages." I sensed how obvious the flattery sounded. "You can go down there." I gestured outside the camp to where a rutted road ran to the river. "And ask one of the fishermen. Please?" My voice was high-pitched, desperate. "For my birthday?" I had wanted it to sound—coy, winning.

"Fa-aith." There was a warning in his tone. "You shouldn't always think of yourself."

My face burned. I knew better than to ask for presents when the country was at war, children crying in the forest. My throat closed up. The river blurred. I turned and walked on numb feet to the long barracks lit by bare bulbs. Moms rinsed their children's feet in basins, washed the day's clothes with blue-marbled bar soap and hung them to dry at the foot of their cots.

Mom switched out the lights and, in the boulevard-lit gray, changed in that mysterious way she had of pulling things off and putting things on without showing an inch of flesh. She crawled into bed and we spoke our prayers into the darkness. "Now I lay me down to sleep...I pray the Lord my soul to take"— machetes and arrows in the grass. Had the *Jeunesse* killed first before hacking off the priest's hands? I could settle for less this birthday. It wouldn't hurt. At all.

Hope had lengthened her prayer list since we'd come here. "Bless our cousins in Stanleyville, and Marie, Pauline, Musasa, Ilunga and all our friends at Kamayala." Dad had said that with *Jeunesse* spreading to other cities, mission pastors, teachers and students were being forced into violence for the revolution. He was most dismayed that despite Mulele's revolution codes against theft and requiring *Jeunesse* to respect all people, they plundered elders' stores and gouged out their eyes. Long after lights out, the soldiers laughed and clanked bottles, voices rose and fell.

In my dreams, I lifted a slice of three-layer chocolate cake to my mouth, thick fudge frosting gleaming. I opened wide, my tongue quivering, saliva dripping. When I bit down the cake melted away but my tongue clung to its bitter sweetness until morning.

One morning, after it seemed clear we'd be staying awhile, and we'd registered to attend The American School of Leopoldville, we waited at the gate for an American embassy van to pick us up for school. The school was on the Baptist mission compound. It had gone from a two-room brick cottage to an American government school with classes from grades one to twelve, auditorium, basketball court and athletic field. All the different missions ran their own dorms on their own compounds around the city but most didn't take children under grade four anymore.

The students at the American school were missionary kids, international business and embassy kids and military brats from COMISH (the U.S. Military Assistance Mission to Congo). They came from dozens of nations, the U.S., Canada, Britain, Pakistan,

France, Belgium, Nigeria, Congo. Home was everywhere and nowhere, an airplane over the Atlantic. They were global nomads from
thirty-seven nations.

When the van finally stopped inside the U.N. gate, it was already filled with American children who had traveled from the plush
compounds near the parliament and trade buildings. They were
dressed from J.C. Penney catalogues and carried school bags full of
Fritos, Cokes and Baby Ruth bars from the U.S. commissary.

Hope, Charity and I each carried an oatmeal c-ration, thick as
a hockey puck. It had the advantage of thudding to the bottoms of
our stomachs and keeping us full all day.

When I climbed into the van, I looked first for my classmate
Ruth. She usually sat by the back window because she and her sister
got on first. Also, she didn't want to sit next to our classmate who
kept trying to kiss her.

It was impossible not to turn around and watch Ruth. She of
the perfect name and haircut. She often had a toy along for the long
ride to school—a Barbie or Ken doll—from department stores in
the States. I smoothed my hair, straightened my faded pink dress,
stuck my c-ration deep in my skirt pocket, and turned to smile at
her. Her straight hair had been curled with Dippety-Do and smelled
like sweet flowers. It was held in place by a white headband. She
stroked the white-blonde hair of her Barbie. I imagined the soft,
silken strands between my own fingers, the crisp cotton folds of her
doll's skirt. Drifting in this fantasy, out of body, out of time, I lost
fifteen minutes, easily.

"Faith. Faith!" It was Hope. "Faith, we're at school. Get out."

I pulled back sharply. Fifteen minutes gone, blank, without
memory. I could not remember any of it, not a single tree or building
we'd passed, not a word uttered by anyone, even myself. Had I mumbled something embarrassing? Like my Jill doll's name? I couldn't
imagine not pretending to be someone else, but this total loss of me
was scary. Especially since I was starting so early in the morning, with

the whole day ahead of me in a class full of girls I'd rather be. Slip into Jette's new handsewn dress, run my fingers along the rick rack at her waist. Slip into Carolyn's head, color with her 24 shades of pencils. Or Katy's. Touch those dangling earrings.

I walked down the steps to the elementary rooms and my socks slid down and bunched inside my shoes, their elastic gone. I wished I had Ruth's socks instead. I walked in her feet right past my own desk.

Our third grade class at The American School of Leopoldville (TASOL) in 1964 with teacher Leaster Funk. Front row, l to r: Marc Chaponniere, George Kenny, Harold Esau, Louis Armour, Fred Dirks. Row 2: George Stathis, Ted Bliss, Robert Buccianti, Bruce Reed, Warren Schmidt, Christian Martin. Row 3: Sylvia Brooks, Carolyn Brooks, Scot Hoyt, Jeannette Buller, Kristine Reinheimer, Ruth Faul, Katy Troukias, Faith Eidse, Moonira Merali. (TASOL photo)

9

REBEL TERRITORY

"The months of captivity crystalized us children.
It was as though we became statuettes of perfect little adults,
instead of normal, dependent, growing children."
— BARBARA LOEWEN

Dad paced the barracks porch in worn trousers and knit shirt and jingled the keys in his pocket. Mom walked over to him, her auburn hair copper in the morning light. "What is it?"

"Our mission leaders and theology students are in danger. They could be forced to join the revolution. It's not right to leave them there at a time like this."

Mom's eyes flashed behind her cat-eye tortoise glasses, her high forehead wrinkled. "Why not send messages by radio and keep in touch that way? Why return and risk your own life?"

I agreed with Mom. Why risk his life when we were finally all safe together as a family?

"Oh, I'm not worried about me. I can take care of myself. But what about our students far from home with *Jeunesse* rallying?"

"Aren't you—a white man—a bigger target than our students? Besides won't the students know what to do better than we do? Who really knows where the rebels are and where they'll head next?" She hugged her waist protectively.

Dad paused, studied her, but pushed on, "All I know is it's useless sitting here when I could be driving them home. Besides, all I have to do is make it back to Kamayala. We have enough gas barrels buried in the garden to drive us to safety."

It seemed the more Dad discussed the situation with the other fathers, the greater the need to go until it was stronger than safety or family togetherness. Stronger than life itself.

Dad checked the van's tires, oil and gas levels and loaded blankets, gas cans and tools.

Mom looked over at Mrs. Gerber on the barracks porch. "The men are not handling camp well."

"Not at all." Mrs. Gerber brushed slender fingers through her fine curls. "If Ben leaves, Ellis will want to go, too."

Dan and Becky sat, heads bowed, legs tucked. They'd heard about a priest buried to his neck, head run over by a truck. Joanna, age 4, had hidden on the floorboards when their family fled Nyanga. They were flagged down at a road block and held up by soldiers with long guns. They ordered Ellis out of the car and in one smooth move he grabbed and pocketed the keys. A soldier entered the driver's seat but found no keys only tiny Joanna staring up with frightened eyes. Mr. Gerber later said that, but for the children, the soldiers might have stolen their car and left them beside the road.

––––––––––––––

The next morning after breakfast, our Dad gathered us around him. "It's over 500 miles with bridges out and roads trenched between the Kwilu and Loange Rivers so I won't go that way. I'll drive around *Jeunesse* territory. I may even be able to return the Kajiji students home to Tshikapa through Angola."

Mom nodded and clutched Grace on her hip.

Dad pulled us in and laid a hand on our heads. "I'm entrusting you to God's care now." His voice dropped and he intoned his farewell blessing. "The Lord bless you and keep you, the Lord make his face shine on you...and give you peace."

I kissed him goodbye with chin raised. Maybe he'd be back soon. No need to let in the pain until it ambushed me.

Dad drove out the gate, turned into *Boulevard du Trente Juin* and was swallowed by traffic. One by one, over the next days, the other fathers hugged their families and followed him out of camp "to check on the situation upcountry."

After the dads left, the rules against wandering the compound relaxed, or maybe we'd learned from them to live dangerously. Hope and I scooted past the camp's cement wall where the U.N. projected stupefying Disney movies like "The Swiss Family Robinson," a refugee disaster turned into a designer tree house with doilies, china and carpets.

We ranged past the kitchen and discovered sand dunes outside the hurricane fencing behind the kitchen. Hope stood guard and sent me under the fence, which had been pulled and stretched as a back exit for the kitchen workers. I checked the quality of sand, fine. The height of dune, ten feet. The jump and tumble, straight down and fast.

We weren't officially permitted to leave the camp alone. Armed guerillas could cross from Brazzaville—and did later that summer—upriver at Bolobo. But we begged Mom and she rounded up Grace and Charity and came along. Stifling afternoons once spent exhausted in the barracks were consumed with tumbling down wind-swept dunes until the supper gong clanged.

I don't remember my ninth birthday. What lingers is moms and children lounging on sand dunes as if on a beach. It was perfect for sharing birth stories.

Mom may have told again how she was driven to the Catholic hospital in Kahemba, well into labor on February 19, 1955, in a jarring jeep. "I felt every bump. We interrupted the Belgian doctor's lunch tennis match." It was a wrenching birth with me arriving two weeks early weighing just 5 lbs., 3 oz. A card arrived from Kajiji teachers Orv and Ruby Wiebe, "Congratulations on your little Faith."

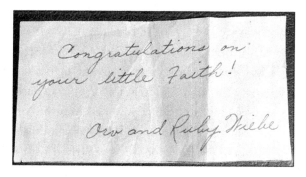

A note from Kajiji teachers, Orv and Ruby Wiebe, after I was born in Kahemba weighing 5 lbs., 3 oz.

Laughter floated over the dunes. Our little sisters romped in the sand.

Several days after my birth, Dad rushed to the hospital from an evangelizing weekend. He kissed Mom, tweaked my ski-jump nose and ran next door to the Bandundu post office to send a telegram—and to receive one. It was black-bordered. Mom's dad, age 56, had died of painful stomach cancer "the same day and, counting back, the same hour Faith was born."

It was such an icy night in Canada, Mom reminded us, that Grandma had to stoke the furnace before daylight. She descended to the basement, knowing she'd have to tell eleven children their father was gone—the three youngest ages eight to ten. *Give me some word just for me,* she whispered. The verse that came was one she shared with me every birthday. Proverbs 3:5 and 6, "Trust in the Lord with all your heart and lean not on your own understanding...."

On the dunes that day, savory scents of chicken and rice wafted over the dunes. Dishes and silverware clattered, tables being set in the U.N. camp dining room.

All of Aunt Edna Gerber's kids were delivered at Mukedi, the first two by Dr. Merle Schwartz. Dan arrived on April 25, 1955, and was left at the hospital when Mrs. Gerber was carried home by stretcher. Uncle Ellis had to fetch him in the front basket of the bicycle. Becky arrived two years later on April 11, 1957, and was carried home with her mom by stretcher. On October 15, 1959, Aunt Edna was driven to the hospital in the literature van, atop books and leaflets. Dr. Elvina Martens told her not to push—to wait while she scrubbed in. Aunt Edna, powerless over the contractions, thought that should be obvious to Dr. Martens who'd just delivered her youngest, Philip, weeks before. Joanna arrived with no one to catch her.

Aunt Edna may have added that Dr. Schwartz and nurse wife Dorothy—who welcomed so much life in Congo—had been given up for dead while sailing to Congo, their ship torpedoed by a German U-boat during World War II. Yet they had been rescued and returned to the U.S., having missed their own memorial service. They then turned around and sailed again for Congo in 1941.

"What about me?" Charity may have asked sifting sand through her fingers.

"Oh yes, Charity, Hope and Grace." Mom would have savored her turn again. "Hope was born April 20, 1953, in Canada—that's three April birthdays we have here. She was six months old when we crossed the Atlantic into 70-foot seas, hurricane force winds. I was afraid we'd lose her overboard. Charity, you weighed ten pounds, *the greatest of us all*," Mom always said.

It was October 28, 1956, at the Kahemba hospital and Charity was so big that the doctor injected Mom with Pitocin to encourage labor. Contractions came so hard and fast that Charity's birth damaged Mom's kidneys. By Christmas week, Mom lay in the hospice

The Kamayala men mixed mortar in a giant mud bowl and added quarried stone to the church arch. (Ben Eidse 1956 photo)

room at the Kahemba hospital. To save her life, the doctor injected her kidneys with anesthesia. He hoped that when the medicine wore off, her kidneys would start working again.

Dad meanwhile read her James 5:16, "Confess your sins... and pray...that you may be healed." Mom couldn't think of any sins. Suddenly Dad could. He sped back to Kamayala where he gathered the workers building the church. "I am so sorry I got angry at you for that crooked wall and cut your meager wages. It was my fault for not supervising better."

The workers were amazed. A white man had never admitted doing wrong, had never apologized to them and never asked their forgiveness. When Dad got back to the hospital, Mom's kidneys were working again. She was advised to leave Congo and never have another baby.

Everyone could see that sunny Grace had arrived safely, though Mom had struggled with high blood pressure during the pregnancy. Grace was born at the Steinbach hospital on November 25, 1961.

Over the dunes, the supper gong clanged. We gathered our shoes and headed back into camp for supper, radiant over our afternoon escape on the dunes that day.

Decades later in Tallahassee, my walking partner, Jean Mauch, would introduce me to her colleague, Myriam Farrar, a fellow nurse anesthetist. Farrar was the daughter of a doctor who served in Kahemba during the mid-fifties. By video chat to Georgia, I was able to thank her and her mother for the late doctor's service in our lives.

I worried when it came time for us to leave the refugee camp. Who would give us food and a place to stay? Who would keep us safe? But I only asked one question aloud. "What if Dad can't find us?"

We had only heard briefly by radio a week after he'd left for Kinshasa. He had a van full of student families from Tshikapa and was in Angola waiting for permission to re-cross into Congo.

"The mission will tell him." Mom pulled me close on the barracks porch. "They're renovating a place for us—a shipworker's dorm purchased from Chanic." Mom stroked my flyaway hair and sang in her melodic Plautdietsch, "*Wüarum düare wan dü bäda kaust?*" (Why worry when you can pray?)

I sang along trying to match the warbling sweetness of Mom's voice. I liked that she didn't try to sugarcoat reality. None of the dads had yet returned but she helped me imagine them alive and whole instead of beaten, cut-up or bleeding to death.

Finally, we moved with the Gerbers to the "old battleship," #5 *Avenue de l'avenir* (Avenue of the Future). The green two story had a ground floor kitchen, dining and living area and second-floor bedrooms divided by metal gunwales with ship-rail balconies. A stench rose from the old latrine downstairs but balconies ran its length, front and back catching river breezes. Across the street, the ancient Congo flowed steadily by.

The "old battleship" Chanic shipworker's dorm became our second refugee home before being converted to a mission boys' dorm. (Painting by Mark Janz, 2022)

Mom's 36th birthday (March 3) and 12th wedding anniversary (March 30) came and went with no word from Dad.

One day Hope led me over the balcony railing and dared me to jump. She tucked her skirt and flew down. "You have to roll forward when you land or you'll hurt your feet." She grimaced but ran round to the back door and up the ship ladder steps.

I climbed over the rail, perched on the very edge of the balcony, looked down into the deep rolling grass ten feet below and plunged—my stomach rushing into my throat. I landed in the moist waves with a slight sting to my bare feet, a tingle in my tummy. The tingle was worth the sting every time.

Our families were still working out the kinks in the old ship, which was purchased to expand the children's dorm on the other end of the block. In the first-floor kitchen, we stored groceries from local stores and cooked our own meals in a balky gas stove. One morning Mrs. Gerber preheated the oven, perhaps to bake a cake for the three kids with April birthdays. She opened the oven door and a blocked gas line ignited, shooting flames into her hair and face. She snuffed her singed eyebrows, hair and face with a towel and covered her red face in butter.

All day she sat on the balcony cooling her blistered face in the river breezes. Mom sat beside her and trimmed her singed hair. Mallets on metal clanged from the shipyard, sirens wailed at lunch and closing time. Workers trudged by on the street below, sunset hovered and sank into the river, and, gradually, Aunt Edna's burn subsided.

Joanna later recalled that their mom listened to the news, perhaps Voice of America, and sewed shifts for her daughters on a treadle sewing machine. They may have been simple, matching shifts cut from the same cloth, perhaps purchased at the nearby stores.

Another day, a slender man greeted us from the street carrying several large paintings—and we invited him in. His dark face glowed while he set up several large canvases around our living room of the fishing village nestled along the riverbank nearby. We admired his deep horizons, colorful brushstrokes and silhouetted fishermen poling canoes toward thatched huts under palm and mango trees. He had captured the natural environment, an ancient way of life and the essential Congoness of Congo. His name was Tambu and he was prolific among Congo's painters. It was hard to choose among his many lush scenes—broad daylights, rosy sunsets and moody nightscapes. We eventually bought paintings for all twenty-four of Mom and Dad's siblings. They became gifts handed down, generation to generation—preserving forever our extended family's involvement in Congo.

We lived a block from the American school, which was next to the shipyard. I studied French and read *Le Petit Prince* in a small brick classroom where Henry Morton Stanley had once slept while overseeing the missionaries' settlement. However, they soon distanced

Tambu painted the fishing village near us in the capital and we bought dozens for our extended family in Canada.

themselves from him due to his harsh treatment of Africans. So excessive were Leopold's taxes on the local people that Chief Ngaliema abandoned the area and moved his entire village across the river to Congo, Brazzaville ("Kinshasa Then and Now," 2016).

Our old ship house was surrounded up and down the shady street by other mission and embassy families in tin-roof brick houses. Sometimes we had sleepovers or played jacks with brown-eyed Leola, our Kajiji neighbor whose family had fled and settled with the Petersons nearby. She was nine, old enough to remember a soldier sticking a gun in her back when she was five and trying to separate her from family during independence wars.

The bouncing ball and falling jacks echoed through our empty rooms.

From our balcony one day, Hope yelped, "Whoo-hoo! There's Dad!" and jumped down.

He was barely visible through the smeared windows of our VW van, slowing and turning into our driveway.

I jumped down, too, and ran to greet him.

The van sputtered into the compound, smoke pouring from its tailpipe. Red clay plastered the wheels and side panels; the engine choked and died.

Dad opened the door and stepped out, trim, whole and alive— our prayers answered.

He reached for Mom and gathered us all in a group hug. "Guess we'll have to rebuild the engine before we return upcountry."

"How was it?" Mom searched his craggy, stubbled face.

"There were bridges out and kilometers of detours." Dad flipped his long dark hair from eyes shiny blue behind thick glasses. "We couldn't get permission from Angola to cross the border to the east so we had to go back the way we came. We tried to cross the Manzala River bridge by laying planks across a washout but it was too unstable. If we had, we would have run into *Jeunesse* on the other side of the Kwilu!"

"Amazing." Mom's broad smile radiated like the noonday sun.

"Instead we drove for Leopoldville along roads that were sometimes just two tracks in the woods. Other places were so sandy they were almost impassable without a four-wheel drive. But the VW was light and the students got out and pushed."

Mom led us into the shady living room, our family intact, together again.

"We were in danger of ambush the whole way. But we sang choruses and felt assured of God's protection."

Mom beamed, hazel eyes sparkling behind glinting glasses.

"When we reached the capital," Dad added, "the mission flew the students home via Air Congo to Tshikapa, high over rebel hold-outs—"

Curly-haired Grace tugged his hands. "Horsey!"

"Yes, horsey!" Charity echoed, though she was already eight with gangly legs.

Dad got down on all fours, neighed and bucked like an old horse and carried them around the cement floor.

With Dad back, we tuned into BBC broadcasts. He had been a radio announcer in graduate school and paced the dining room with his portable radio, adjusting knobs and antenna to cut the static. The *Simbas* had opened headquarters near the Chinese embassy in Burundi on Congo's eastern border.... They had received military weapons and overtaken two-thirds of the country.... U.S. fighter pilots were running covert bombing missions on *Simba* forest camps.

Daily we prayed for our cousins, the Mel Loewens, who were caught in the war while founding a university in Stanleyville. Gerry (Jake), 13, Barbara, 12, and Margaret, 10, were close in age to Hope and me. We had spent time together at their home in Leopoldville and felt close through our grandmas in Steinbach who were sisters. Johnny, 6, and James, 5, were younger and more mischievous and had chased us into hiding in more carefree times. Aunt Elfrieda, always alert and serving others, was pregnant with Lisa and we prayed for their safety.

Later we heard that James and Johnny were playing in their sandbox when several men with AK-47s marched up. One pointed his machine gun at Johnny and demanded his toy dump truck.

Uncle Mel, ever the diplomat, invited the men into his home office. He showed them the wall map and his Canadian passport. Canada was different from America, he said, slipping his wife's American passport into his back pocket. It wasn't as capitalistic; it was more socialist.

One *Simba* noted that Canada was colored pink like the Soviet Union and spared the family. By the end of July, *Simbas* were keeping the Loewens under house arrest and had moved into the Loewen's house and yard, keeping themselves safe and our cousins on edge.

By August 1964, Stanleyville had become headquarters of the *Simbas'* "People's Republic of Congo." But U.S. President Lyndon Johnson refused to meet with the Organization for African Unity (OAU) to broker peace or consider the *Simbas'* demands against a corrupt Congolese government. Nor would the American Embassy risk any hostage-freeing until Johnson's reelection was assured. The Bay of Tonka incident in Vietnam was bad enough. From July until Johnson's landslide victory in November 1964, the U.S. blocked or delayed every attempt by Congo's leaders to free Stanleyville (Kelly, p. 125ff).

The summer of 1964, we moved back to Kamayala where conflicts had ended when the *Jeunesse* were defeated fifteen miles away at Tshifwameso. To save precious fuel, we sat around lamplight rather than running the electric generator to eat supper, read and write letters.

"We have to work ourselves out of a job." Dad passed a plate of *Tata* Michel's fresh buns. "The Congolese want to run their own country, with their own pastors, teachers and nurses." Dad had returned from bicycling to surrounding villages with student pastors and teachers.

"And they have asked us to walk alongside." Mom handed me a platter of fresh tomatoes. "That may take a while but we are committed to achieving it." She had returned from training interns at the clinic and leprosarium.

After supper we played Scrabble and Chinese Checkers in the flickering lantern light until bedtime.

At the orphanage across the street, there was a new girl my age, Hélène. Her dark eyes sparkled, her face and form were taller and narrower than Marie's. Perhaps she was from tribes further East. But like Marie, she had a bubbly, infectious laugh and trim, close-cropped hair. I didn't know if she was a survivor of the revolution but she had arrived without family and became my *ndoyi*. She knew all the clapping games and her callused hands met mine, ringing through the mission. All summer we clapped until we had the chants, partner claps, self-claps and hand flips down. We created a special handshake that was our secret code whenever we met or parted—shake, clap, snap—laugh.

Back from the river, our chores done until supper preparations, we clapped in the sandy, palm-lined avenue and sang the afternoon away.

> *Mande, Mande, ndoyi, Mande, Mande.*
> Mande, my friend, Mande.
> *Mande, obuti mwana ya kala-e, Mande.*
> Mande, you gave birth to a child a long time ago, Mande.
> *Mande, kisalu kenyi sukumbe, Mande.*
> Mande, the work is no fun, Mande.
> *Nakututa, nakulamba, mono moshi-e, Mande.*
> I pound and I cook by myself, Mande.

- Translated by Charity Schellenberg

In other words, "My friend, ever since you had your baby, I am left to do the tiresome work by myself." It was a lament, but Hélène taught me to lean into the syncopation, move with the beat. When we were warmed up, we opened our partner-clapping to circle clapping, letting in Hope and Marie, Charity and Sala, Grace and Lumbu. Like the women of the village we paired off, or joined together, a common sisterhood.

The work was constant but it lightened our moods to sing and clap about it, turning it into play. Still, it pointed to the days when we'd need each other just to get through the hoeing, washing, water carrying, pounding, meal making and childcare. And when we didn't have each other, we'd need the muscle memory of rhythm and song just to get through the drudgery by ourselves.

In early September 1964, MAF's single-prop Cessna 180 circled over the station, signaling its arrival at Kahemba airstrip to take Hope and me to the Mennonite mission hostel for school in the capital. We had adapted "Red Sails in the Sunset" to "White Wings in the Sunrise...we dread to see you" as our parting anthem.

Yet I didn't cry when we piled into the van with our *ndoyis* and raced to the airstrip, didn't wipe my eyes when we loaded our bags into the plane's cargo hold. I couldn't permit sadness or any admission of it. I knew what was expected of me—a smooth, tearless farewell.

I hugged and kissed Mom and Dad goodbye, a hard, quick hug, a brushing of soft cheeks. I traded a special handshake with Hélène, hugged my little sisters Grace and Charity a moment and let go.

There was not even a hint of tears or a lump to swallow when I buckled in the middle row beside Hope. Leola, onboard from Kajiji, was already in the favored front passenger seat and flashed us her gleaming smile.

The plane shivered, rattled and revved its engines spraying dust. Outside Charity shielded Grace's eyes with a corner of her skirt and waved. The plane raced fast as a sports car down the bumpy dirt runway and all I felt were butterflies. I looked ahead as we'd been taught, not back. The savanna filled the windscreen and then there was only blue sky with puffs of cloud here and there and the steady hum of the engine.

I may have been grinning when I turned to look at Hope, her

neck craned backward, both hands on the window sill. Only then did I realize she was crying. Buckets.

Somewhere, sometime I'd known the agony of leaving. Perhaps buried in the excitement of the TWA flight from Canada, or the adrenaline rush of leaving Mukedi. I tried to blink out a tear or two. Nothing. I had pushed them down so deep, all I could feel was a soaring from the pit of my stomach that rose up and up and filled the cabin.

10

RIVERBED CITY

When we arrived at the Mennonite hostel in lower Leopold-ville, all the windows were screened and barred—no glass. The afternoon heat seeped in like a hot, wet breath. It would never get cool enough in this riverbed city to shiver in the tub like we did on the high plateau at Kamayala.

Someone had organized the girls' dorm into a grade school side and junior high and high school side for students arriving from the scattered stations of our mission. In the "little girls" bathroom, I plunked my toothbrush into a plastic cup labeled "Faith." There were cups for Vangie, Becky and Leola, too—some I had met and played with—others I barely knew yet.

I shared a room with Leola and was captivated by her dark eyes and short, curly hair. She was a fifth grader, already in her second year at the hostel, and she sewed her own clothes.

"You need to lower your hem," a hostel parent scolded in the hallway. "I just hemmed this with my mom," she retorted and shot me a look. It was our mom who had proposed the new rule and I ducked, knowing that would win me no popularity awards. Leola was soon out reconnecting with other kids, unconcerned about un-packing, organizing and settling in.

Barred windows threw a stark pattern over a wooden table and two chairs. In the empty closet, I hung my four knee-length dresses—three for weekdays, one for Sunday. They were lightly worn hand-me-downs from Hope who always changed into play clothes

96

before pounding down dirt paths, shimmying up rough trees or plunging through elephant grass.

I stepped back and considered which to wear the first day of grade four. The plaid was dressier, the flowered shift more comfortable. It was new for me to debate myself like this, to talk with myself almost audibly in my own head. Now that I was nine and in charge of me, I would spend hours holding court with myself.

I made mental lists to stop my looping thoughts. What I would need for the first day of school (pencil, ruler, notebook), what I had to do before dinner (unpack, make bed, wash hands), what I had to do before school on Monday (make bed, dust, sweep). The cleaning duties posted on a chart by the door were checked off by a dorm parent after we left for school. If we didn't get a single "demerit," bad mark, we would get candy on Friday night after supper.

I thought that might be hard to do, keep a clean room for a whole week. I struggled against worry to stay happy. How would I get everything done every day before school? But this sadness wasn't right. I wasn't supposed to get upset or "down-hearted," as Dad always said. Yet during those first days, I struggled with concern over neatness and perfection.

We were to dust our rooms daily, shake the rag outside on the step, fold it and place it back on the shelf. Rags were ripped-up threadbare towels that didn't fold into perfect squares. I tried it and ran back to the linen shelf five times to refold a crooked rag—then broke into a prickly sweat, afraid I was going insane.

I had to "keep on the sunny side," as Dad said, but I didn't always know how. Maybe by thinking of others? I spread my sheets on the bottom bunk as a courtesy to Leola who might want the top. Also, it made me feel better, safer, more secure to be enclosed on the bottom, like snuggling into a warm, dry cave. So maybe I was being selfish, after all?

I laid my underwear and socks in the second bureau drawer, mindful not to take the top. It was only the first day but already I was thinking of the group—burying the need to know myself.

True, Mom had marked my initials, F.E., with indelible ink on each item. Yet we had to throw them into a huge laundry basket where they'd get mixed in the wash. It seemed crucial that they all return to me to lie neatly and separately in my drawer again, no matter how scrambled they got in the alphabet soup of F.E.-L.F.-E.C-B.Z.

The laundry schedule posted in the kitchen divided ten girls into teams to fold linens on Mondays, boys' wash Tuesdays, girls' wash Thursdays. I would have yet more work to do, but I didn't question why the girls had to fold the boys' laundry. It would be years before any of us thought to ask, and years beyond that before the rule changed to fold-your-own. Instead we girls would circle the folding table, reaching, flipping, stroking—like clapping under palms at Kamayala.

I was shoving flat sheet corners under my mattress when Aunt Jenny Bertsche walked in (though others say she came later when her daughter Linda got sick). She had hosted us at their family home in Kandale before it burned. Their work had been destroyed, yet her face remained soft, her eyes kind.

"Oh you don't know how to square the corners?" She had lost everything—dishes, sheets, pillowcases—yet she was here to help me. She stroked a dangling sheet corner, folded and tucked it, as though she were wrapping a gift.

She helped spread and tuck the top sheet and quilt, too. How could I tell her I'd never made a bed properly with top and bottom sheets? Mom sometimes made "hospital corners"—after all she was a nurse. But she let us be children and just shove sheets under mattresses, straighten our blankets, and put on our own pillowcases—especially when they came off in pillow fights.

I pushed my suitcase under the bed and sat stiffly on the straightened quilt. It was tucked in tightly at the toes. In my dreams my legs often went numb just when I needed to run. Now they'd be bound, too.

The Bertsches had written a letter to church women in Ohio requesting sponsors for us children. "Children are separated from the love of family nine months of the year but there are benefits, too. They learn to care for themselves." So compelling was the letter, that these women had sent fresh towels, sheets, and handmade quilts for the 1964-65 school year. They also sent Tootsie Rolls and Mars Bars for Friday after supper if we got no demerits.

One of our favorite quilts was appliqued with Holly Hobbies. At first we had to circulate them so everyone had a chance to sleep under their favorites. But eventually Leola got that quilt more than anyone else. She loved to lie beneath it, thinking about the women who cared enough to spend the time making something special for us missionary kids.

———————

"Koko." A boy's voice sounded at the door. It was Timmy with a pack of cards here with his parents to help us settle in. He'd played checkers with us at Kandale before it burned and the missionaries had held a toy drive for him after Christmas.

I hesitated. I had never played cards before and thought it was a sin.

"This is Rook. It's okay." He shuffled and divided cards and taught me how to build a hand, remember suits and count cards played.

The dinner gong clanged through the compound like a decree. We put down our cards and Tim put them away. "You did good for your first time."

I felt encouraged when Leola joined us in her crisp new hand-sewn dress and we crossed the lot to the old battleship. Near the garage, two German shepherds, chained to a dog line, sat up and wagged thick tails.

"Hi, doggie." I dropped to my knees in the dirt beside the first one. "Lonely are you? No one to pet you?" His thick tail thumped the ground. I wrapped my arms around his neck and burrowed into his scruff. A place of comfort.

That is, until two men passed in the street. Then a low rumble started deep in his throat. The dog knocked me off my knees and lunged along his chain at them.

"Guard dogs—not pets." Leola's thick dark curls bounced when she laughed. "They have German names, Schnitzle and Schnetke. That's so passersby will have trouble saying their names and won't tease them."

That didn't seem right. Why would missionaries have guard dogs to chase away neighbors? Also, there was a padlocked gate and fence to cage us in.

For my sister and me there was about to be another shock. Boys—ten instant "brothers." When we arrived at the old battleship dining room there were little ones my age, big boys in high school and more in-between. The big ones seemed loud and rough and sure of themselves.

We gawked when they raised their legs like dogs to climb into long benches around dining tables while we tucked our skirts and slid in from one end or the other. Hope had said we hated boys, and I believed her since we hardly knew any yet.

One of them, Ricky Thorn, mimed the boys' awkward bench-sitting contortions. He caught the eyes of us younger kids and cranked an invisible shaft to jerk his joints and limbs into a rigid sitting position—just when we bowed for prayer. We laughed out loud—and were silenced with a frown from the dorm parent. Ricky had arrived from a different mission and seemed a lot more fun than we serious Mennonites.

The other boys hunched over their plates and spread their elbows as if protecting their food. Yet if I so much as lit my elbows on the table they jumped at me. The first time, I thought I'd touched a hot element.

"Uh-uh!" A boy scolded around a mouthful of bread. "Faith, Faith, strong and able, get your elbows off the table."

I had never heard such nonsense before, but I quickly tucked my elbows against my sides.

"I caught you!" The boy took another bite of bread. "Now you have to do k.p. for me."

Ugh, k.p., kitchen patrol. It meant I had to wash and dry dishes out of turn and do extra for *him.*

After supper I was handed a dish towel and directed to the sticky hot wash tubs the last free hour before sunset, drying two dozen bowls, cups, forks, knives and spoons until the towel was drenched.

Over the next few days, I discovered that the boys on k.p. duty squirmed out by catching the girls breaking some small table rule. But if a girl on k.p. duty ever mentioned some gross violation by a boy—talking with his mouth full—she got shouted down as "unfair" until she blushed for mentioning it. Also the couple in charge, "Uncle" Hector and "Aunt" Clara seemed to back the boys.

The rule about not taking the last cookie without asking got twisted by the big boys, too. "Does anyone want this cookie more than I do?" Everyone laughed. As a "little girl," I was learning to suppress my needs while the boys were learning to express theirs.

Even when it came to the Coke we got once a week, the girls quickly gave up their half-tasted bottles to the boys who seemed to have a deadly thirst. I tried not to drink too much, just a few tangy swallows before offering it up. The boy who got my Coke swung it high and crowed, "Look how much Faith left me." It made me momentarily visible but I watched with a dry throat while he guzzled it down.

One of the big boys had brought a record player and rock'n'roll albums from the States. We sneaked under the balcony and listened to the Beatles. "I wanna hold your ha-a-a-and." And though I had jumped from that very balcony a few months before, I could not

imagine speaking to such a big person. If he came out, we little kids
scuttled away.

At dinner, I chewed dry bread and glanced at the bowl of home-
ground peanut butter parked near him, his shoulders hunched, his
arms stretched around his bowl. I could not find a voice to ask for the
peanut butter until I had rehearsed silently several times.

"Please pass the peanut butter." My voice sounded strained
even to myself.

"What? Speak up."

It was harder to say it again. If I could hear the right volume
in my head and say it clearly the first time, I didn't have to repeat
myself. So I rehearsed each word and inflection. "Please." They could
hold out 'til girls said the "magic word" though they themselves rou-
tinely forgot it.

A boy my age, Carl, had only brothers. He seemed just as
stumped about girls as I was about boys. One night, hiding at "sardines," we eluded the seeker by sneaking together from one hiding
place to another until he crushed me against the rough bark of a
mango tree. I stopped breathing. I had nothing to say, had not rehearsed this. He had no words either. He just crouched against me
watching for the seeker. Perhaps Carl rehearsed action the way I rehearsed words.

Days passed and Carl got bolder—walked right up in broad
daylight, with the big boys standing around—and threw an arm over
my shoulder. I said nothing, tried to act natural and in control, a rising
heat in my cheeks. His older brother and the other big boys, exchanged
secret grins, scraped their feet in the sand and laughed out loud.

Carl removed his arm.

———————

At the American school, classes filled to overflowing. Chairs
for extra children lined classrooms and four-square and volleyball

courts filled with players. The auditorium was partitioned for classes that disbanded for general assemblies. American embassy staff met with parents about building a new school up on the hill near the president's mansion. It would serve an expected 800 students, kindergarten to grade twelve. The flow came from the expanding U.S. military base in Leopoldville and international companies piling in.

Also, missionaries who once worked upcountry noticed that the capital had become "the new population center" and were moving theology schools and planting churches in the capital. Thousands of people poured in, looking for jobs, building cardboard lean-tos onto tin lean-tos onto relatives' concrete block houses.

Outside the hostel compound, shipyard workers passed each morning to assemble jig-sawed U.S. gunboats for the continuing *Simba* clash in the east. (Kelly, p. 164) Each carried a lunch baguette and supported a whole clan of displaced villagers.

At school, I shared a desk with a marine kid who wore American flag tee-shirts. Sometimes it felt like this school was more firmly American than any school in the U.S. where Dad had attended Goshen College and Wheaton Graduate School.

I squirmed at talk of limiting enrollment to sixty percent Americans and tried to blend in. I honored the American Civil War with my classmates and blinked misty eyes over, "Tenting Tonight," as though the old battleground were my own. "We are tired of the war on the old campground, many are lying near, some are dead and some are dying, many are in tears."

Even at the hostel where most of us were from the same mission, Hope and I were teased for our Canadian "aboot," "garawje" or "zed." Hope refused to change and chanted, "Canada-is-better-than-America."

Four boys countered at once. "We've got a bigger army."

"Better T.V."

"More people."

"Summer!"

Hope tipped up her delicate chin. "Canadians aren't as mean." "Canadians are stronger." Another Canadian kid piped up. "Smell isn't everything." Witty Loren Roth said, shuffling and grinning. We all laughed, but I could see how Hope's protests made it harder for her to fit in. I tried even harder to blend with the group. I tried to say "abouwt" and "zee." All my trying failed, though, when I was defeated in the class spelling bee for "colour." The teacher was kind enough to say it was Canadian but made me sit down anyway before I confused everyone with "aeroplane" or "cheque."

My room after school was a warm humid cell behind twisted window bars. I sweated over American spelling and long division since we had to show all our work. Mom had taught me all the short-cuts and I did so much math in my head that I skipped baby steps and had to erase and add them until I'd erased a hole in the page. The figures blurred, the pencil shook. It wasn't right to be so sad. I dared not tell anyone.

When mid-quarter marks came back I had a C in math and "Aunt" Nettie, the girls' dorm parent, asked to check my work. If she found a mistake, she asked, "Why didn't you see that?"

I didn't know. I usually got A's and had never scored worse than a B before. At night, after lights out, I sometimes allowed a small trickle of tears to soak my pillow. But then I had to toss quietly to find a dry spot, or turn the pillow over, all without waking my roommate. It felt terrible to feel so bad so I vowed to stop feeling and whispered a prayer for help to my mother-father god.

Aunt Nettie taught us to knit later that year. At first it was just simple squares that could be folded on the diagonal and stitched into pointy-toed triangle elf slippers. They made great Christmas gifts for our parents.

But while Aunt Nettie was showing me how to cast off, she noticed my writing callus. "No boy will want to hold your hand."

I was puzzled at why that should bother me. Still, she set down the needles and seated me at the central table—with all the girls gawking—to practice holding my pencil with a three-finger-tipped grip.

At recess, I gravitated towards the other non-Americans —Angelique from France and Asifa from Pakistan, who hung out under the steps. Sometimes I felt so different next to my buzzcut seatmate that I slid to the seat edge, tuned out and curled up inside.

The teacher called me up at recess. "Is something wrong?"

"I don't know. Maybe I'm sick?"

The teacher gave me a new seat next to Patience from Nigeria. "Patience can help you with math and you can help her with reading." She smiled brightly.

We put our heads together, tight black curls against thin pale strands, and worked the problems, until I realized Patience was helping me feel at home. Her lilting voice, her ease with being the only African in class, the way she rushed out—laughing, at recess—all melted anxiety.

————————

Upcountry, the military tightened around *Jeunesse* who controlled Mukedi and Kandale between the Kwilu and Loange Rivers. The *Jeunesse* traveled barefoot and bare-chested, carried handmade weapons and chanted "*meya, meya*" (water, water) to turn bullets to water. CIA rockets and machine guns felled hundreds of *Jeunesse* marching on Gungu, Idiofa and Kikwit. International Red Cross representatives found too many bodies to bury, so they piled them up, doused them with gasoline and set them on fire (Bertsche 1998, p. 136).

————————

Sunday evenings we gathered with other mission families for picnics on the grounds of Sims Chapel, the oldest permanent building in Leopoldville. While the sun set over Ngaliema Bay and bats flew from nearby attics, we heard about *Simba* hostage takings and slayings.

Dr. Helen Roseveare was captured, brutally beaten and raped on October 29, 1964. Feeling God had failed her, she heard instead, "These are not your sufferings. They're Mine." She wrote, "God never uses a person greatly until he has wounded him deeply. The privilege He offers you is greater than the price you have to pay" (Taylor).

In Stanleyville, our Loewen cousins were still hostages under house arrest by *Simbas*. Gerry, 13, and Uncle Mel sneaked around, eluded their captors and hid valuables in their attic. We longed for their rescue but did not know how we could help or when that would happen.

Two Mennonite PAX men, Gene Bergman and Jon Snyder, who worked with the Loewens had been taken by *Simbas* to a hotel and kept under guard. PAX was an alternative service program of the Mennonite Central Committee (MCC) relief service that started when the U.S. imposed a draft for the Korean War and continued through the Vietnam War.

On November 18, Bergman and Snyder were driven, along with U.S. Consul Michael Hoyt (our classmate's father), four of his staff and Dr. Paul Carlson to be executed at the Lumumba monument. The men were lined up amid boisterous crowds shouting for "meat." That is, until *Simba* General Olenga parted the crowd. He argued with the *Simba* in charge, knocked him to the ground and ordered the men released (Bertsche 1998, p. 141).

American Thanksgiving, November 26, 1964, approached and we hostel girls requested construction paper and scissors to decorate for a special dinner. We cut dozens of orange, yellow and red maple and oak leaves. Though there were none like them on the landscape, we patterned them from the *Childcraft Encyclopedia.* We would not be going home for the holiday, and did not yet know all we would be thankful for.

On Monday, November 24, American cargo planes dropped 320 Belgian para-commandos at the Stanleyville airport, but a plane load of armored jeeps needed to rush them to the hostages in center city had been delayed. Without vehicles, the paratroopers had to run two miles into the city. A column of mercenaries had been delayed in their ground approach from the East and, when paratroopers took the control tower, the phone rang. It was the hostages downtown calling the paratroopers to hurry. The *Simbas* had started the executions. Two-hundred-fifty hostages were lined up in the streets and twenty-seven killed. One of them was Dr. Carlson who was climbing a verandah to safety (Kelly, p. 147). He would be featured in the *Reader's Digest* and on the cover of *Life* and *Time* magazines.

The morning of the Stanleyville rescue, American mercenaries drove to my cousins' house and Kilometer 8 to rescue several missionary families. But across the river, twenty-eight missionaries were murdered, including nuns and priests.

Uncle Mel appeared on TV to thank the commandos and add that he hoped his wife would have a safe delivery. Years later, when I visited the Loewens in Maryland, Uncle Mel found it hard to tell me about their rescue. The mercenaries had told him to keep his head down in the jeep while they fired a continual barrage into the frantic crowds. He was haunted by dozens of Congolese—women and children—running to the rescue jeeps, shouting, *"Nos sauveurs!"* (Our saviors!), only to be cut down.

At the American school, an assembly was called to receive the survivors of the Stanleyville massacre before their midnight flight to the U.S., courtesy of Pan Am. Some of them still seemed dazed and

The Mel Loewen family a year after being freed from the Simbas, *Christmas 1965 (l to r): baby Lisa, Elfrieda, Gerry, James, Johnny, Mel, Margaret, Barbara.*

shell-shocked. They told stories of dodging bullets, scaling walls and jumping high power lines.

Ken and Paul McMillan, Canadian missionary kids who'd been rescued from Kilometer 8, were shot in the face and arm. Their father had been executed by *Simbas*, yet the McMillans sang for us, "God leads his dear children along":

> *Some through the water, some through the flood,*
> *Some through the fire, but all through the blood;*
> *Some through great sorrow, but God gives a song,*
> *In the night season and all the day long* (Young 1903).

My throat ached with unswallowed tears. The piercing lament seemed the only way to make sense of events so severe. Their hymn became our searing survival anthem, sung at gatherings of Congo missionary kids for decades.

Christmas vacation 1964 arrived and our Grandma Reimer joined us from Steinbach, Manitoba, to spend five months at Kamayala. The only white on the landscape streamed from a tropical moon and glinted off the aluminum rooftops of the mission or landed with wings on our front lawn. Migrating snowy white egrets gathered each morning under our green *fungu* tree to eat its purple fruit.

About that time, a boy my age ran away from the mission orphanage. A white patch had appeared on the back of his shoulder. He couldn't see it but the other kids pointed and jeered. He had raced the mile to his mother's home at the leprosarium and my mom did not send him back. She started him on sulfone medicine instead.

Grace, age 3, wearing another new dress from Grandma. When we couldn't visit Grandma, she came to us in December 1964—soon after Jeunesse were routed. (Ben Eidse photo)

Grandma had brought colorful quilts for the patients for Christmas. They had been handsewn by her friends in Canada and the boy smiled to receive one for himself.

Grandma also held sewing classes on the back porch and women and girls flocked from the village to learn new shortcuts. They received cloth, needles and thread and, in turn, taught Grandma a few words and phrases in Chokwe.

During rest hour in our bedroom, Grandma taught us the tenor descant of her favorite German chorus, "*Gott ist die Liebe*" ("God's Love Eternal"). We sang it with such excruciating harmony, as only sisters can do, that our parents eventually toured us as the four sisters who sang in five languages— English, French, German, Kituba and Kipende.

For Christmas, Grandma also sewed Charity and me identical shifts with ruffled hems. Grandma's feet blurred on a treadle Singer machine in Mom's bedroom. It was a machine Grandma knew from childhood, when she'd been kept home in grade four—crying and pleading to join her friends in class. Her tireless industry was needed to help her mother, Katherina Penner Friesen, run a boarding house in Steinbach.

The only problem with the dresses, Grandma said, when Charity and I tried them on, was that they looked identical. Charity, twenty months younger, had caught up and was passing me in height. Grandma had to add ruffles to my bodice so we could tell them apart.

Charity was tall for her age, but barely eight to my almost ten. She still soaked up all the loving and hugging from parents and grandparents I had steeled myself against since moving to the hostel and becoming a visitor at home. I was looking for love and acceptance elsewhere—from girls and boys my age at school.

"Boy crazy," Hope called me. She saw my constant hair-combing as somehow false, a betrayal of our sisterhood. It was disloyal to her and Mom because their love didn't require fake beauty or wasted

Grace helped Grandma distribute handmade quilts for Christmas, one especially for the new boy at the leprosarium. (Ben Eidse photo)

Grandma Reimer joined us in Kamayala from December 1964 to April 1965. Charity was 8 and passing me in height but still loved leaning-in and holding hands. Dad, 36, Hope, 11, and me, 9, stand unattached. Mom, 36, holds Grace, age 3. (Ben Eidse photo)

emotions of fear and worry. Unlike me, Hope never wanted to marry. She had never been "a cuddler" like I had at five pounds, Dad said, but held her back straight, head high from infancy.

———————

After the fall of Stanleyville, President Kasa-Vubu's shiny black motorcade glided through our neighborhood of Kintambo, blue flags flying from polished Mercedes. America had backed him against the *Simbas* and he had plans for reelection. He dismissed popular Prime Minister Tshombe and tried to patch up relations with other African leaders in the OAU, declaring that he'd get rid of foreign mercenaries. This "leftward drift" perceived by American Ambassador G. Godley, caused the CIA to encourage Mobutu's self-selection as eventual president (Kelly, p. 167).

11

UNDER THE WATERFALL

During the September 1965 school year, my classmate Patience was gone and an American flag stood at the front of the room. Non-Americans had to get special permission to attend. Asifa, Angelique, and myself were all expected to pledge allegiance to a flag that was not our own. "One nation, under God, *invisible*." We were the invisible, our nations brushed aside, unseen.

We did this every day until Teddy returned from England. He refused to pledge anything to America. Our teacher, Miss Celia Gerber from Ohio, paused. "At least rise in respect." This was, after all, an over-crowded American government school.

Around the room hands went up. "May I be excused? May I? Me, too?"

"Me, too?" I finally asked.

"Where are you from?" Miss Gerber seemed surprised.

"Canada." I felt almost disloyal making the distinction. We were neighbors, allies, tuned in to "Dick Tracy" and "Donald Duck." Even my African friends didn't separate the two; Canada, America, it was all *putu* (far-off land). Canadian kids still sang, "God Save the Queen." I was used to honoring more powerful nations. Did I have the right to resist a loyalty pledge to the U.S.?

"Well, all right." Miss Gerber nodded. "But stand at attention."

The chant went on, thinner, quieter, and even then not all the chanters were American. The others, perhaps feeling vulnerable like I did, continued trying to blend in.

At school, one of the grade six teachers was the musical Helen Boldt from British Columbia, Canada, who taught us hits from a new musical movie, "The Sound of Music." My spirit soared with her lilting voice like a bird winging over hills and babbling brooks. Singing along with her, soothed my musical ear and transported me to the snow-capped Alps of Switzerland where we had picnicked with our Peters cousins. Though many of us had not seen the movie and did not know its dark Nazi backstory, we could sing "Doe a Deer" and "Edelweiss" like the von Trapps.

After I'd declared myself Canadian, the American girls stopped inviting me to their slumber parties. Peter, whom the teacher had seated with me—since I was so quiet, and he so rowdy—brought rubber bands to class and *flitzed* me under the desk until my thighs turned red. Or he dug his long nails into my bare leg leaving cuts and bruises. I was too ashamed to tell anyone.

When I raised my hand to answer a question, Peter thought I would tell on him. He didn't know how sick I felt inside, how much I needed to answer questions to get the teacher's approval. He leaned close and whispered, "I'll pinch 'til it bleeds."

Charity had joined Hope and me at the hostel for grade four and roomed with Joanne Janz, daughter of another family from Steinbach. They were mission representatives and Joanne got regular care packages from home thanks to the mission's frequent flights to Tshikapa. Plus, Joanne's big brothers, Larry and Mark, came every night to tuck her in. Charity sometimes felt left out but was unaware of her unconscious coping effort.

One day, Aunt Nettie announced that she'd caught Charity sucking her thumb in her sleep. Charity felt blindsided and publicly shamed. She didn't even know she still sucked her thumb. The reprimand was almost more than she could bear, especially since she already felt so sidelined.

Each week, I dreaded our piano teacher's footfall at the door and the squeak-clap of its tight spring. While I played, he joined me on the bench, put his arm around me, repositioned my hands and stroked my fingers in a sticky way with large hairy hands.

His touch scalded long after he was gone so that it constricted my throat. I never wanted to see him again, didn't want to be in the same room with him. Yet his rule was that no one was to interrupt or even cross the living room while lessons were in session. We girls deliberately broke it. Every ten or fifteen minutes, one of us walked through to keep the teacher from moving too close, reaching too far. When that didn't seem to work, Hope, especially, lingered at the bookcase.

I wanted to stop the lessons, but Mom and Dad were 500 kilometers away, and there were no telephone lines, no buses to catch, barely any flights that far from the capital. There were only commercial trucks that took weeks on deteriorating roads. There were only the letters we wrote each Sunday as meal tickets, proofread and edited for spelling and complaints. I stopped writing my true feelings. I stopped knowing them.

One day I became so upset when the piano teacher tromped up the steps that I refused to take my lesson. Aunt Nettie asked me what was wrong.

"It's icky—the way he touches me."

She pulled back, eyes icy behind her glasses. "But he's getting married—it will solve everything. You could ruin that for him."

I had to let him touch me so I wouldn't ruin *his* life? When my turn came again hot tears scalded my face and I could not leave my room.

Aunt Nettie urged me on. "You should take your lesson anyway. Besides your mom and dad already paid for them."

If I had to take every lesson they had paid for, I would rather die. I kept crying and couldn't stop. Hope tried to calm me down, said she dreaded the way he touched her, too. She asked Aunt Nettie to please tell my parents on the next radio broadcast that I wanted to stop. I tried to calm down enough to slip into the schedule when Hope or Leola had finished. But when it came to leaving my room, I started crying again until the room spun out of control and was drained of oxygen. For an hour I wept until I had upset the entire lesson schedule. Finally, still sniffling, I was sent to take my lesson anyway.

But why had I been sent at all when I protested so hard? Leola had received an escort to afternoon French classes when she complained about African men whistling at her on the river road. Why were some of us not protected better from the men in our own community? When I heard, years later, of other children's sufferings, I wished there had been some adult listening and acting for us children all along, someone who would have acknowledged our feelings and shielded us better.

In January, we had a new piano teacher, Wanda Kroeker. She was a slim woman with curly brown hair and kind eyes, the mother of our classmates. She gave me a recital piece, "Country Garden," but puzzled over my slow progress and said I needed to practice more. I took the music home to memorize over Easter week and played it so often that Charity sat down one day and played it through entirely by ear. I realized that she had easily surpassed me—without training or lessons.

Our recital was in the school auditorium with a small audience of parents, teachers and friends. I climbed the stage steps, curtsied and sat down at the keyboard. I played the introduction and then entered a black tunnel. My hands moved automatically over the ivories but my brain was a complete blank. Everyone clapped politely as though something had gone wrong. When I asked my teacher, she said I'd only played the introduction and conclusion—that I had left out the entire middle of the song.

———————

At school, we had a substitute teacher who spoke sternly and gave us math tests. She permitted no talking, no hands raised. I couldn't help it, I had to go to the bathroom. But no matter how I waved my hand and pleaded with my eyes, she wouldn't call on me. Finally I could hold it no longer. It trickled down my legs and puddled under the bench.

"Eww." Peter scooted away.

"What's the problem?" The teacher seemed puzzled.

I rehearsed the words before I spoke, the right volume and tone. "I think some water spilled."

"Where did it come from?"

I pointed to our labeled water tumblers, upside down on the shelf beside me.

The rest of the class stood and craned to see. The boy behind me held his nose. "She peed her pants."

"No. Uh-uh." Some other kids protected me.

The teacher puzzled over the spilled water until the recess bell. I waited for the others to leave so no one would see the dark patch on my skirt. Then I stood and inched into the sunlight outside to dry.

———————

There were places of shelter during those first years at the hostel. On Saturdays we went swimming at the Funa Club or to the Little Falls on the Lukaya River just south of the city. There, a brown river dropped a meter over a rocky ledge and frothed up white and bubbly beneath. I swam around the pounding water and came up under the falls, where I climbed a mossy rock and stood behind a translucent sheet of water. It was my own private cave, warm, humid and soft under foot. Through the veiled curtain, soft bright shapes drifted where hard-edged people had moved before.

At the hostel, there was the dog's scruff, rich and deep, to burrow in; the long sweep of the tire swing, its dip and twirl to soothe and excite me; the "torn heart hedge" where I could pick heart-shaped leaves, tear them apart and hold them together—whole again. There was the garage roof, flooded with hot light, where I climbed to read the Psalms. "He will cover you with his pinions, and under his wings you will find refuge." I could jump down for a satisfying tummy tingle. There was my pillow to lean into, like Dad's muscled shoulder and Mom's soft cheek.

In the girls' dorm, Aunt Nettie had progressed to teaching us purling and sophisticated slipper patterns. Children from other missions came to take lessons with us. Leola and Linda were experts, so

On weekends, we dove and swam at Les Petites Chutes de la Lukaya (Little Falls of the Lukaya River) south of Kinshasa. (Dr. Wayne Meyers 1969-70 photo)

advanced they were making sweaters for their mothers for Christmas. Besides, Linda was quarantined with hepatitis so it was nice Leola could spend time in her room—at a safe distance.

The ache of my accident at school lingered. At night I lay awake in the close and holy darkness and begged only for myself. "Forgive me. Make me good, so I can go to heaven." I would buy presents to win back the American girls. The local stores at Kintambo were just two blocks away across the boulevard, but I couldn't go by myself. It wasn't safe being a white girl alone in the *cite* (city), the hostel parents said. We had to go in pairs, little girls with big girls and big girls with each other.

I found Mary Henk, a round, bubbly tenth grader. We slipped money in our pockets—purses begged to be snatched—and slapped out the screen door to the dirt road that curved under mango trees to the boulevard. We waited at the Gulf station for a break in speeding traffic and crossed quickly.

On the other side, bar-windowed shops lined the street and, from their shadows, men made kissing sounds at us. This was the polite way of calling girls but it made my neck prickle. Congolese women at street corners sold bread, soap, matches, anything for a few *makuta*. We called *"Mbote"* (hello) to them but ignored the men's calls, though I felt rude doing so. Upcountry we'd at least say *"Moyo!"* (Life!) We'd shake hands, ask if everyone got up well. But here we didn't know names and had planks to walk for our easy lives.

The stores were cool and shaded inside. Multi-colored *batiks* hung ceiling to floor patterned in drums, flowers, vines and birds. I didn't have money for wax-print cloth and looked instead at pen knives, accordion wallets, and candy. Finally I selected a box of Chicklets. How simple it would be to share these American treats and win my friends back.

Back at the boulevard, we waited for a break in the cars. Behind us, a group of tall, thin men descended and trapped us at the curb. One of them walked right up behind Mary, grabbed her wrist and tried to pull her away. She struggled. He gripped harder. I pulled uselessly on Mary's other wrist, lessons of turning the other cheek and loving your enemy ringing in my ears.

He bent her wrist and clutched at her breasts. She struggled and cried out. He bent her wrist harder and ripped her blouse open. She tried to bite him, but he gripped harder with muscled arms.

When I finally moved, it was not the way I'd been taught—gently—but the way I'd learned from the early years when my sisters and I still fought. I leaped and scratched at the man's eyes. He raised his arms, Mary between us. Long grey streaks of skin curled under my fingernails. He wouldn't let go.

The men closed in. "Take her. Make her your woman."

I felt cartoonish and small, jumping and scratching like an animal. Drivers on the boulevard stopped to watch. Several Kinois women appeared, bowls of baguettes on their heads.

I screamed, *"Mamans, assistez-nous!"* (Mothers help us!)

They looked us over. *"Tika ye akende!"* (Let her go!)

But the men just laughed.

Mary gripped at her shredded blouse with one arm and pulled away with the other. Her eyes behind her glasses grew big and jumpy. Again I lunged for the man's eyes. My fingernails collected blood, skin and tears all in one claw. He let go, hands to his face, doubled over, shouting. *"Opesi ngai pasi, yo nyama!"* (You hurt me, you animal!)

Seeing his pain, I forgot myself for a moment. He had just called me the worst insult on the streets and I felt badly. But Mary grabbed my arm and rushed us across the boulevard. We didn't stop running until we got home.

I scrubbed with a nail brush to rid the man's skin and eyeballs under my fingernails. To dull the trauma, I broke off the candy coating of a few Chicklets, a treat so rare and sweet, I chewed a couple whole before stopping myself. At school the next day, I placed several denuded Chicklets on each of the American girls' desks. I added a note. What did it say? "I'm sorry. Please, let's be friends again." I can't remember, but it must have been a plea so direct, they had to huddle and take me back. At recess, the American girls called from the outstretched limb of a mango tree and offered me Frito chips.

———

Mary later said she doesn't remember me clawing her attacker or why he let go. "I was shocked more than scared. His eyes were filled with such hatred. We weren't used to that. I thought he might be mentally ill."

She remembered another little girl with us as well. Perhaps Joanne? After that, Mary said, she became more cautious about leaving the hostel. "I was always afraid for anyone I was with." Before coming to our hostel, she had been sexually molested by her dorm parent, Rev. Bill Pruitt, at Central School in Lubondai. "I was already under a tremendous cloud of depression." At night, Mary paced our dorm, unable to sleep. She shed twenty pounds, forty. "In the pitch dark, I kept my sanity by walking."

She padded endlessly around the living room and dining room ping pong table, blue eyes wide and wary. "That's how I warded off nightmares. It was better than going to sleep." Her cheeks hollowed, her elbows and collarbones pointed, her soft curves and bubbly laughter vanished. She lost fifty-five pounds and contracted hepatitis. She was flown home yellow and skeletal weighing eighty pounds. Her mother, when she saw Mary, nearly fainted on the runway.

Pruitt's method, Mary said, was to show films like "King of Kings," and, while everyone was engrossed, seek out stray children. Mary, 13 at the time, suffering from malaria in her room, welcomed his visit. He knew magic tricks. He used hypnosis to help his two hemophiliac sons through their pain. "We were enchanted by his ability. He was the beloved Uncle Bill."

Mary blames her vulnerability on a lack of sexual information. "We weren't given language or knowledge. It was a failing of our parents. I didn't know what was happening when my first period arrived. I would never leave that teaching to anyone else."

Not until Mary returned to the U.S. for nurse's training and experienced a total collapse did her psychiatrist tell her parents of the abuse. "They left the mission field and moved to the States…but by then the damage had been done," Mary said (Turnbull).

In mid-May 1965, Jim Bertsche and my dad returned to Kandale and Mukedi with a truck full of food and clothing. The Baphende people had been deceived. Youth bands had secretly given charge of Phende villages to leaders from another tribe. The youth looted, maimed and killed respected elders and kidnapped young girls for "wives." They permitted only church services that preached Jesus as a revolutionary, then banned services entirely for months (Bertsche 1965 "Kwilu Report").

When Chief Nzamba found his name on a *Jeunesse* hit list, he sent a message via a teen girl—a custom that guaranteed her protection. Instead she was executed and her head mounted on a spike along a path the Mukedi women took home from the fields.

Chief Nzamba rallied his men and burned out the *Jeunesse* camp. Skirmishes continued until the villages around Mukedi were torched to cinders. The mission clinic, hospital and everything remaining were charred and ruined. The people fled south to Kandale having lost their territory and everything they owned (Bertsche 1965 "Kwilu Report").

Dad found the pastors and teachers tested by threats and beatings yet clinging to their faith. Samuel Kakhenda told his family when they fled Kandale, "If the Lord has not written it down, we cannot die." Pastor Wayindama saw the church "tottering in the balances" but, as in the time of Elijah, God had hidden 7,000 faithful who had not bowed their knees to Baal. The church would not die. (Eidse 1965)

On November 25, 1965, Mobutu surprised even the CIA when he declared a coup on the 5 a.m. broadcast and later that day announced his five-year presidency. For 32 years he ruled by decree, killing or coopting his critics, like Mulele and Tshombe. (Kelly, p. 184) Although Mobutu offered Mulele amnesty, it was only to lure him to his public torture and execution in 1968. His eyes, ears and genitals were ripped out, his limbs amputated one-by-one and his trunk thrown into the Congo River. (Close, p. 208; Wrong, p. 90)

In authenticity campaigns, Mobutu changed colonial names to precolonial names. The capital became Kinshasa, Stanleyville became Kisangani, Elizabethville became Lubumbashi, the country, river, and currency all became Zaire (from the Kikongo *nzadi* (river). The changes were meant to free the nation from colonial symbols, but King Leopold II still sat stonily on his high horse at city center for six more years. He was toppled—not by Mobutu who had become an autocrat saying, "A village only needs one chief"—but by the people who had to live under Mobutu's repressive regime.

A joke circulated from the university where Uncle Mel was academic dean (later the Université Protestant au Congo, Kinshasa) where graduates wore Mobutu's signature leopard print on their green hoods and gowns. "Green is for experience, yellow is for courage, black is for the future."

We didn't know then how, in twenty-five years, Mobutu under student pressure to hold democratic elections, would shut off the electricity at the University of Lubumbashi and send his *Garde Civile* to massacre 50 students in the night.

We heard from mission news sources that despite Mukedi church services being banned by *Jeunesse*, the people met to celebrate Christmas 1965 unopposed. The grip of revolutionaries in Kwilu province was loosening. (Bertsche 1965 "Kwilu Report")

At The American School of Kinshasa (TASOK) our music teacher, Ms. Boldt, drew colorful mountain scenes on the blackboard, led us in singing and hit all the high notes. She held auditions for a grades five and six musical, the 19th-century Engelbert Humperdinck's "Hansel and Gretel." I was pleased to be selected as one of 14 angels to sing the beatific Evening Hymn, "When at Night I Go to Sleep."

I enjoyed rehearsing with the sixth graders like my cousin Margaret (the children's mother) and her friend Dawn Wiebe who

Margaret Loewen, Mary Dirks, Charity Eidse, Linda Bertsche, Becky Gerber, Barbara Loewen and me gathered at the Loewen's in 1966.

made a great witch with her long, dark hair all tousled and ratty. I also painted sets that year with my artistic classmate Evelyn Brown.

All our singing with Ms. Boldt, Grandma and our musical parents got us Eidse sisters selected for the talent show. Our fluid voices blended through intricate woven harmonies of "His Sheep Am I." We may have also sung Tommy Dorsey's "Precious Lord, Take My Hand." It was a lament written after he lost his wife and infant son in childbirth and it helped us grieve our many disruptions, separations and losses of friends, families and homelands.

While flying home from school, perhaps at Christmas 1965, a massive monsoon blew up and blocked our flight path. The pilot was slender and serious by Leola's recollection, perhaps her classmate's father John Strash. Or Bob Gordon. She sat in the copilot's seat in the Cesna 180 while we Eidse girls sat in the middle and her little brother Marvin sat on a cushion in the upper cargo-hold desperate to shift his cramped legs.

In December 1965, an MAF flight arrived at Kajiji with Rodney Schmidt, Marvin and Leola Falk, Charity (holding Grace), me (holding Polly) and Hope. Grace joined us after we'd landed for the photo. (Peter Falk photo)

Our pilot first tried to reach a military post outside the capital, then the airstrip at Sona Bata but nowhere was it clear enough for passage or landing. We headed further East trying to circle around the system. Turbulence buffeted us, air pockets dropped us. The gas dwindled.

At last, flying on empty, our pilot coasted into Vanga, its runway neglected perhaps since the Kwilu rebellion. Sweating and white-knuckled, he set the plane down hard on a bumpy airstrip—so hard a flight instrument shook loose and fell into Leola's lap.

The pilot sat still for a while then popped the instrument back in, got out and surveyed the grass, woodlands and thatch huts on a nearby ridge. Rebels were still active in some areas of the Kwilu. He then stared straight ahead, Leola recalled, "probably praying."

"Only when I decided to get out of the plane did he turn to help us," she added.

Finally, the pilot opened our doors. We girls, who had been desperate for a bathroom break, dashed across rain-wet ground for the deep grass while the pilot pieced the plane back together.

From mud and thatch huts, naked children crept close to examine the plane, followed by adults in worn clothing. The pilot motioned that he needed a key for the gas that MAF kept there in a locked enclosure. We waited an hour while villagers searched for the man with the keys.

The children gradually crept up and examined every strut, wing, wheel and propeller. All over Congo, kids built balsa models of passing trucks, motorbikes, boats and planes. Many they only saw at a distance. Here, with the plane at a standstill, they were able to touch, feel and memorize every detail. Finally a man arrived, rolling a barrel of gas. He helped the pilot fill up and we jolted down the airstrip, lifted off and headed South.

That evening, the pilot landed safely at Kamayala, then Kajiji, relieved to deliver us safely to our parents. Too late to fly back to Kinshasa, he spent the night at Kajiji where he recounted every detail of his search for safe landing. He was elated to make it to Vanga and the stored gas.

Leola felt guilty, however, that the children waiting in the capital would be delayed in returning home. The ripple effect would throw off the short school vacation for kids and their families.

An excerpt from pilot John Strash's unpublished autobiography (Strash 2012) reveals the risks of flying us home. It added many hours in the air during winter's rainy season when the sun heated the unstable humid atmosphere and built massive cloud fronts. In a chapter titled "Singing in the Rain," Strash fetched us Eidse sisters from the dorm on an undated morning hoping to make it out early, ahead of the monsoons. He drove twenty minutes past city center markets to Kinshasa's secondary airport, *N'Dolo* ("little insect," used by lighter planes). He weighed us and loaded our luggage in the "pregnant" belly pod of "Mama" Cesna 206 (in the Congolese view); and double-checked the fuel tanks. Here, in his words:

> The flight to Kamayala was 365 miles, or about 2:30 hours in duration; I needed all 84 gallons for the round trip.
>
> We then proceeded to the opposite side of the airport to file a flight plan and have the girls go through...immigration and customs. These procedures had been instituted shortly after the execution of Patrice Lumumba by the forces of the breakaway province of Katanga. No one was trusted, not even young expatriate students!
>
> The flight went smoothly to Popokabaka, a distance of 120 miles. Looking beyond the government post, I saw a huge wall of sinister-looking cumulus clouds. They topped an estimated 30,000 feet and stretched from horizon to horizon. The base of the cloud wall was a threatening gray-black; there was no way around, or under this front. The airport was still in the clear; however, without mission personnel there, it was not a safe place for these youngsters. There was only one thing to do, return to Kinshasa. As we flew back, I noted that the clouds

were building up ahead of us; it was going to be a race all the way back to Kinshasa!

At the control boundary, I called N'Djili flight control [and] got an immediate response.... "Weather is threatening, conditions deteriorating. Call back [when] field in sight." That didn't sound too encouraging; I would call back in 10 minutes....

We were paralleling a huge wall of clouds that stretched all the way to Kinshasa. [When I called back, *N'djili* flight controls said,] "The field is closed. Ceiling 300 feet, rain, visibility one quarter mile. Wind north across runway at 30 knots."

...It wasn't good. Storms have been known to last for several hours.... I then heard another transmission.... It was Bob Gordon calling..., "John, I'm on the ground at Kimpoko, on the other side of the storm. If you can get through, you can wait it out here."

...I made a broad turn away from the storm to get a better look in the direction of Popokabaka. As I retraced my track, I kept looking at the cloud wall to see if there was a lighter area. Storms are not stationary; they will keep moving on. A half hour passed since my first contact with the flight control; there must be something, somewhere. Then I saw a lighter gray area; this was it! I immediately headed into the storm. It was dark, the rain pounded the aluminum skin of the 206 with a deafening roar, visibility was straight down; I couldn't see anything ahead of me.

Suddenly, from behind me I could hear the girls singing, "He's got the whole world in His hands...." They sang the second stanza: "He's got you and me sister, in His hands..." Then finally, "He's got the pilot-man, in His hands..." I had completely forgotten the sisters and wondered how they felt flying through the storm. It wasn't rough, just dark and gloomy with the loud pounding raindrops on the aluminum.

Within ten minutes, or so, we were out of it under a huge dark canopy of clouds. The air was cool and the wind calm; down below the terrain was soaked from the heavy downpour, the visibility was excellent. I contacted the flight control and told them that we were continuing on to Kamayala....

The flight…took us five hours. When we landed at Kamayala, the girls' parents were waiting at the airstrip with big smiles and warm embraces. They had been following my radio transmissions with [my wife] Erna, on the mission network, and knew the predicament we were in. I knew that they would really be celebrating a joyous Christmas!

What we often didn't realize in our Missionary Kid (MK) privilege was the risk we faced that certain adults protected us from. Why not land at Popokabaka in the face of descending monsoons? In diamond-rich Tshikapa, some of our teen dormmates had reported the abuse of strip-searches and were provided mission escorts to their planes. Even at villages near our small airstrip between Kahemba and Kamayala, some military men pressed girls and women into services. My parents and other mission leaders were actively working, through verse-memorizing programs, to prevent these abuses.

12

BAOBAB DREAMS

Jette returned to the hostel from Princeton, New Jersey, in September 1966 to be our roommate in grade six. She arrived with a suitcase full of squat troll dolls with unruly, neon hair and Tame hair rinse. "For my own hair," she grinned and stroked her smooth blonde hair.

We were so giddy at being together again—she, Charity and I—that we rolled on the floor, laughing, tumbling and turning somersaults, hugging each other with our legs.

It must have been a rare sound at the hostel because it brought Aunt Nettie running. When she found us, legs entwined, heads back, she blanched.

"Girls! Sit up properly."

We did, wrapped in a tight group, still grinning.

"Not on the floor." She sounded frustrated, arms crossed, and when we moved to the bed, "Not all on the same bed. Not so close. Girls mustn't sit too close. Bad things can happen if they start touching each other."

What was she saying about girls touching each other in a bad way? I crossed to my own bed. Jette and Charity slid apart. We shot each other sly grins. Was our girlfriend love somehow wrong? What bad things could happen? At least not pregnancy, the condition mom had warned us about. Was Aunt Nettie saying we should already forget each other and turn our interest to boys instead?

When she left, we choked back laughter, thinking her strange. How could our happy hugging and tumbling be like sex? We helped

Jette hang her dresses and fill her dresser drawer, wondering if we really were as bad as Aunt Nettie said. That night we prayed aloud together again, taking turns stringing together "*Lieber Heiland*" and "Now-I-lay-me." I faced the room, then the wall and groaned my sharpened guilt to my pillow.

One afternoon when Jette and I had the room to ourselves and were talking sixth grade stuff, she told me about sex with boys. She curled the fingers of one hand into a tunnel and jabbed the index finger of her other hand back and forth inside it. We had no words or labels, no maps or diagrams, only crude finger-play. A boy could come close enough to jab us? It was alarming.

"Don't touch" was still the rule about our bodies and became more so under Aunt Nettie. We were saving the sensations of touch for a husband who would show them to us after we were properly married. Without marriage we had no hope of discovering pleasant touch. Aunt Nettie required us to bathe, not with bare hands, but with washcloths that she'd marked with our names in indelible marker. She called at the closed bathroom door for us to "get out now" if we had played with our troll dolls too long in the tub.

In the rec room, the big girls pushed the ping pong table aside and rolled on the cement floor like rolling pins. They had read in our new *Seventeen* magazines that you could shrink your hips that way. The fashion magazine was a gift from a well-intention church sponsor, an effort to usher backward MKs into the 20th century. In it, the girls were impossibly thin, long-legged and boy-crazy and that was how we pictured the perfect American girls.

The big girls no longer told the boys to move over on the basketball court so they could teach us little girls to shoot. It was as though we had become anxious to please boys instead of ourselves.

On Saturday night all ten girls gathered in the living room for popcorn and devotions. Each little girl, fresh out of the bath, hair still damp, paired off with her "big sister" who combed and styled her hair, wrapping it around pink sponge rollers. We nestled in the crook of a big girl's knees, the gentle tug of rattail combs dividing and brushing our hair over our faces like waterfalls.

Aunt Nettie did her equivalent of sex education, or "girls' talk," which was to read from Ephesians on marriage. "Wives, submit yourselves to your husbands as to the Lord. For the husband has authority over his wife just as Christ has authority over the church."

Submitting ourselves, Aunt Nettie said, meant being available to our husbands, cooking, cleaning and making the home pleasant for him. It meant meeting him at the door with a joyful kiss. If we did all this, our husbands couldn't help but love us. She knew this because she had been a good and faithful wife and her husband loved her— 'til his early death. Submission was the only way to keep a man's love. It was our life's ambition. If we didn't, we were unworthy of love and would remain single and sidelined.

For some reason Uncle Hector started coming to the girls' hostel at bedtime. Had we resisted getting to bed? Had Aunt Nettie asked him to help her enforce lights out?

We little girls poked our heads out, excited by his low voice in the living room, sinewed limbs splayed in an easy chair while he

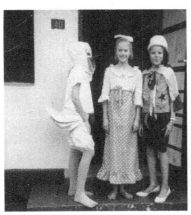

Left: Halloween 1966 fell on a Sunday and we dressed up for dinner, me as Donald Duck, Jette as Sleeping Beauty and Charity as a fortune teller. (Jette Buller photo) Right: Marcia Buller, Hope Eidse and Leola Falk dressed as the Beatles. (Leola Falk photo)

talked to Aunt Nettie. The bigger girls across the hall teased him about whiskering them. But he said they were too old.

"Get to bed. Lights out!" he barked.

I glanced at Charity and Jette hovering with me at the door. Had there been an incident with the older girls so that he could no longer whisker them?

"I know. Let's get him to whisker *us*!" Jette's eyes twinkled.

We three little girls hesitated only a moment. "Uncle Hector come whisker *us*!"

Hector called out rules. "You have to be in your nighties, in bed, lights out."

We scrambled out of our clothes, threw on our nighties, rushed for the light switch and jumped into bed. "Ready."

Hawk-like, Hector filled the door with talons raised. He hovered between our beds and sent us diving for deeper cover. He lunged, pinning me like some helpless chick. His jaw pricked like a steel brush and ripped. The sting brought tears to my eyes.

"Say uncle." His whiskers stuck and ripped again from the top of my cheek to my chin.

"Uncle!" I gasped.

"What? I can't hear you." His serrated jaw sliced again.

"Uncle, uncle, uncle!" When he pulled away the sting kept burning. I felt both relieved and defeated while he whiskered Charity. I should have been able to take it, should have submitted more.

Uncle Hector kept coming to whisker us goodnight. We said "Uncle" sometimes before he touched us, but until we really screamed it, he kept right on ripping.

I grew achy breasts and felt exposed under his grasp. One night, I squirmed and struggled, trying to free myself, and he drew back a moment. I kicked at the binding sheets and rolled. He dove again, but I got away, wedged between mattress and wall.

Jette, was leaning over the top bunk, watching me and Hector grabbed for her. She dodged. "Uncle!" she said before he caught her, but he whiskered her anyway.

She cried out, "Ouch, that hurts!"

I winced, guilty for having triggered his rage with my escape.

When Hector left, banging out the screen door to the boys' dorm, I crawled back to the center of my bed. Jette whimpered softly into her pillow. "It really hurts."

We dared not turn on the lights to check. We all lay quietly until Jette fell asleep. In the morning there was blood on her pillow and a welted purple rash on her silky cheek.

On our way through the compound to breakfast, Jette whispered, "Walk in front of me, Faith."

I did and she stepped on my heels.

"Not smack in front of me, silly." We both laughed. "Here on my right so no one will see my cheek." Then, she placed a hand on my shoulder and groaned. "Oh Faith, how can I go to school this way? What will I say?"

I helped her make up a story about tree branches scratching her. And that was the story we told when we got to the dining room and ran into Aunt Clara. With Jette injured, we couldn't risk worse punishment. Aunt Clara took us into her bathroom, opened the medicine cabinet, and dabbed Jette's cheek with cotton balls and disinfectant.

Hector didn't whisker us again after that. For a few weeks, while her cheek healed, he seemed extra friendly. But then he feint-punched us instead. For reasons we didn't understand, he aimed his knuckles at our faces and laughed when we dodged. "Made you duck."

When we didn't dodge—or didn't see it coming from behind us—it stung. "Suck-er!"

That was a sucker punch and it was our fault for getting in the way.

After that, Jette and I spent hours drawing pictures of teens with perfect faces—smooth cheeks, long bangs, flowing hair, wide eyes, pert noses and parted lips. I imagined an older, more perfect self, not the bruised and ducking girl at the hostel, but the glamorous model I would one day become. We kept notebooks just for drawing and writing and got brave carrying them in our teeth, up the notched knobs of a large silver baobab.

The baobab trunk was five people around stretched fingertip-to-fingertip, and grew straight up twenty feet before branching. Its trunk was scarred with initials and gashed for toe holds. The gashes oozed green and yellow pulp that hardened into climbing notches. These were the minuscule grips we clung to, hearts pounding, to reach the high cradle of its branches.

I knew Charity couldn't climb the baobab, but I kept on, completely wrapped up in the romantic lives Jette and I were dreaming. Charity said she couldn't draw and wanted to play dolls instead. In her doll world, she pampered her friends, went on family adventures and stood up to bullies. At Kamayala she had carried orphan toddlers on her hip around the village, had cuddled up and read to four-year-old Grace or rested her head in Mom's lap at bedtime. She missed this loving togetherness and family bonding at the hostel. Sometimes she played dolls with the dorm parents' little girl and I hoped she was happy.

However, often at night she cried and said she felt left out. Jette and I put aside our notebooks and dressed Barbie and troll dolls with her for days at a time. We designed dresses, cut patterns, crushed on colors like brown and pink or black and yellow. We stitched and knitted troll robes, Barbie shifts and sweaters. Our Barbies danced at balls with dashing men, something that could only happen for Mennonite girls in elaborate make believe.

Yet soon enough, Jette and I sneaked back to our hideout in the baobab and drew rugged, wild hippy boyfriends with angular noses, long hair and headbands.

We girls cycled four to two bicycles around Kamayala. (Ben Eidse photo)

The Christmas break brought relief when we made it safely through angry monsoons. It was a joy to be back home with Mom, Dad and our little sister Grace. It was exhilarating to bike around the village, see our friends, range the grasslands, bound downhill to the river and plunge into spring-fed currents with them.

One day a doll-sized two-year-old was brought from the orphanage for milk. Terry Lee had thin legs and arms, and a swollen belly. Tears had dried on his gray cheeks and his large, observant eyes looked sad. Ever since his mother died, he had been sickly and not eaten well. He had stopped growing or developing and could not yet walk.

Mom realized he needed focused care and we all took turns holding him, finding him cuddly, warm and responsive. But Charity especially related to him. She mashed bananas and filled bottles with milk for him. With her constant care, he ate happily and became so attached she carried him around for hours. His gray skin began to shine and his eyes sparkled when she reached for him.

She became so intent on his bright expressions that her surroundings faded. One day, while she carried him on her hip, she didn't notice the rotting lid on our abandoned underground water cistern and fell in with him, scattering rats. We lifted them both out, stunned and covered in stinking mud. We helped wash them off and Terry Lee recovered quickly from the shock. He continued to reach eagerly for Charity whenever he saw her. His arms and legs grew chubby and he smiled constantly. Before long, he could balance on his muscled legs and even take steps.

Sometime that holiday season, we drove two hours to Kajiji to visit the Falks, Schmidts and Bullers. Jette and her family had moved there so her father could help Mr. Falk teach at the seminary. They lived at *Ecole Belle Vue* (Beautiful View School), a campus on a high ridge overlooking the dramatic Mabete peaks of Congo and Angola. We kids rehearsed several carols and performed for the gathered families in a spontaneous Christmas celebration.

Leola and Marvin gave us a ghost tour, ushering us into the long dorm hallway lined with empty rooms once filled with missionary kids before school moved to the capital. What ghosts still lingered here? There had been lions circling, frightened children taken on hunts in the night. Or thorny branches soaked in rain barrels to

Jette and her family moved to Kajiji in 1966, here with Mom Gladys, brothers James and Charles with puppy and Dad Pete. (Buller family photo)

flay the legs of rowdy boys. We sat in their old dorm rooms on bare mattresses while "ghosts" rattled windows in first one room and then another. Finally we realized Marvin was creating the window-rattling effect by softly opening and closing the doors.

On New Year's Eve, we headed back to Kamayala, bumped down a rutted, red dirt road through the river forests below Kajiji and crossed on the ferry. Somewhere along the way, past the ferry and the Catholic honey farm of Chiwalwa, we picked up a soldier in full dress uniform and metal helmet. His belt cinched a narrow waist and he grinned broadly as he slid in beside Hope and me in the middle seat of the VW van. He greeted Mom and Dad in the front and turned to shake hands with Charity and Grace in the back. He was happy, he said, to be getting home to his family in Kahemba for New Year's Eve. For our part, we were happy to have a military man along in case of unscheduled roadblocks with men taking pay-offs from clueless drivers.

There was little traffic on the road, perhaps a merchant truck or army jeep. When we entered Kahemba Territory the jostling ride

Charity, Hope, Leola, Karen Schmidt, James Buller, Rodney, Jeannette, Charles, me and Marvin sing a carol during our 1966 Christmas-New Year service in Kajiji. (Peter Falk photo)

Dad with our VW van before it rolled. Hope, age 13, squeezed through the wing window of the crunched-in front passenger door to safety. (Peter Falk photo)

gave way to smooth, well-packed and maintained sand roads. Dad stopped the car so Hope, age 13, could practice driving. Mom got out to join us in the middle seat and the soldier got out to let her slide in beside me. He wanted to be close to the door when we dropped him at his home.

We flew along with Hope at the helm, headlights revealing packed white sand roads and grassy woodlands, no cars in sight. We were jolted by a stump in the road and after that Hope could hardly hold the steering wheel straight. What was wrong? Would we make it home?

Dad took over again but the steering column was just as balky under his hands. He tried to direct the car evenly but any bump wobbled the car. Another rut in the road launched the car over a high embankment.

Gravity broke loose and we spun through crunching metal, shattering glass and falling bodies. The car rolled all the way over and settled on its wheels again, the motor still running. Skinny Hope could not open the crunched front passenger door and scrambled through the wing window instead.

Dad called each of us by name. "Grace, Charity, Faith, Mom are you hurt?"

Someone, maybe Charity, said she had a headache. My shoulder was bruised but nothing more. The soldier sitting by the crunched door looked fine, protected by his helmet.

But Mom could not move. "I think my hip's broken. I may have hit the soldier's helmet."

Dad got out and circled the van to yank open the door and help the soldier and Mom out. But she couldn't stand. He flipped the middle door seat forward to let out Charity and Grace from the back. Both seemed uninjured; no bloody cuts or obvious bruises. Dad settled Mom back in the seat as comfortably as possible. We had no two-way radio, no way to get help. But the soldier offered to run ahead to Kahemba, maybe even find a bicyclist along the way to speed his journey. He jogged down the road and disappeared into the night.

Dad circled the car again. It was undrivable, totaled. At the back, the plywood wall he'd installed behind the back seat had prevented his busted toolbox from launching wrenches, hammers and screwdrivers forward and impaling his family.

We stood beside the silent road under a dark sky studded with stars. Overhead the southern cross gleamed, its four points once a vision for sailors navigating home.

At last, we heard the throaty labor of a loaded truck cresting the plateau. It was an army truck full of celebrating soldiers waving Primus bottles. They jumped down and gently carried Mom to the front seat. The rest of us climbed in the back where the soldiers permitted us to shelter behind the cab from the cool wind. We were their service project for the Bonne Année.

The next day Dr. Schwartz flew in from Kalonda to examine Mom. He found one leg shorter than the other and diagnosed a fractured pelvis. She was to lie still for six weeks between rigid supports. Dad carried in two ten-pound sacks of salt to wedge her in as though she were in a cast. She would need daily management and care—but which of us sisters would it be?

It could be me since I was capable and proficient, but I hesitated. Deep down I wanted to get back to grade six, Jette and our baobab dreams.

Before I could speak up, Charity begged to stay home. She offered to finish grade five by correspondence, teach Grace preschool, answer medical questions at the door and manage the daily shortwave radio broadcast. She pushed on. She also wanted to take in Terry Lee. Mom and Dad agreed and she pushed together two living room armchairs for his crib.

New Year's Day 1967, we had just survived a car accident that broke mom's hip and Charity had agreed to stay home and help Mom, teach Grace and take in orphan Terry Lee. (Ben Eidse photo)

I folded my pink flowered dress into my suitcase, relieved at not having to ease Charity's life at the hostel anymore, her persistent longing to play dolls. What I could not see was how this experience would change Charity's trajectory. She would sharpen her language skills, learn Chokwe hymns and lead choirs. She would help raise Terry Lee into a happy walking toddler. She would return with her husband to monitor Congo's 2006 elections and join his work with Wildlife Works Carbon to save the Earth's second lung, the Congo rainforest.

From the high cradle of the baobab Jette and I could see any action in the compound without being seen. And we could dream of houses with deep shag carpets and fountains flowing in sunken living rooms. I added textural detail like brickwork, quarried stone, relief, texture, wet splashes.

In her creations, Jette installed boys from grade seven with kind eyes and muscled shoulders to pillow against. She, who had two brothers and was the princess of the family, seemed to enjoy being a girl, although an athletic one for sure. I followed her into her fantasies but sometimes still imagined being a boy—to fill Dad's need, Mom's wish.

At school, we played varsity soccer while delicate girls watched from the sidelines. At times Jette and I were both reluctant to give up our tomboy ways. I practiced lay-ups, Jette practiced chin-ups, and neither of us actually spoke to the seventh grade boys we watched. That might spoil our make believe.

Home and family were the enticements dangled for us. So we even envisioned children—twins—so they always had each other, even if the family moved, which it never did. We made up schools nearby for the twins to walk to, friends they would never have to leave through junior high or high school. In weeks we'd filled our notebooks and started new ones.

Meanwhile, books circulated in the hostel and we discovered *The Chronicles of Narnia* and a book about a World War II orphan. I was so caught up in the young girl's abandonment that my tears wet the page and made it hard to read. I didn't notice a stranger walk under our window, past the barking cocker spaniel, Dixie, right into the house. He went straight to the hostel typewriter on the ping pong table across from my room, paused to take a half-typed assignment out of the carriage, and walked back out with the typewriter. If I had glanced up, I would have seen the whole thing.

My dormmate who later found her half-finished report on the table was bewildered. "Where's the typewriter?" No one had taken it to their room or put it away in the cupboard. It was just gone, taken by a passerby while she was out at school watching a basketball game.

"Oh no, how am I going to finish my report? Weren't you sitting right there?" She gestured at my bed in full view of the table.

"What were you reading that you didn't notice some guy walk in and take a typewriter?"

Mom had sometimes warned us about the dangers of reading. Certain fantastical books could grip us and take us far from duty and purpose. They'd absorb us in unreality and cause us to forget our place of service. "You are a part of all that you have met." She said it as though some things we met could prevent us from accomplishing the good works we were created for. At the same time, she loved hearing, reading and writing real life stories of struggle and survival. She had published in the *Congo Missionary Messenger* stories of the mission freeing Kamena from slavery and Pastor Wayindama's suffering for his stand against rebels.

To me it seemed books improved understanding and restored order to the chaos around us. Anne Frank and Corrie Ten Boom had helped me access World War II with its swastika flags and death camps. But I still couldn't make sense of someone climbing over a locked gate, edging past a barking dog right into a well-lit house to take a typewriter. Perhaps he was a writer like me, desperate to tell his story; or just a person in need, desperate to sell the typewriter and feed his family.

Why did some people live in such need and some in such privilege? And why couldn't Congo with its kingly President Mobutu, do more for the people? Mobutu lived large, buying mansions in Switzerland, France and Spain that could have housed whole tribes. He traveled to twelve countries a year by jumbo jet to win international support for his absolute power and authority (Kelly, p. 199).

Copper prices were rising, foreign investors were extending credit and Mobutu was paying himself $75 million a year from the national treasury. Without leaving tracks, he was sucking over $5 billion from a nation with an average wage of a dollar a day (Kelly, p. 199).

———————————

It was easier to write and draw and play make believe than to try and make sense of politics in Congo. There was the tire swing where we played Batman and Robin—a show Jette had seen on TV. With my imaginary cape flying, I was the boy my parents had always wanted. There was pick-up basketball and, beside the court, a Zairian family to talk with across the fence. Uncle Hector called them "squatters" but they seemed like ordinary kids to us.

A boy and girl our age came running and shouting home from school every afternoon just like we did. They kicked a soccer ball around their sandy yard in plastic shoes and faded cotton shirts and dresses. Jette and I called them to the fence and tried to speak Lingala with them. We asked Aunt Nettie if we could invite them over to play soccer or attend Good News Club with us.

Aunt Nettie led the weekly child evangelism club at our hostel and gave us prizes if we invited our school friends. She even trained an African couple to run the same program in the city neighborhoods. But our neighbor kids were somehow different.

"No, you shouldn't even talk to them. They live there illegally."

I didn't understand. Had they just found an empty house and moved in?

That was fine with me. It seemed wasteful to let good tin roof, concrete houses sit empty, especially in this city where people lived on top of each other. We kept talking over the fence when no one was looking. But after a while we noticed, the neighbor kids had stopped talking to us. Aunt Nettie said the mission had bought the lot and asked them to move. Hector wanted them out by the end of the month.

It turned out the family resisted going for months. Aunt Nettie's Siamese cat, Willie, disappeared for a day or two and came back with its whiskers cut. The Congolese man who ran our laundry said the family was probably using the whiskers in powerful witchcraft medicine against us. We could only imagine what form that might take. But we felt sorry for them. Jette and I exchanged hangdog looks whenever we passed their house.

Later when I asked Mom, she said the mission had found them another house.

After New Year's 1967, Aunt Nettie told me it was time to wear a bra. I couldn't continue bouncing around in my shirtwaists for all the world to see. She added that there were things I could no longer do when I became a woman, like strenuous sports. I'd have to taper off my running and basketball, or I might lose my period. Then, I couldn't have babies. Why did I want babies at age 12 anyway?

She and the physical education teacher agreed, girls should not run more than a mile or they might drop their uterus or stop getting periods and become "infertile." I slowed down and grew more cautious, even though I was a strong runner and swimmer and sometimes shot baskets for hours.

Hope wouldn't listen to the rules. "What about the African women?" she asked me, defiance glinting in her blue eyes. "They run morning, noon and night, out to their fields, back and forth to the river. They cut firewood and haul water uphill, all while pregnant. They do it pregnant with babies on their backs!"

Hope loved running and jumping. During track and field, she set the girls' mile record and won the running broad jump. She ran far more than Coach Cornelsen allowed and said she didn't care "two hoots" what "they" said. Even if they were quoting the International Olympic Committee, which had decreed that races of more than a mile could permanently ruin women's reproductive systems.

"Who wants babies?" She squinted at the high jump bar, hands on her bony hips. "Who wants to get married? I'd rather stay single and adopt orphans."

In this I knew I was different. I was excited by the possibility of babies—some time far in the future. I thought it might make me somehow central and powerful. But I wasn't sure, was growing less sure of everything all the time. I cut back to a mile a day and worried that I was getting flabby. I told Jette I was going on a diet. "I'm only going to eat five pieces of bread at dinner."

Jette laughed out loud.

I didn't like the way my body was turning soft and round and didn't recognize it as a sign of approaching womanhood. At school we had divided up into boys' and girls' classes for physical education and watched a diagram filmstrip about menstruating. Still, I was not anticipating my first period and so was horrified at my first bleeding. It happened at school but no one had the courage to tell me about the stain. Or perhaps they didn't notice since I was wearing red plaid. I didn't have a clue until I got to my dorm room and stuck to my wooden chair. I'd never seen so much blood caked into a dress. I had thought menstruation would be discrete, a small leakage now and then. The film strip showed a tablespoon or two over a week. I couldn't believe the wreckage. My dress was ruined, and I had none to spare.

Aunt Nettie showed me how to soak it in cold water and gave me a sanitary belt and pad. Sitting under the barred window in the bathroom, threading my first pad, I saw my female life with unusual clarity. Already at age twelve I could produce babies years before I wanted to. I was only a child myself. But the weight of womanhood rested heavily on me and made me fear being invaded against my will. The whole somber possibility of growing a new person inside me thudded like a c-ration in my gut.

I stood and crossed to the sink, my stride stiff and stuffy. How could I walk with a mattress between my legs? How could I run, climb, swim, bounce basketballs, make jump shots in this new life? Even if I wanted to? Even if "they" let me?

I swallowed hard and tried to walk naturally across the living room to the big girls' rooms, looking for my *yaya*. Hope was at her table, science or math book open in a beam of sunlight. Dust mites glittered in her glasses when she glanced up.

"I got my period." I was miserable, didn't even dare sit down. "How do you wear these mattress pads?"

"I don't."

"What? How not?"

"I stopped getting my period. If you exercise hard enough you can stop it."

Oh, so that's how she spit on the messenger announcing her womanhood and turned the message on its head?

She handed me a long piece of thread. "Here, swallow this but hang onto the end. Then when you pull it up you can feel it glide up your esophagus."

Esophagus? She was always doing experiments like some mad nurse scientist. She demonstrated and I copied her. Sure enough, we could tug and feel it glide up our throats as if mapping our insides.

Hope swallowed hers again but this time let go of the end. "Oops!"

"What now?" I laughed. "No, wait. Don't tell me."

I realized she wouldn't say another word about menstrual periods. Not with Aunt Nettie's room next door and the older girls around the corner. She had been angry about getting her period. She had declared she would not become a "lady," that no one could make her like boys or give up running and swimming. The other big girls often didn't even come along to the FUNA Club swimming pool or the falls when they got their periods. They said girls could get cramps from cold water or collapse from exertion. When Uncle Hector sat behind the wheel beeping for them, they sent messages that they were "sick."

To me, the most obvious reason not to go swimming was that you couldn't wear a pad in the pool. But Hope didn't believe any of the rules or she purposely disobeyed them. She said cold water stopped bleeding and she swam all the more—without a pad. No way would she let the boys or Uncle Hector think she was "sick." She would never chose to stay in when she could be out exercising and building her muscles.

That evening, Hector pulled me out of supper line and shook my hand. "Congratulations, Faith. I hear you're a young lady now."

My cheeks burned. Who gave him the right to know? A man who had pinned me down, breasts achy under my nightie, stuck me with his whiskers and ripped my cheek. I didn't even get to talk to my mother about menstruating, there being no telephone lines. Yet Aunt Nettie had given this grown man, the deepest, most private, sexual knowledge about me. I choked down white rice and chicken gravy and skipped dessert. I had to stop the dark feeling that filled me. I hurried back to change my pad and hunker down over homework while basketballs bounced on the court outside

Leola, too, later revealed that her menstruation news was shared with Uncle Hector. He had told her privately she could no longer roughhouse with him now that she was a young lady. One prohibition at a time, we learned how we would be limited as young ladies.

Mom had let us know—with rules about knee-length skirts, buttoning our blouses to the neck, and sitting with knees together—

that womanhood was a burden. We didn't like being singled out as sexual. It wasn't fun or welcome. It didn't make us powerful and we should not let gender get in the way of who we were or interrupt our good works.

Yet Jette had received a different message. She seemed jealous of my period, seemed to want curves and attention from boys. She asked how she would know when her period came. Would there be cramps? Would it hurt? She seemed eager to enter the mysterious passage. Also, she enjoyed combing her hair, dressing up, stretching her long legs. Evenings on the lawn, she and Leola practiced springing handstands and cartwheels on their way to becoming varsity cheerleaders.

Below the Little Falls, where the hostel picnicked on Saturdays, a brown river flowed past a sandy beach around a deep bend and into a canopied forest. You could dangle inside an inner tube and let the river carry you into its shaded cathedral, breathe its woodsy, decaying warmth. When you went far enough, you beached on a log in the dappled shade, and listened for the begging call of the long-tailed whydah bird. You could at least hope for a smooth ride through womanhood.

Yet, after rainstorms, there could be a whirlpool undertow at the base of the Little Falls and once Leola was caught in it, unable to escape. She had been swept under, surfaced and pulled under again. It was Hope who noticed, braced herself on the bottom, grabbed Leola's arm and tugged her to safety.

However, Hope also lost a dear friend that year. Her classmate, Lanie Lindland, a sweet, curly blonde, was flown with her Baptist family to the States to be treated for cancer. The doctor suspected mosquito control trucks that weekly drove through our compounds, spraying DDT while kids ran behind in the mist. We heard that

Lanie had rallied, received skates for Christmas and skated that winter. We had high hopes for her return. Instead, on Valentine's Day, 1966, she died and left our hearts pierced.

———————

A new hostel was going up in place of the boys' dorm. The commotion and stress reached Jette and me high out-of-sight in the baobab tree. Uncle Hector strode out of the boys' dorm and threw punches at the boys. "Made you duck!" Or with a shout, called them to some chore—haul bricks, cut down a tree, shovel sand, wash the van. "Get out here, you little peckers!"

Jette and I cringed. Our pencils froze on our floorplans. Wasn't calling the boys "peckers" the same as calling them penises? How did that make them feel? How did that make them feel about their peckers? I knew how it made me feel. Low down, dirty, nasty, mean.

Once several little boys were assigned to lift the lid and clean out the smelly battleship septic tank. Cockroaches swarmed—all sizes and colors—up their shorts, in their shirts and hair. We shuddered over dinner when they described it.

Rather than feeling cut down to shameful, sexual things it seemed easier to numb out and stop feeling at all.

There was no sense of power in knowing these things. It actually made us feel smaller, less special, hollowed out. It crushed who we were trying to become. Yet if I didn't try to fit in and accept things the way they were, I might go crazy or get sick and be sent home—a failure.

Jette and I sketched and didn't say much about what we'd seen and heard in the hostel yard. We sealed it up as though it had never happened, or as though it were somehow normal. We stuffed it away and vowed never to cross Uncle Hector if we could help it.

It was clear something was happening to the little boys, too. They became silent and sullen. They couldn't talk back to Uncle

Hector, couldn't let go their rage except by flicking open pocket knives and slashing at the old baobab. Thick yellow sap oozed from its silvery bark—in the shape of swastikas.

———————————

We flew home for ten days at Easter break and Dad gave us each a fresh *cahier* (notebook). It was for research and note taking. He piled encyclopedias on the dining room table. We were planning a camping trip through Europe on $5 a day on our way to Canada. Also, he had bought passage aboard a Russian liner, the *Alexander Pushkin*, to Expo '67 in Montreal. Canada had won the world's fair celebration for its centennial after Russia gave it up for its fiftieth anniversary of the Revolution. However, Russia had refurbished the ship for passage to the fair in a show of openness and had christened it for its famous anti-establishment author.

Dad wanted us to travel with spirits and eyes wide open, minds buzzing with details, connecting every image to history, architecture, science, religion. We started with I for Italy, R for Rome, G for Germany, B for Berlin, N for Netherlands, A for Amsterdam. I drew and wrote about tulips with high hopes of seeing brightly-colored fields of them. We would visit Friesland, where our grandmas' ancestors came from. Dad wanted us to find and suggest stops along the way. I longed to see Anne Frank's narrow attic hideaway where she had written her candid journal, knowing at age 12 she wanted to be a writer.

Back at school, our two grade six classes moved uphill to our new campus carved from jungle. Instead of getting pinched by Peter, I sat next to Carl and learned to draw shooting missiles, exploding planes, parachuting pilots—"fighting soldiers from the sky." "The Ballad of the Green Berets" and the Vietnam War were popular for several months before war footage and coffins filled the news.

That year, the school talent show peaked with Ted Ericson and Dan Culp on guitar, Donna McMillan and Beth Hester singing the

Hope, Charity and I waded rivers and climbed trees—even in our Sunday dresses. (Ben Eidse photo)

spirited Caribbean calypso, "Jamaica, Farewell." It was clear that new international rhythms were penetrating the school. The Green Beret Anthem was being replaced by more diverse sentiments.

I would have to leave Jette that summer for a year that would stretch to two in Canada when Dad's stumbling and falling was misdiagnosed. But high in the baobab, Jette and I were as close as we'd ever been. Our friendship was intense, a race against time.

Deep down we guarded our friendship, not daring to get too wrapped up in each other for fear it would hurt to tear apart. At school we sometimes separated and played with other girls, practicing a ranging friendship that cushioned us against losing each other and prepared us for all the losses of our lives. After dark on the hostel grounds, we played king's base with all the little kids—hiding behind old garages and giant trees—racing the seeker for home base.

We loved it when the high schoolers joined in. One who stood out was Paul Brower, a trim, muscled guy with a wicked grin and glass eye. He had lost his in a kitchen knife accident when he was little. He liked to pretend he had no depth perception and missed the cup when he poured or us kids when he lunged at us. He once took out his glass eye as a special gesture for Jette and she never forgot it. He seemed resilient and spirited despite trauma. How could we know how quickly we'd lose him?

13

GHOSTS AND BONES

In June 1967, our family caught a flight from Kinshasa to Rome and it was like landing on another planet where psychedelics had replaced a dusty city. Teens in bright tie-dye shirts, beads, bell bottoms and peace signs lounged in Italy's parks and shared flowers and tokes. Transistors played The Mamas and Papas. "If you are going to San Francisco…summertime will be a love-in there…" It was the "Summer of Love," for 100,000 flower children descending on Haight-Ashbury. Another 100,000 turned on, tuned in and dropped out all over Europe.

The Beatles' "Penny Lane" played on the bus to the Vatican. The wistful strings and trumpet crescendos expressed our longing for friends left in Congo and the thrill of new adventures. Charity had wept to leave Terry Lee, whom we'd sent back to the village with his aunts. National policy at that time would not permit expatriates to adopt Congolese children. Yet we hoped to be back next year and trusted he'd be well-cared for with his aunts.

Ahead of us was the promise of ancient wonders, grand castles, the Rhine River and our ancestral roots in Holland and Canada. At the Vatican, we joined throngs in the courtyard. Jewelry hawkers selling necklaces to be blessed by the pope circled among men in suits, nuns in habits, women in pastel suits and pillbox hats. The hawkers got no purchase from us plain Mennonites. My parents didn't even wear wedding rings.

But I did note that I was wearing my aqua dress with puffed sleeves—handed down from Hope—in case some magic came of it.

The papal balcony doors opened and Pope John Paul II appeared in white pointy hat and robes. He was hailed for ushering in Vatican II, a time of dialogue among faiths, spiritual renewal and unity—even in Congo. He intoned a Latin blessing, raised two fingers and traced a cross over us.

We surged into the Sistine Chapel and I tried not to stare at the naked marble David. Michelangelo's painting of God and Adam touching fingers on the ceiling held me spellbound a moment. But it was "La Pieta," Mary's veiled head bowed, her arms holding the lifeless, alabaster Jesus that caught my breath. That moment of grief must have seemed bottomless and Michelangelo had dedicated hours to carving it.

At the Colosseum we soaked in the warm June sun and contemplated the open stone subfloor that once held Christians and the roaring lions who shredded them. Those Christians had refused to recant the faith and had not escaped the lions. *Simbas.*

To escape the *Simbas* in Congo, we'd heard, a student, Mayambi Sosthene, had hidden his family with wild gorillas in the forest beyond Stanleyville. The large apes had challenged the huddled humans but the family had escaped both gorillas and *Simbas.* Realizing that not all escaped, Sosthene had settled on this wisdom: "Nothing happens to any of his children without his knowledge" (Bertsche 1965, p. 11).

We drove the Appian way under ancient pines and toured the catacombs where skeletons lay behind glass in wall niches. Here Christians hid in limestone tunnels five stories deep and buried their martyrs in caves.

Back above ground, graffiti read "US out of Vietnam" and tie-dye shirts displayed "Make love not war." U.S teens had turned in their draft cards in mass refusal and their backpacks displayed Canadian flags. Young people gazed openly at each other and I gazed back. My cheeks burned if I caught the devouring eyes of some dark-haired stranger. It seemed that in this new era of love and unity, revolution could be sparked in an instant. I was twelve and traveling with my family but the air sizzled with possibilities.

Over hotel menus in Rome, we laughed at "smashed potatoes" but ordered pizza in one place and cheese fondu in another. In the lobby, our dashing Dad was approached by a painted lady whom he politely turned down. Hope and I exchanged secret glances. We had never seen him so openly propositioned.

We flew next to Frankfurt where we picked up a shiny black VW station wagon with red leather interior. In this, Dad had splurged when he ordered the car, tax- and duty-free, from the Wolfsburg factory through friends in MCC. It was perfect for a family of six camping in Europe for a month. We visited medieval-gothic Frankfurt, home of coronations, poets and composers, and bought a six-person tent and sleeping bags.

That evening we camped in a huge field of tents and Westphalia campers surrounding a large bath house that offered toilets and cold showers. Our neighbors were traveling by camper van to Turkey and the Soviet Union. They seemed cheerful about visiting "behind the iron curtain." I worried for them and wondered if I was just ignorant or prejudiced. The Soviet-supported rebellion in Congo had cost our friends dearly. Yet the western-supported capitalist strong man who followed was also cruel and murderous.

I shivered that night, though it was summer in Europe. I layered on all my thin summer dresses but could not sleep. They were no barrier to the damp, seeping cold. We older sisters finally huddled together—in the back of the VW wagon with the passenger seat folded down—and leached one another's body heat.

The next morning we entered the autobahn wary of the traffic blurring past on the superhighway. There was no speed limit but a black sports car bore down on us blowing its horn.

Dad was sweating it. "I'm already going as fast as I dare."

The speed demon roared past, careened into the ditch and rolled. When the dust settled, a man emerged and walked away as though it were a daily occurrence.

Mom looked back to make sure he was okay but there were few pull-offs or turnarounds. Besides, Dad had a spinal cord injury high in his neck and dared not make any sudden moves. As it was, he walked on numb feet and held handrails with dull hands. That night, well after dark, we set up our tent near the Brandenburg Gate in West Berlin. In the morning, we snapped our last permitted photos at the classic arch, and waited to cross through Checkpoint Charlie to East Berlin. A high wall topped by razor wire marked a sterile strip of no man's land. Men in green helmets watched from towers, rifles ready. German shepherds paced on chains. Before the wall was built in 1961, East Germans had left stark lives under Soviet rule and walked to freedom. After the wall, many risked their lives to escape.

At some point we visited the *Gedachtniskirche* (Memorial church). It was a cathedral bombed by Allies in 1943 and was better known by Berliners as "the hollow tooth" since all that was left was a hollow tower. In that space, I was grateful for the many who'd given their lives to free the death camps. But I also felt the wreckage of ongoing wars—the U.S. bombing North Vietnam.

Two decades later, President Reagan issued his famous challenge: "Mr. Gorbachev, tear down this wall." Yet it would take until November 9, 1989, before the soviet grip collapsed and people swarmed the wall, hacking it to pieces with pickaxes. That year my eldest son was attending kindergarten in Arlington, Massachusetts, with a close friend from Germany. The whole class acted out the drama. First they built a block wall, separating the class into two groups unable to connect. Then they knocked down the wall and joined together in celebration.

We left Berlin and drove through towering pines of the Black Forest and up into the high mountain lakes of Austria. Dad had read about a family of septuplets, seven look-alike sisters. Because their parents were struggling to run a restaurant, they baptized only three and the girls took turns going to school and helping in the kitchen as though they were triplets. We found the family restaurant and parked in the back. Through the kitchen window we saw two young women washing dishes; one looked just like the other.

I understood in that moment how identified Dad was with multiple births. He had been his mother's eleventh single birth before four sets of twins (though only one pair survived and one each of two other pairs). By the time Dad was born, his parents had also adopted orphaned cousin Martha. So Dad was the twelfth, born on October 12, 1928, weighing 12 pounds. We were returning to Canada in its centennial year, 1967, and Grandma won a senior citizen award for the large family she'd raised.

Near Stuttgart, we drove up a high hill to the massive Hohenzollern Castle with its soaring turrets, pinnacles and pennants. We walked across a draw bridge, past a kill zone and into a ribvaulted hall with red marble columns. Hardly a ray of light shot through heavy brocade drapes or warmed its cold stone walls and yellowed tiles. There was no flowing fountain or deep plush rug, no rugged prince in headband standing by. If that's all there was, I could not imagine living in such a palace—as a princess or kitchen maid.

Still we had visited a real castle. In the gift shop, my caring Dad bought me a castle key chain that I have cherished. It has stayed with me through 40 years of moves across states, nations, oceans and continents. It reminds me of clouded turrets, fortress walls and reality piercing my baobab dreams.

We drove along the ancient Rhine River, marveling at its massive flow, towering cliffs, old castles and glinting waterways filled with riverboat cruisers. Dad sang a mournful German folksong, *"Die Loralei,"* in his mellow bass voice. It described a sunset cliff where a mermaid sang and combed her long blonde hair luring boatmen to their deaths on the rocks below. With a twinkle in his eye, Dad ended the lament with its sarcastic flourish. All this, with the power of her song.

We left the Rhine valley for Münster, West Germany, a stop Charity, age 10, especially recalled. She remembered the three human-sized, iron cages hanging from the medieval St. Lambert's Church steeple. The cages represented the city's religious tolerance policy that had led to an Anabaptist rebellion during the Protestant Reformation ("Munster"). A peasant uprising against powerful elites of the Catholic Church drew radical reformer Jan of Lieden, Holland. Dad said they had tried to reestablish a New Testament church, which held all things in common and practiced equal distribution of wealth.

But Jan went further. He and his followers drove out the city council and townsfolk who refused re-baptism. Jan declared himself monarch of a millennial kingdom and announced women should marry. Since there were three for every man, he declared polygamy acceptable and accrued for himself 16 wives and personal wealth—beheading one wife with his own hand in the town square for criticizing his hypocrisy. In response to all this, Münster's expelled bishop laid siege and put down the rebellion with a combined Catholic-Protestant army.

After that disaster, Anabaptists defined their pacifist positions more clearly in the writings of reformed priest Menno Simons who preached at Witmarsum, East Holland. Simons' words, "The regenerate do not go to war," echoed through the 1960s among Mennonite conscientious objectors to the Vietnam War.

We entered the Netherlands on a pilgrimage to our ancestral home in Friesland where both our grandmas got their family name, Friesen. We paid tribute to Simons for several hours, sitting in wooden pews of the old Mennonite church and circling the obelisk that bore his beloved verses. "No foundation can be laid other than the one already laid—Jesus." And, "Endure hardships as discipline; God is treating you as his children." Dad walked around the memorial on numb feet and gripped the wrought iron fence with numb hands.

We drove along the Zuiderzee Dam. High on the other side, the sea sparkled, seemingly stretching above us endlessly. Here some wandering Irish sailor may have inserted himself into our Dutch lineage. At least grandma liked to say, touching her wavy red hair, "That's the Irish in us." Here the legendery Peter (I always thought of our Uncle Peter) stuck his finger in the dike to save his country—its glistening white farmhouses with sparkling windows, women scrubbing driveways on their hands and knees. Signs in fields invited us to pitch our tent and we did, spending the night and taking cold showers in the morning. There was no hot and, our hostess explained, it makes you feel warm when you get out. Again, it was Charity who recalled that remark distinctly.

The next morning, we passed white picket fences, canals, windmills, Holsteins and cheese farms. We drove up to one farm store, parked the car and asked in our Canadian Plautdietsch for "*kjeis*." The rosy-cheeked farmers understood and offered us a variety, from Gouda to Edam. It had been years since we tasted cheese so fresh and fine.

We toured the fishing wharfs of Volendam and visited a photographer who specialized in artistic stylings. His studio was hung

Hope, Charity and me in traditional Dutch dress.

with the sensual prints of Renoir who had painted in this village. The photographer described Renoir's fascination with the play of light and shadow and captured the three of us older sisters in crisp Dutch costumes.

In Amsterdam, we kept the tent packed and splurged on a *gasthaus* room with soft beds, heavy feather blankets and lace curtains. We rose to a continental breakfast with five kinds of fresh breads, cheeses and jams. I ate the rich food of my ancestors as though I were not on a continual diet.

That morning, I lost my loafer heel in the cobblestone streets and hesitated to tell mom lest I overrun our budget. This was not Europe on $40 a day was it? At last, limping along with shoe tacks piercing my heel, I alerted her to the catastrophe. She found a cobbler nearby and averted total calamity.

We visited Anne Frank's stark attic hideaway, directed up the narrow, ladder-like steps by a woman who had known the family. In that space with its hazy windows, I understood how close her first love must have felt with Peter and how tense her riffs with her mother. We recalled her early commitment to writing, no matter how personal and private the ordeal, and her tragic end in the death camps. If she could write her truth in such a short lifespan, in these raw wooden confines and under such stress, then so could I.

In The Hague, we visited Maduradam, a miniature city named for a Dutch resistance fighter who had died at Dachau. It pleased us to mark its twenty-fifth anniversary, an enduring tribute to our Dutch ancestors' resistance to the Nazis and rescue of Jewish refugees. We marveled at the 1-to-25 scale model of the common and extraordinary. There was the Binnenhof house of government, lighted ships in the port, airliners at the Shiphol airport, bicycle jams in rush hour traffic and miniature secretaries at tiny typewriters in knee-high office buildings.

We left before we'd absorbed every detail under threatening skies. Mom must have noticed us shivering in our thin summer dresses because something spurred her on when the storm hit. We entered Belgium in a deluge, yet she searched along the famous dress shops of Antwerp for parking. Mom dashed ahead of us through the rain into glittering boutiques to examine fine woolen plaids. She found Charity a cute red plaid wraparound kilt and had Hope and me sized and tailored in woolen plaid, lined skirts. Mom had revealed herself to be the dressmaker's daughter after all.

We spent that stormy night in an old Brussels hotel, radiator pumping out heat under tall windows with sheer curtains. Under the deluge, I was grateful and amazed that our thrifty parents had sprung for such once-in-a-lifetime luxury for our family.

The storm clouds lifted and a cool sunny morning dawned in Paris the next day. We strolled the manicured grounds of the Eiffel Tower, dwarfed by the iron goliath. Eiffel, who'd built the iron ribs of the Statue of Liberty, had designed France's tower for the 1889 World's Fair—a marvel of strength in its day. In the gift store, I selected an Eiffel Tower key chain, symbol of solidity and permanence in my traveling life.

In contrast to that monolith, the Notre Dame Cathedral was a patchwork of many hands over eight centuries. Its famous rib vaulting, flying buttresses, rose windows and carved gargoyles were a triumph of many different, unknown artists. Even its towers were not twins, one was larger and featured different carvings than the other.

We bought tickets to Le Louvre and my callused sketch finger no longer mattered. Here were more of the impressionists we loved—Manet, Monet and Renoir. Another hall was full of religious paintings, images of a skeletal, ashen Christ, one foot in the grave. How had some painter decided on such a ghastly depiction? I could not fathom. At Kamayala once in reverie, I had summoned a kind-eyed, square-lipped, long-haired Jesus to paint on Dad's birthday card.

We waited our turn to see Leonardo da Vinci's "Mona Lisa," valued at $100 million. In the room dedicated to her image, we were permitted a silent turn to gaze on her almost living presence. Her secret smile and unbroken gaze followed us to every corner of the room. Da Vinci had, perhaps, received the lady's flirtations and achieved this image by painting her full-fleshed—without outlines—seated above a receding landscape from an unusual aerial perspective.

I wanted to see and do so much more among esplanade art exhibits, violin solos and cafes but it was time to catch a ferry for England. We landed beneath the chalky White Cliffs of Dover. Cawing seagulls welcomed us and we piled into our VW wagon to see England. We drove off the boat in the left lane but a few turns later faced a large truck bearing down on us, horn blaring. At the last instant, Dad realized he was on the right. The driver shouted down at us, "Foreigner!" He threw back his head and laughed at the scare we'd given ourselves.

We camped in the countryside south of London where Cockney accents were so heavy that Dad switched to French when asking directions. It kept things simple, even elementary. We toured London from the safety of a cushioned tour bus and Dad grinned at seeing his namesake, the massive Big Ben clock tower. We paused beneath the "Bloody Tower" of London to learn about the royals beheaded there amid religious and political intrigues.

Finally we boarded the *Aleksander Pushkin* with our VW wagon for Montreal and Expo '67. Our parents' cabin was next door to ours and provided us girls privacy in bunks with curtains. Here, Charity crawled up and pulled the curtains to play with her souvenir dolls while Hope and I laid out my key chains and her souvenir spoons to remember our once-in-a-lifetime trip.

The seas were rough our first day and Mom stayed below with the youngest while Dad took the others to the formal dining room. The captain came to our table amused by so many passengers below decks. He showed us how to pour a bit of water from our glasses onto the linen tablecloth to keep our dishes from sliding. Beneath

During the ship's talent show the crew closed in with microphone and video camera to capture our village clapping games.

the table linens, a metal bar edged the table to prevent the real china from sliding off. We ate hot soup, fresh fish and our first salty black caviar. We lined up for dessert tables of cakes, custards and pastries, unable to choose just one.

After the first day, Dad disappeared into a smoky lounge behind the dining room where men puffed cigars and played chess—his passion.

Dad also signed us up for Russian language lessons and the talent show. It seemed a fitting cultural exchange for us to perform our village clapping games. The crew's cameramen zoomed in and the emcees circled close with their microphones. We ended with "God's Love Eternal" in five languages sung in our exquisite harmonies practiced over kilometers of Congo roads.

Our first sight of Canada after four years brought our family joyously to the ship's rail. We sailed up the Saint Lawrence Seaway, a system of locks, canals and channels. Each successive lock filled and emptied raising our ocean-going ship upriver to Montreal.

We crossed the Atlantic on the Aleksander Pushkin *and sailed up the Saint Lawrence Seaway. For our missionary family photo, Grace clutched a pack of soggy cigarettes she found on deck, refusing to give them up. (Eidse family photo)*

Dad had learned through BBC newscasts that Montreal families around the fairgrounds were hosting campers for a few dollars a night. We drove the perimeter of the world's fair and found a hand-written yard sign and tent site in walking distance of the fairground. It was perfect for spending maximum time in the pavilions.

We pitched our tent and navigated the spaghetti turnpike to tour the world's most successful fair in the twentieth century—for three full days. Throngs of people (fifty million) from around the world visited sixty-seven pavilions featuring sixty-two nations and technical advancements, such as air travel, color photography and video phones. We marveled at architectural wonders like the U.S. geodesic dome (pierced and ridden through by skyrail) and Habitat 67, futuristic modular homes later offered for sale to private citizens. I especially loved the video phone featured in the Telephone Pavilion. Such an invention would one day bring us closer to our

loved ones across oceans and around the world in our global nomad lives.

We were all permitted one special ride or souvenir. Dad chose
a hovercraft trip, a new technology in 1967, and wanted me to tag
along. But I fancied an old technology I had never tried before and
rode my first ferris wheel. Grace rode a miniature Model T around a
track and Charity got a monogramed hat featuring her favorite nickname, Cherilen. Coined by Dad, it combined her first and middle
names, Charity and Helen. Hope preferred to join Mom in watching
out for our safety. In fact, it was Hope who fluttered on the edges
of my jittery vision when the ferris wheel stopped high above the
lighted midway and I struggled with vertigo. In this way, she stepped
up her role as my backup guardian angel.

14

GLIDING

That summer, amid cool prairie breezes and woodsy-scented evergreen wind breaks, I practiced smooth pumping and gliding on a *shuckle* (bench swing). We shuckled and chuckled with our cousins on Grandma's farm near Rosenort, Manitoba. Their newsy letters had laced Congo's tropical nights with winter blizzards and snow forts and we were together again at last.

They had grown into busty teens in clingy sweaters with shag haircuts and were full of scandalous riddles about wild farm boys—some of them our cousins who play-dated them. I smiled at what seemed funny to them, waiting to be translated into their secret world. Irene, Marlene, Liz and LaVerna had been our faithful pen pals for four years and we had spoken their names in bedtime prayers. But how could I catch up with their mysterious racy boys knowledge? They were kind and funny yet I could barely keep up with their low German inside jokes. If I nudged Marlene, eyebrow raised, she might whisper clues to me, fill me in on the mischief of suave cousins. How they made mudslides in the pond or skinny-dipped in the river, treading water endlessly when some girls showed up teasing them about *knjiepa* (pinchers).

After dark, we sisters snuggled into shared beds in the trailer beside lush gardens—now run by Grandma's youngest son George and wife Elma since Grandma had moved to town. We pieced together puzzle bits of stories trying to make sense of it all.

"Would river beetles or turtles pinch your butt?"

"I'm not gonna try it," Hope said. "Silly boys."

"What about kissing cousins. What do you think?" I asked.

"Yuck. That's the worst!" Hope turned and faced the wall. Even though several older cousins were dating second cousins, she didn't like young uncles or older cousins kissing her at all. I had never had "the pleasure" so I had to trust her.

Would I ever make up for my years away? And when we returned to Congo would all my new knowing grow old and fade away?

For the school year, we bought an old house in Steinbach with vaulted roof and dormers that wasn't too showy or expensive for missionaries—only about $2,400. It was on Highway 12 a block from the Bible college where Dad was dean of students and taught Evangelism. The location was perfect for catching students sneaking out of the dorm at night. We'd just turn out the light, stand behind the living room curtain and watch while they passed under the streetlight.

It was also in walking distance of Grandma Reimer's and schools for us girls.

A scratched upright piano canted on the sloped living room floor and—surrounded by loving family—I started playing again. My favorite was not from the hymnal but from a big band collection. "There Is a Tavern in the Town." Mom had objected to music that made her *hoopsich* (hoppy or dancey). But even she took her turn at the piano to render her version. Yes, and quite *hoopsich* it was!

Grandma Reimer's neighbor was a much-loved and gentle piano teacher and my parents signed us up for lessons. She puzzled over my "music block." Why, when I could read music and play fine while she was out of the room, did I mess up when she sat next to me? Just when I was playing beautifully, I'd bungle it as though some thick, hairy hand had reached in to stroke me.

"We're going to break your music block," she said. And slowly, gently, by leaving the teacher's chair and praising me from the hallway, she did.

One summer day I caught a ride downtown with Dad. On Main Street, the red-maple-leaf flag luffed over the post office. It was just one of the many changes in the four years I'd been gone. Canada had replaced the Union Jack, symbol of allegiance to the Crown, and was celebrating 100 years of confederation with Great Britain.

On the car radio, Pierre Elliott Trudeau campaigned for Prime Minister. He promised to repatriate our constitution, bring it back from London, rewrite it and make it our own. It was unacceptable to go "hat in hand to a foreign government to edit our own constitution."

I looked over at Dad who grinned behind the wheel. "Who are you voting for?"

Dad braked at a stop sign. He'd been a British subject until 1948, had sung "God Save the King" from boyhood, and I could tell he thought getting our constitution back was a gutsy thing to do.

Skillfully, like the diplomat he was, itinerating among conservative or progressive Mennonite churches all over the U.S. and Canada, he eased out of a direct answer. "Mennonites don't vote."

"Why not?" Canadian politics were new to me, and we had not participated in elections in Congo.

"We believe in separation of church and state." Dad raised an eyebrow as though inviting further questions. "Also, the Mennonite peace vote was blocked by the government in World War I."

"Really? But how can we not vote when we're citizens here?"

"Well some do. Others believe they obey a higher law."

Oh, so Mennonites thought they could live in Canada and be separate from it too? "But what if the issues really matter, like getting our constitution back?"

"What do you think?" Dad braked for the light on Main Street.

"I'd vote—for Trudeau."

Our house on Highway 12, wedged between farm implement dealers, was a timeline of wallpaper patterns we'd missed while we were away. In the three bedrooms we four girls shared under the eaves, the roof slanted close and low and we could peel a hidden corner of wallpaper patterns or walk through the slanted house across five patterns of linoleum. We felt no urgency to strip and redecorate but I became aware—each time we entered a modern bungalow—of pile carpets, neat lines, true corners.

Yet we became conscious of cars slowing just in front of our house as though we were the toast of the town. Not so, Mom pointed out. Traffic reached residential speeds right at our yard, which meant we attracted the passing gaze of all arrivals. This became especially important when hanging laundry. The outer two lines were for sheets and towels, the inner two for bras and panties. "We don't want to embarrass anyone."

Between flapping sheets, I pinned bras and underwear and wondered at our changed attitudes. In Zaire, if a woman owned a bra, she pulled down a blouse sleeve to show off her lingerie. If her children owned good underwear, why cover them with shorts? Since we had come back to Canada, Mom gasped at miniskirts and tube tops as though we hadn't overlooked stark nakedness in Congo. Here we missionary daughters were expected to set new standards in modesty with hems to our knees.

In the kitchen, we snacked on soda crackers and butter, processed foods we'd never had in Zaire. Hope, Charity, Grace and I gathered after school, sprawled on the counters and surfed radio stations for shocking or maudlin pop tunes. "Just call me angel of the morning…" We missed our simple lives in Congo where we'd worn hand-me-downs like everyone else and not fretted too much about skirt lengths. Here we tended to be the most outmoded kids at school—our dresses longer, our collars higher. That is, except for the conservative Holdeman Mennonites whose dresses covered the knee by decree. Little sister Grace had worn a dress the first day of school and was mistaken for a Holdeman. It took her weeks to change that impression until she'd worn the same jeans every day without variation the entire year.

Given my outdated hem lengths, I resorted to rolling up skirt bands or buying chain belts to blouse up my dresses. But I also tried to distinguish myself by studying harder, reading more, and speaking out more in class. Fortunately, we'd just toured Europe, had seen historic landmarks in real life. So I described them in fuller detail for the class, driven to stamp out any impression I was backward or ignorant. Around me the more modern Mennonite, Lutheran and United Church girls seemed to talk less, check their pocket compacts more and arrange their orange-fish-net legs prettier under their desks.

My friend in grade seven was natural, down-to-earth Brenda Friesen, a smart, dimpled, bouncy-haired farm girl who rode the bus. Her plaid dresses, like mine, contrasted with the other girls' fashionable grape and pink miniskirts. In her father's shed, Brenda taught me to hammer straight, and at school, to ignore the boys who followed me around singing Sunday School choruses "Have Faith, Hope and Charity…."

In this way, the boys discovered we missionary daughters were named out of biblical order. Their discovery drew an audience. "Hey, don't you have an older sister? You're not supposed to be Faith! You're supposed to be Hope. Your missionary parents named you wrong!"

I squirmed. How could I explain our mis-ordered names? "My parents didn't expect to have only girls. So they started with the name they liked—Hope."

"Yeah, you morons." Brenda was feisty and I liked that.

I needed Brenda to interpret recess for me, too. I'd been to the Berlin Wall, had toured the Colosseum and Catacombs, but didn't understand nonsense phrases parroted in nasal tones around me such as "What's up doc?" They whistled or shot me a finger and I didn't know the difference.

Brenda whispered, "That's the bad finger, ignore it. They're giving you the peace sign—it's okay, sign back."

Gerald, the nerdy, mouthy, class president, was as locally adept as I was ignorant, and for some reason he went crazy for my naiveté. After school he dawdled while I waited with Brenda 'til she caught her bus. Then he followed me out the door. But I couldn't tell whether he was teasing or flirting with me.

Gerald tried to walk me to the corner, take my books, hold my hand. I thought him silly so I sped up or slowed down, making his attempts to share the sidewalk graceless. Shy, quiet Lyndon sometimes trailed us and the two of them tried to teach me "good girlfriend etiquette."

"You're supposed to let me carry your books." Gerald reached for my homework.

"Why?" In Congo women did all the carrying. "I only have two. I can carry them myself."

"You're supposed to hold his hand," Lyndon prompted if Gerald's hand brushed mine.

Gerald's hands were scarred from a childhood burn and I worried I might hurt them. Besides hand-holding was for girlfriends. In Zaire I walked arm-over-shoulder with my *ndoyi*, Hélène, and boys held hands while they strolled through the village. For a boy to hold a girl's hand was just weird.

Since I didn't fall for Gerald's boyfriend style, he and Lyndon flanked me and sang silly chorus songs, substituting my name. "For all my fancy dwells with Faithee, I'll sing tally-ho." I suspected they were making fun of me and was relieved when we got to the corner where Gerald turned for home across from the funeral parlor and I continued a mile to the highway. Residential lawns gave way to farm implement dealers and I assured myself that Gerald was just teasing me, not despising or falling for me.

But when I reached home, the phone rang and it was Gerald—full of chitchat. The Beatles this, the Monkees that, the Liberals this, Progressive Conservatives that. Hope said he was worse than a girl. Deep down I realized he knew how badly out-of-tune I was and he was giving me a crash course in pop culture. It felt a lot safer at a distance. I could talk, or listen, and not worry about what that meant about possession and control.

At school, Brenda said we didn't need boyfriends and I agreed. Yet Gerald's mini-lectures and my own drive to learn Canadian culture must have worked because later that year I ran as Pierre Elliott Trudeau, P.E.T., in mock elections at school.

We assembled a campaign committee, girls in tights and miniskirts—Candy, Kathy, Karen, Phyllis, June, Ruby and Evelyn among them. They kicked up a Trudeaumania can-can in miniskirts on stage around a giant stuffed dog labeled "P.E.T." I delivered a speech practiced from Trudeau on the radio—and we won by a landslide.

Brenda was learning some smooth moves of her own at folk dance classes with our cool young gym teacher, Henry Kroeker. Moves that would prepare her for a starring role in Steinbach's world-renowned "Treble Teens." Mr. Kroeker taught classes before school that Brenda attended because she caught the early bus. The Kroekers even invited seventh graders over and taught us the Charleston. Two years later, while Henry was teaching with our cousin Larry Eidse, the principal at Lowe Farm, he and his wife Lynn, both 24, were lost in a canoeing accident leaving a two-year-old son to be raised by his aunt and uncle.

Tragic losses occurred in Congo, too. In November 1967 we received word that our little orphan brother, Terry Lee, had died of measles in the village. The promise of seeing him again, delighting in his flashing smile and joyful dance was gone. We would never again, in this life, see the child Charity had nursed to laughing, singing, sparkling health. Recognizing the depth of her grief, Mom and Dad bought her a commemorative wristwatch. Charity and her children would continue to adopt Congolese family and sponsor their immigration to Canada throughout their lives. In this they became more rooted in several nationalities than I ever was.

On Epiphany, January 6, 1968, we received a call from our hostel big sister, Linda Bertsche. Our dorm brother, Paul Brower, had been in a truck accident outside Kikwit on December 29, 1967. He was riding in the back when the truck hit a soft shoulder on a new road, rolled down an embankment and crushed his chest and good eye. My classmate Becky Grings—who had lost her aunt in the revolution two years before—was in the open truck bed with him but escaped serious injury. Paul could not see at all. His parents, who had been in the cab, wanted to know if he was ready to go. Yes, he assured them, he would *see* Jesus. During his short life he had cherished us as though he were living on borrowed time. His death pulled us back to a time when life had been lived closer to survival, closer to a larger calling and purpose.

Our new favorite radio tune became, "We had joy, we had fun, we had season in the sun," by the Kingston Trio. Perhaps to nurture ourselves following deep loss, my sisters and I baked and sang and ate. We seemed to be making up for all the controlled eating we'd done at the hostel. In old Nigeria, young girls were housed in "fattening rooms" and taught to nourish themselves into attractive marriage partners. Our Canadian kitchen would have made a great fattening room, if we had not recalled the sunken eyes, rail arms and legs, and bloated stomachs at Mom's clinic in Kamayala.

We couldn't accept our weight gain with those images burned on our retinas, so Hope led us to the pink-and-black-tiled bathroom and told me to lean over the green toilet. But no matter how far down my throat I stuck my finger, I couldn't gag. If I choked at all, it was a sissy cough.

Charity could gag but didn't want to. She was growing so fast, her legs ached constantly. She seemed to need every calorie she ate.

Grace, who was not yet six, and still free with her opinions, said, "You're crazy!" and flounced up the stairs.

Next, Hope led me in the early dusk to Townline Road. Together we raced the mile at the western edge of town. Gliding against the wind brought back exhilarating descents to the Kamayala River, just me and my pumping arms and legs against the wind. I sped straight down the gravel road, past farms framed by evergreens and into scrub prairie. We ran a mile down Townline Road, fast, turned around and ran back. I learned to love this punishment on legs, arms and lungs. It seemed to purge the guilt. Plus there was the cool wind in my face to bring the senses alive. I could get addicted to such motion and speed. I missed it on the days we couldn't run and felt a new guilt. After I ran two miles, I paced off the burn while Hope ran four.

She was always setting a higher standard for both of us. We Eidse daughters should be more perfect, more disciplined, more fit, more modestly dressed, more heroic and nobler. And just when she cranked her standards, I relaxed mine. Just when she tucked her white blouses deeper into her Belgian plaid skirt, combed her hair into a longer, thicker braid, I wore a baggy yellow sweatshirt from Uncle Henry over my Belgian skirt, my hair loose and free.

Sometimes my sloppiness bugged Hope so much she left the table when I sat down. "Like a hippie!"

"Exactly."

Flower children filled Winnipeg parks in 1968, vagabond teens giving out flowers as symbols of love and unity. It was my second summer in Canada, our return to Congo delayed by Dad seeking treatment for his numb feet. So on Thursday evenings, I rode into the city with Pentecostal friends to meet these peace-loving youth.

When we approached a group lounging in a park, they easily shared the grass, moving over to let us into their circle. It was like Kamayala where we were easily received by the youth.

"Peace man." A couple of bronzed First Nations guys with flowing black hair flashed the peace sign.

"Peace!" We flashed it back.

A pixie-faced, wavy-haired girl—barely thirteen—handed me some flowering clover.

"Thanks!" I handed her a dandelion. "You new here?"

"Yeah, just passing through." She pulled her leather vest closer in the gathering shadows and crossed her legs.

"Where to?"

"West."

"Oh, Raincouver!" An older teen in headband, khaki shirt and beads lit a cigarette and passed it. "Why not hang here with us awhile"

"Okay." She brightened and moved in closer, accepting the smoke.

"Where're you from?" I asked. She appeared relaxed, at ease with coping on her own.

"TO, my parents kicked me out."

"Why'd they do that?" I didn't understand; she was still a school girl.

"Didn't want a hippy for a kid."

"Yeah, sucks." The older teen and several others nodded. "Bummer. Bad scene."

Several in the park joined us at a nearby Pentecostal chapel afterwards. They swayed and tapped along with the singing, circled up for prayer, hung out and told stories. Like fluffy seeds from a dandelion blowball, they had spread across Canada and joined thousands of U.S. draft dodgers fleeing Nixon's cancelled college deferment.

Summer lengthened, sunsets flamed across prairie skies and we spread out from local parks inviting folks to chapel services from surrounding bungalows and overcrowded rentals thick with marijuana smoke. We were Youth with a Mission and we welcomed all seekers. Canada had just opened its borders to U.S. emigrants regardless of military status—even deserters. I knew in my gut their war on rigidity and expectation. I knew their need for freedom, purpose and adventure.

Later that summer, Hope proposed a bike ride across southern Manitoba. In Congo's far more challenging terrain, we had pedaled ninety kilometers through sun-seared savanna and teeming river jungle to visit the Falks in Kajiji. We were no strangers to roughing the elements and challenging expectations.

Dad had assembled several bikes from rusty parts left in our Steinbach garage. He had worked cautiously on numb feet to build us swift sturdy one-speeds that rivaled the three-speeds sold new at McCleod's. We girls welcomed long rides in the country, recalling endless jaunts on Congo's open grasslands. It was but a small leap to plan a ninety-mile bicycle trip on our trusty rusties to see the Falks in Morden, Manitoba.

We started out early, wearing orange squall jackets and signs duct-taped to our backs, "Steinbach-Morden." We headed west on Highway 52 and turned toward Otterburne. There, we met a Steinbach radio CHSM van with my classmate Ruby Kehler's dad at the wheel. He noticed our Steinbach-Morden signs and flagged us down for an interview. The story aired that afternoon and the following morning.

"If you're on the road between Steinbach and Morden this weekend, keep an eye out for Hope and Faith Eidse. They are pedaling the ninety miles just for fun. Hope is 15 and Faith is 13. Way to go, Faith and Hope!"

We passed farms at a pace that brought dogs running. One big black dog nipped our heels happy to finally catch his prey—but then confused about what to do with our churning feet. We spent the night at our cheerful, athletic Aunt Rosie's on Meridian Road south of Rosenort. Widowed mom of five sporty kids, she was thrilled to be part of our epic journey. We were grateful for her homecooked meal, fresh baking, warm beds and cheery breakfast.

We started out again before sunrise and pedaled against a biting wind that pasted our windbreakers to our arms. My muscles ached with lactic acid build-up; my inner thighs stung with each stroke against the bruising bike seat. I needed Hope's encouragement all the way to Highway 23.

"We can do it. Come on, stay close. I'll break the wind for you."

"Haha." We laughed together and it lightened our journey.

The sun crested the horizon and rose on acres of green sunflowers turning yellow faces to greet it. Our names caught on the gusts of passing drivers while we cycled west through Lowe Farm, Kane and Myrtle. Truckers leaned out and shouted, "Way to go Hope and Faith! Thirty more miles!" Sedans slowed to let us turn south to Winkler. "Keep the Faith, Hope, twenty more miles."

We arrived wind-blown and sore and may have stopped at Aunt Grace and Uncle Wilf Warkentin's manicured yard and accepted water, hugs and congratulations. We then rode down the street and around the corner to the Falk's. They were returning to Zaire

Grace picked some weed for this family photo. Hope and I were sun-burned after pedaling 90 miles from Steinbach to see the Falks in Morden in 1968. (Peter Falk photo)

and we had made it in time for a farewell visit. Mom, Dad, Charity and Grace had arrived in our VW wagon and Mom brought the matching dresses Grandma had sewed us sisters that summer. Peter Falk took our photo in their backyard and captured Hope's and my sun-burned cheeks.

———————

On Sundays our family traveled near and far to Mennonite churches in cities and farming communities. We four sisters sat on raised platforms, objects of curiosity.

When the preacher called on us we circled-up, clapped and swayed in syncopated rhythms as though we were back in our beloved Kamayala with our cherished *ndoyis.* Sometimes Mom cautioned us. "Tone it down. These people aren't used to so much jig in their music." From 1967 to 1969, our village games were the jazziest music in many prairie Mennonite churches, where instruments were still forbidden.

Later Grace would coin a term to describe our role on those stages. Proselytutes.

By the time our traveling show reached my cousin Lois Reimer's church in Winnipeg, we had added a culture shock skit. It was a daring thing to do among a people who traditionally considered play-acting lying and foolishness, certainly not appropriate for church. But this was a culturally advanced audience, so we pushed the limits.

It wasn't for that reason I wished I could walk down the block and disappear into a park full of flower children. It was because, for the first time, there was someone in the audience I cared about and wanted to impress—someone suave, dignified and going steady at thirteen—my tall, red-haired cousin Lois.

I picked a chair behind the pulpit, and when it came time for us to act out our reentry shock, I turned carmine as the knee-length, drop-waist dress Grandma had sewed me. My prop was a bathroom scale. I had to hold it up for all to see, set it down and step on it, then let my hands fly to my mouth. This usually brought down the house. But in front of Lois, I felt like a freak on parade, someone who would always stick out. I went through the motions, looking as pained as I felt.

Afterward I waited in the lobby hoping I had not humiliated Lois or lost her as my friend. She finally appeared, not with her new steady boyfriend, but alone. She'd already been replaced, she said.

Well then good riddance, I wanted to say but Lois didn't seem too smitten.

Without status dividing us, we linked arms and walked outside. Later, lounging in her attic room, her red hair copper in the dormer light, Lois handed me some small pink plastic flowers. "Here, have some of these." A slight smile played on her lips. "I've been hanging out with the flower children. They are some of the cutest on the planet."

15

WALKING PICKET FENCES

At the Steinbach post office, three bushy-haired Mennonite teens and a girl with dark flowing hair, leaned against a picket fence. A gangly boy with Beatle-cut blonde hair walked picket fence points. His work boots rocked over one picket after another, balancing a moment and wobbling on. One misstep and he'd be a eunuch. Dad braked at the light and I watched the boy's rocking boots through our VW windscreen holding my breath. "Drop me off here."

"Here?" Dad's eyes widened at the boy tottering on fence points.

"Yep." I jumped out and closed the door. "Your light's green. Bye."

I leaped to the curb, my shoulders radiating heat and smarting under a clinging yellow tank top. I'd just come off my summer job hoeing sugar beets and my long mop was knotted and windblown. I joined the fence-leaners knowing that my face was familiar to them, in a younger, primmer version. I grinned big to erase the old black-and-white prayer card stuck to their fridges.

"I told you to hoe beets, not turn into one." Brad jumped down. He was the same smart-mouthed punk I knew from Red Rock Bible Camp the month before. A giant grin lit his angular joker face. He had passed me racy poetry during evening chapel to make me blush.

I laughed, happy to break out of my missionary kid straight jacket. I enjoyed being the new girl, still, in this square-mile prairie town. That worked as long as I didn't get stuck too long in any one group.

Maggie tossed her long dark hair, grinned at me, blew smoke and ashed her cigarette. She'd been a prim girl on a prayer card once, too, and we could probably show these fence-sitters how to have fun. Catch some of those bullfrogs croaking in Stony Brook—the creek the town was named for—and roast us some frog legs.

Except for crazy Brad, these guys stood still as stones, barely looked at each other and uttered short, monosyllable bursts.

"There goes Moose."

"Cool mags."

"Check out that *Schmäa.*" (Grease.)

"*Schmäa?*" I was puzzled. Wasn't that what you put on your toast?

"Yeah, Greaser."

"Fuzz dice."

"Rug dash."

"Keep Truck'n' sticker."

"Hick radio."

They reached into their plaid flannel work shirts, shook out du Maurier cigarettes and handed them down the line. "*Schmieek?*" (Smoke?)

I passed it on. The Plautdietsch lingo was simple street slang exaggerated to sound hick, a parody of a parody of themselves. It had come from the lowlands of Holland and Poland, survived migrations to Russia, treks across Canada. More than those flat, twangy phrases, the kids seemed unwilling to speak.

Maggie slid over and said in a low voice, "It's the silence at home that drove me out here."

"And this is better?"

"Yeah, my parents don't talk. Not to each other, not to us kids. They don't say what they like, they don't say what they don't like. They just don't talk."

I had seen this among some prairie families, entire conversations in a series of guttural bursts. Mom called through a silent bungalow, "*Meddach!*" (Lunch.) Dad and the kids wandered in for lunch. "*Na, waut sajst?*" (So, whaddya say?)

"*Nuscht, du?*" (Nothing; you?)

They pulled up chairs, bowed and recited, "*Alle gooten Gaben.*" (All good gifts.) The prayer was standard, the ritual automatic.

Silence had haunted Mennonites for centuries, from secret re-baptisms in 1540s Holland to drownings in rivers and canals, burnings at the stake and escapes to the Polish lowlands where their singing drew so many converts that they were forbidden to sing for 100 years. They bent to their work, avoiding utterance. *Let your ayes be ayes, your nays, nays.*

The silence drove spikes of worry into Maggie's chest. "*Do Mom and Dad hate me? Do they like me? Will I ever know?*" She found herself struggling to breathe, her palms sweaty, her pulse racing. She grabbed her jean jacket and fled to the picket fence.

At home some kids observed a silence more terrifying than speech. Away from home they were too cool for words. *Steena.* (Stones.)

"There goes Grease."

"Here comes Rat."

A young Rod Stuart sauntered up to us.

"Hey Rat. *Jet it?*" (Goes it?)

"It goes."

"*Schmieek?*"

Rat accepted a cigarette, bent to light it, sucked deeply, raised his chin, shot a wispy column into the vast prairie sky. He was bolder, more daring among us than he could be at home where smoking was forbidden.

By hanging out with them, I was accepting exclusion in this town of rule-abiding Mennonites. It was like admitting I, too, lived on the edges—on the edges of the edges.

A red sports car pulled to the curb in front of Maggie. "Wanta ride?" The dark-haired boys spoke in lilting French accents, probably from neighboring La Broquerie or Ste. Anne.

"Going north?" Maggie asked.

"Sure."

"Say hi to the Eskimos for me!" She raised her chin and tossed her flowing hair.

The muscle car screeched off into the purple light that would linger until 10 p.m.

The fence-leaners laughed, sucked du Mauriers and exhaled.

The light turned green and a sedan-load of girls in neat page boys passed. All around me wolf whistles split the summer air. Perhaps I should find a more talkative group. I would in time. Learning what I didn't know was all part of being an outsider becoming an insider in a new town. Then, I'd launch myself out again, because "outsider" was who I was, and what I did best. I didn't want to get too attached or too involved with any one set of friends. Or maybe I didn't know how to keep friendships going long enough to weather all the tension and silence.

This group was more adept than I at biting down on speech. They could lean for hours on the fence and bare nothing. They avoided any but the most surface expressions. I was used to telling my life story in fifteen seconds, creating friendships that were a race against time. I over-shared and didn't care that I did. I'd soon be gone, better leave a lasting impression.

Brad sidled up to me, making a play for the crowd, daring to speak two-syllable words, break the monotony. "I've always wanted a girl to ask me to say something soft and mushy in her ear."

The other kids waited. I considered Brad, his brown eyes dancing, his Joker's mouth grinning. Perhaps the other kids had heard this joke before, but how would I unless I asked?

"Okay," I said, "say something soft and mushy in my ear."

He leaned close, smelling of stale smoke, cupped my ear, and stage whispered, "Shiiit."

The fence shook with their laughter. I grinned, my prim, pinched smile gone, replaced with a groan and memory of bitter hand soap.

Summer mornings at six, Hope, Charity and I filled gallon jars with ice water, fetched our hoes, and got Dad to drive us to the beet fields. The sun was just climbing the horizon, a hard-boiled egg. The black dirt was still cold and hard, and our hoes hit it with a clang. This was a job Hope had scouted for us. One that would give us muscles, tans and money—as much money as we could hoe. A buck a quarter-mile row. Even the farmer didn't much value this work but Hope was on a mission to teach us the importance of physical labor. She wanted us to feel the character we built when every row hoed meant another loaf of bread.

We hoed, not for the farmer, but to build our own strength and to help our parents pay for our first house, our slope-floored, wood-frame with dormers among tractors and combines. In my thirteen years, every place I'd lived had been temporary, from student housing in Goshen, Wheaton or Steinbach to a cabin or trailer on Grandma Eidse's farm, to various mission houses, refugee barracks or transitional dorms on the Congo River. We had averaged a move or two a year. The $900 we raised hoeing beets that summer would cover nearly half the cost of a home we owned.

We gathered on the farmer's field with the immigrants from Mexico and Paraguay and listened to their pure Plautdietsch. Most of the women could not read or write but they used no English where low German should be. When we spoke, we often just made English words sound low German, like *coffee-gonna-tiet* (coffee-going-time).

The Mexicans were conservative Mennonites whose grandparents had trekked south to avoid Canadian nationalism and conscription in World War I. Now they were trickling back, weary of their hardscrabble lives. They had shunned worldly knowledge and had bent to the hoe in Cuauhtémoc, where some of their sons would serve time for growing pot—shipped across the border in homemade furniture (Corchado 1995).

The Paraguayans had come from the semiarid lowlands of the Gran Chaco, where they were so isolated they had become laws unto themselves. Governments had to stop public hose-whippings of church members. Or in Bolivia, to prosecute men for drugging and raping their own colony women and children (Friedman-Rudovsky 2023).

We field hands had common origins in Russia, where Catherine the Great invited the hard-working, silent Mennonites of Poland to farm the East Reserve. Common roots and common language but the women's lives, cut from the jungles of the Chaco or the desert of Cuauhtémoc, had made them tougher. They worked harder and expected less than we did. Their work was as relentless as any water carrying or manioc pounding we'd done with the girls or women of Congo and we felt a kinship with both cultures.

Still, other farmers used beet-thinning machines instead of field hands. Why should anyone have to do this back-breaking work? Did no one want to help these women improve their lives? Why should they have to struggle, feet splayed, fingers callused? I knew Mennonites distrusted education—too much could cause you to lose your faith. But a little would go a long way for these immigrants. Charity would one day teach and coauthor a literacy textbook and workbook for them (Tiessen 1995). Even the African women wanted to trade their hoes for books, an opportunity granted by Dayspring Christian Ministries funding Kamayala initiatives in the 2000s (Goertzen).

The sun reached its midday slant and family groups of mothers and children gathered in the shade of a hydro-electric pole around reusable tin honey pails filled with sandwiches. Their men were probably parking forklifts and eating the same lunches of homemade bread and spun honey at Penner Lumber, Loewen Windows, Steinbach Feed Mill. They washed down lunch with lukewarm water and returned, refueled. The women and children hoed two or three rows to our one. They swung their hoes steadily and never leaned on the handles or raised their eyes to gauge the distance to the end of the row.

When the season deepened, the beets grew big and tough as callused fingers. I had to hack at a single beet plant several times, and went periodically nuts, my loose hair flying, my chopping frenzied. At night the rows came back at me in my dreams and I hacked at raised fingers, flesh and bone, blood and spatter.

Unlike Hope who gloried in her growing muscles—her sore back, legs and arms—I could not see much reward in such work. Perhaps there was virtue in wielding a hoe, if only to identify with women around the globe who produced eighty percent of the world's food.

———————

Each morning the farmer drove out from his gleaming white two-story home, a mug of steaming coffee in his work gloves and dispatched us. "These rows need to be done today. When you finish, cross the road and start on the other side." The reward for getting done early was more work. Sometimes he loaded us into his pick-up and dropped us far from town in distant fields. Even if we finished early, we were stuck under the beating sun until he came to pick us up. Charity suffered the most with her fair complexion and, one day felt she had suffered sunstroke. She was hot, dizzy, pale, thirsty, crampy and sick. We encouraged her to stay home after that while Hope and I returned for our workout and pay days. On Saturdays, the farmer peeled bills off wads he pulled from deep coverall pockets.

On Fridays, the farmer took off on shopping trips to Winnipeg, Manitoba's windy capital. Each trip a different tire would blow. Hope and I watched the migrant boys stride to the farmhouse to refill water jars on Thursdays and return at a buoyant pace. At season's end, three of the farmer's tires blew at once. He had to be towed home, past the beet fields where his workers ducked and smiled. After he passed, the boys yipped across the field to each other as though it were payback day.

———————

Weekends we continued to sing and run skits at prairie churches. So I wasn't at all shy at school, where geography, social studies and art had come alive in family travels. Many of the places in our textbook I had seen on our camping trip through Europe: the sub-floor cells of the Coliseum; the dark paneled parlor at Le Louvre where Mona Lisa's subtle, flirting eyes tracked her visitors around the room; the Berlin Wall with its guard towers, concertina wire and mined no man's land.

My friendship with Brenda teetered through educational tracking when I was placed in grade 8A (later, after student protests, 8M for our teacher Mr. Martens) in a dingy corner of the Kornelson school basement, and Brenda was placed in 8B. Perhaps the principal thought that by putting the A students in the smallest, darkest room, he could curb the insult to the others being divided by grade point average. But Brenda protested at being separated into 8B when we had performed neck-and-neck the year before. And she had proven herself a genius in so many ways.

One snowy morning, she and I huddled in stockings and boots in the lobby waiting for the doors to open. A tall, face-powdered girl asked me about Europe. I could see from her thick orange hair yarn, glistening lipstick and blue eye shadow, that she led the styles at school. It would take months, but by spring all the girls would dress like that, and she would have to start something new.

"Why were you in Europe?" Her voice was dripping honey. "Did you live there?"

"Oh no, we were just traveling through."

"Coool. How long were you there?"

"A month."

"She lived in Africa." Brenda's voice was measured, matter-of-fact.

"Africa, too?" The girl cooed.

"Her parents are missionaries." Brenda set the girl straight. We didn't travel the world because we had money and leisure, we weren't tourists traveling on sight-seeing packages. We were plain folks who worked overseas and had camped through Europe on our way home on $5 a day.

Contempt rose in the girl's brown eyes. I smarted at being regarded as zealous and backward.

"Humph!" The girl crossed her arms and turned her back, flouncing her orange-yarned curly hair in my face.

There was so much these kids could not understand about our lives in Congo, such depths of meaning, adventure and sacrifice they would never know.

16

FOOT WASHING

"We are all just walking each other home."
— RAM DASS

Winter 1968-69 howled in like a timber wolf, rattling the doors and whistling through loose sills. We rose numb and shivering in the dark and struggled into school-required skirts and stockings.

One morning I ran late to school and popped my garters, hid behind bare bushes and pulled up my stockings. Headlights shone out my blanched thighs and I was livid with indignation. Crazy women's fashions, stupid school dress codes. How would I survive months of dressing trauma in such a rage? In sunny Congo, none of this would be necessary.

Perhaps I needed an attitude adjustment. Our Evangelical Mennonite Church on Steinbach's Main Street called for baptismal candidates and I signed up.

"Don't you think you're a little young?" Mom looked up from the church bulletin.

I was surprised she'd object. What was she referring to? My age, maturity, ability to mess up? Or just that I was the youngest by two years? "I'll be fourteen in February."

We ranged from my youth group friends (Corinne and Gloria Reimer) to my Friesen and Loewen second cousins (Yvonne and James, CheAnn and Paul), singles (Aunt Betty Friesen) and young marrieds to senior citizens. We were thirty-six candidates in all that year and the church may have mimeographed extra instruction manuals for us.

Pastor Fast's eyes behind black-rimmed glasses shone with approval. "You have made an important decision to confess your faith publicly and take an open step of obedience. Mennonites follow the New Testament—baptism on the confession of faith. So you will prepare your testimony to give in front of the church."

No one blinked. Most of us had grown up in the church so were familiar with the one-page statements by baptismal candidates describing how and why they decided to turn from sin and follow Jesus.

The class dipped into the instruction manual, recalling the early Mennonite martyrs during the Reformation who had been secretly rebaptized after the state church had already christened them as babies. For refusing to recant their Anabaptist (adult baptism) faith they had been burned at the stake in Holland or drowned by "Zwingli's baptism" in Switzerland.

"We don't baptize babies," Pastor Fast pointed out. "We dedicate them."

Fat snowflakes fell past the window and I tucked in my stockinged legs.

"The first Anabaptists were calling out the corruption of the church," the pastor explained. "They were seeking renewal, a revival of the New Testament church. The authorities pursued and imprisoned them, drowned them in rivers and canals, or burned them at the stake."

Our lessons also taught us expected behaviors. "These are advised so we don't cause weaker Christians to stumble and fall," the pastor said. Mennonites shouldn't drink alcohol, dance or gamble.

To his credit, Pastor Fast did not hew closely to the old manual; things had changed. But I read ahead and learned we once didn't play cards either, though we had played plenty of cards in Congo. We reviewed how the church "disciplines" its members by sending pastors or deacons to confront them if they are caught in sin. If members in error didn't confess and repent, they could be excommunicated.

That meant if I joined the church, I would be accountable for all my behavior, public and private. We were surrounded by examples of what that might mean. A friend's sister required to publicly confess her pregnancy by a married man, the unnamed father nowhere to be seen.

Why would I go through with this? Did I consider myself inerrant? A handmaiden of the church? Perhaps Mom was right. I was too young.

Shunning was still practiced by some congregations, like the Holdeman church near our house. There Hope's friend, age 16, was being isolated for getting pregnant outside of marriage. She could not eat at the same table with her family and church members were not permitted to talk to her until her child was born and put up for adoption. Again, the father was nowhere to be seen.

I also learned from the baptismal manual that Mennonites don't wear jewelry or make-up, though I saw plenty of it—a gash of lipstick or puff of blush here, a rock diamond there. A gold Harley Davidson ring on some guy's hand. The instruction booklet was outdated, perhaps? Or members lived in denial and let their girls use lip gloss, their sons race motorcycles and *sew their wild oats*. It was understood, boys had to get the partying out of their systems before they could join a strict church. Girls rebelled more subtly.

I was baptized by water one snowy Sunday morning flanked by cousins and friends. I knelt on a rubber runner in front of the large Evangelical Mennonite Church on Main Street. The pastor poured a tablespoon from a measuring cup and trapped the runoff in my hair with his other hand. It was a warm, caring touch. No woolen jumpers would be ruined that day. "I baptize you in the name of the Father, Son and Holy Ghost."

The baptism was contained and symbolic in the iconoclastic Mennonite way. Barely a drop escaped to my white blouse. The pastor took my right hand and lifted me up. "I raise you to membership with the right hand of fellowship."

I felt received even though I had not been immersed the way Hope was the year before, when she was dunked by Pastor Mark in the Kamayala River.

Dozens of friends and family filed past to hug and "holy kiss" me after the service, and later that afternoon I received my first communion. Only the baptized could attend the hour-long service that included silent confession and foot washing. The ceremony was considered so grave that it was conducted only twice a year. Because of

Hope was baptized at age 14 in the Kamayala River by Pastor Mark. (Faith Eidse 1967 photo)

the intimacy suggested by foot washing, the men, in dark suits and clean socks, sat at the front left; the women at the back right.

The grape juice and cubed bread came around first, and I gulped the bread without thinking, only to notice that everyone else cradled a square of bread and jigger of grape juice. The pastor read, not Jesus's words, "take and eat," but Paul's, "Anyone who eats and drinks unworthily, eats and drinks his own condemnation."

The dry bread scraped down my throat. Had I forgotten to confess some forbidden card game, some joyful dancing? Had I eaten my own condemnation? Had I made myself worthy of Christ when "there is no one worthy, no not one"? I sagged at the weight of the grape juice. I shut my eyes and pleaded silently. *Please don't condemn me. Don't punish me. Don't make this hurt.*

I was amazed to see large white enamel bowls arrive, white towels, and women going down on their knees, washing each other's feet. A bowl arrived at our bench and I noticed that the women didn't bother removing their nylons. They just reached out their pointy toes and dunked them, nylons and all. Then they submitted to a vigorous drying and slipped their heels back on. I had not yet worn my first nylons, my mother perhaps thinking to ward off womanhood in that way. I sweated, knowing how soaking heavy my stockings would get if I dunked them for foot washing.

Next to me, my Sunday School teacher whispered, "Go down to the bathroom and take off your stockings." I slipped into the basement, grateful for Ms. Brown's guidance and annoyed at my stupidity. I unsnapped my garters and wondered how everyone could have forgotten this critical matter in their glow at my baptism that morning. I crept back upstairs barefoot, shivering in bare, blue-blotched legs and clutched crumpled stockings in white-knuckled fists.

My teacher washed my feet first, to demonstrate how it was done, before I washed hers. She quickly dunked my blue toes in cooling water and then rubbed them pink again with a white towel. She seemed to linger an extra minute to bring back their color. Then

I got down on my knees and lifted hers gently into the basin. I tried not to breathe in her private, closed-shoe musk and lingered over her webbed toes until she said, "That's okay." The Apostle Peter had objected, too, but his was pure shame at the real dirt and grime Jesus scrubbed off after hours walking dirt roads.

Ahead of us on the left, men pulled on dark dress socks and gripped each other in a "brotherly" hug and "holy kiss."

My teacher hugged me, a quick "sisterly" clutch. Then I padded downstairs to pull my stockings back on. I could not leave the basement in anger after communion. So I counseled myself to speak gently to my mother about being old enough to wear nylons, no matter how they showed the leg. I needed them for communion.

———————————

At school I was editor of the junior high newspaper and took up the debate over the dress code. Girls in grades seven and eight were considered "young ladies now" and had to wear dresses to school. We weren't permitted to wear pants in class—had to take them off if we'd walked to school in them—even on sub-zero days when our knees turned to ice. And yet there were dozens of Holdeman girls among us who were not permitted to wear pants at all. How would relaxing the dress code affect them? Would they feel even more separate?

Before I wrote a word, I talked to girls in the hallway and after school.

"Do you want the dress code changed?" I asked a hefty girl in pancake make-up.

"I don't look good in pants. Please don't let them change the rules."

"Do you want the dress code changed?" I asked a tall, leggy girl.

"Oh please no. I'm too short-waisted. Jeans make my legs look impossibly long, my body squat and fat."

The more I talked to the girls, the more I realized that many of them were hiding behind the dress code. They were trusting the rules to be the great equalizer, not with boys, but with other girls. I talked to so many girls and sympathized with all of them, including the ones who thought it only reasonable to wear pants on cold days that I couldn't take one tack on the topic. Instead I presented the entire debate as fully as I could. Our newspaper advisor, Gus Reimer, was nearing 70, white-haired and rotund, but he was also our art teacher and I appreciated his zeal for the liberal arts. He said I was weakening my argument by taking two sides. "Stick to the argument that girls should wear dresses. That bit about some girls preferring dresses is your strongest argument."

My gut kicked over when I realized he wouldn't let me speak for the students who opposed the dress code and wanted to wear slacks.

After the paper came out, several of my old friends from the grade seven Trudeau campaign stopped me in the hallway.

"Look what we get for wearing skirts to school." June stamped her foot, her orange fishnet stockings and green miniskirt shaking.

I had seldom permitted myself such anger.

"What happened to your Trudeau politics?" She was not even trying to restrain hers.

They had cheered and chanted in their miniskirts when I delivered my Trudeau speech.

"I had to stand up in front of class for the whole period." She shook her thick dark hair out of her green eyes.

"Why?" I was puzzled.

"The teacher said if I wanted to be 'ogled' in my short skirt, I could stand up in front of the whole class."

"Yeah." Candy pursed her pink-frosted lips. "And I said her skirt was as short as mine, and if she had to stand, so should I."

"Then I joined them, too," Kathy added.

"Incredible!" I knew June with her brave temper had never been a teacher's pet, but Candy and Kathy tended to sweet-talk their way through everything. Now they had staged their own protest and it was more powerful than anything I'd be permitted to write in the school paper.

Candy, Kathy and I grew close that year and I soon preferred walking to school with them rather than my own sister. When Charity reminded me of this later, I asked who she'd walked with. Orlando, a Holdeman with a smuggled transistor radio, who loved discussing pop music. As sisters raised among worlds, it turned out, we were united in efforts to loosen our strict cultural traditions.

It was February 1969, leap year, and that meant girls could invite boys to a Sadie Hawkins party at school. My classmates told me to go for bookish Mallory, the boy we'd successfully promoted as student council president, "Our pal Mal."

So I waited for a private moment, a solitary meeting in the school hall. Mallory came toward me, slender, blue-eyed, longish blonde hair.

I rehearsed the right tone and timber before I spoke. "Hi, Mallory."

"Hi, Faith." He paused in the hallway.

"Are you going with anyone to the Sadie Hawkins party?"

"Not yet."

"Would you like to come with me?"

"Sure."

I could tell by his raised eyebrows and giant grin that he meant it.

The conversation reminded me that I could, at times, speak up and get what I wanted even if I was censored in the school paper. When I had nothing else to recommend me, dresses too long, nose too big, editorials too one-sided, I could speak smoothly and clearly. I had learned to face fear and jump. I could manage moments like this.

For the date, I had to make a silly corsage but I wasn't sweating it like my girlfriends were. I had maybe $2 to spend and one store in mind. I was so lacking in shopping savvy, I didn't even think to get ideas at a flower or gift shop. I went straight to the five-and-dime on Main Street and walked home with a bag full of yellow ribbon and white crêpe paper. The only pop culture motif that came to mind was an odd-petaled daisy, "He loves me, he loves me not...."

When I told Mom about the party, I sensed she wanted to know more. *How well did I know Mallory? How would we spend the evening? Did I need a ride to school?*

But she only asked one question: "What church does he go to?"

I hesitated. Was she going to categorize him with one question? Only in Steinbach could you even ask such a thing, just assume that everyone belonged to some church or other and identify them by that alone. The renegade Mennonites went to the United or Pentecostal Church. I had gone to those churches myself during the free-ranging year before baptism. The United Church had been lively and informal with children singing choruses I'd never heard in church. "If I were a butterfly..." The Pentecostal Church was spirited but I was disappointed when I couldn't speak in tongues. I just couldn't loosen up enough, my friend said. *Throw your head back, let your vocal cords go slack and let it flow.*

In a town of fourteen churches, there were one or two other non-Mennonite churches—solid, rational, Christian, all. But none with such strict codes about modest dress and earnest behavior as Mennonites.

"The Emmanuel Evangelical Free Church." A solid, rational church, I thought.

Mom went back to her mending. "Oh," as though that explained something. Later I learned the difference. The Free church made salvation easy—"once-saved-always-saved." It didn't come close to the Mennonite struggle of "working out your salvation with fear and trembling" and proving your faith with good fruit and deeds. No one produced fruit like Mom who, that winter, angered some in the community by moving a homeless First Nations family to an abandoned two-story near the water tower. Grandma had also fostered a First Nations child, my spirited Aunt Marj. So finding them furniture, jobs and school clothes seemed like our legacy. I gladly joined her in fetching and delivering donations and introducing them at church.

The night of the Sadie Hawkins party I met Mallory at the gym, the corsage folded into my five-and-dime bag. He grinned nervously at its limp flower when I unfolded it. I reached inside his grey pullover to pin it on and caught a sweet musky wool scent. We both stopped breathing. I stepped back to size up the huge, single-tiered daisy, each petal a thin piece of nodding crêpe paper. Several lengths of yellow ribbon hung down, weighted by smaller daisies with copper penny centers. It was quite color-coordinated, I thought, and gave him a thumbs up. He grinned crookedly.

But when the other guys entered the gym wearing stuffed teddy bears, and dangling acres of ribbon, loaded with candy bars and dollar bills, "our pal Mal" looked quite diminished. Still, when the boys lined up to have their corsages judged, Mallory stood boldly, even sardonically, with his drooping daisy until his corsage was ruled out.

"Little Arrows" played on the PA system and I felt pricked by what I had put him through. Yet his warmth and wit sparkled among my friends and it seemed he would forgive me for anything—even being a clueless missionary kid.

The thing that saved the evening was the arrival of another new kid in town. She was tall with pixie-cut copper hair and stood uncertainly inside the gym door wearing huge, baggy pants. I felt total sympathy for her odd dress and broke ranks with Mal and my classmates to talk to her.

She brightened and confided, "It's so hard to move to Steinbach where no one appreciates fashion."

I didn't understand until the orange-yarned girls surrounded us and exclaimed over her "new elephant pants."

I introduced her to Mal and my friends and she captivated us with her Winnipeg street smarts and breadth of experience. She got us laughing and glowed with our acceptance.

Ten o'clock approached and Mallory walked me between snow drifts to where we'd part ways for home.

"Strange party." Mallory kicked snow drifts beside the sidewalk. "No one danced."

"No one knows how," I laughed. "Sorry about the corsage."

"That's okay." He pushed a mittened hand through air. "I would've died if I'd had to wear one of those teddy bears."

I accepted his snowflake kiss on my cheek as nothing less than absolution.

———————

Grandma kept picture books of the royal family under her German Bible and opened them over my stockinged knees to point out the finely tailored princesses Margaret and Grace. That spring she sewed me two new cotton-print dresses and confided, "When I was your age, there were no dress shops on Main Street. We sewed our own dresses and when they wore out we wore them as under slips."

Grandma fitted the brown flowered dress on me, frowning through bifocals at her exact top-stitching, her mouth full of straight pins. While I stood on a chair she pinned the skirt two inches above the knee. I held my breath hoping Mom would permit this daring new hem length.

But Mom disagreed, her lips drawn. "The dress should touch the knee."

I was not inclined to argue with Mom, and I feared the hardship I'd create if I did. We had often been isolated as a family, with no back-up relatives or friends around, so I dared not create tension where I could avoid it. Our closeness was honeyed with a politeness that shielded us from one another rather than exposing us to each other. It was a willing cover-up of feelings and emotions rather than bare, honest expression. I knew the promise that went with obeying your parents, "that it may be well with you and that you may live long on the earth." I heard the irony in those ancient words. Why willfully invite a stoning for disobedience? Not arguing was my survival tool in a traveling family.

Instead I silently made my own plans for how to wear dresses with hem lengths painfully out of fashion.

With my babysitting money I went to the five-and-dime and bought a silver chain belt. When I got to school, before I took off my coat, I slipped into the bathroom and bloused my dresses over the belt. It made them puffy and uneven, but at least my hem lengths matched the decade.

Mom softened and bought me my first pair of pantyhose on sidewalk sale, white to match my pink flowered cotton dress. But when I opened the package they had seams down the back, a style from the last century. I tried them on anyway and saw how opalescent they were, how perfectly they fit the leg, not bunching like stockings did. I wore the nylons to school, conscious always of the backs of my legs. I leaned against walls at recess, stood in line with one leg in front of the other and sank, relieved, into my seat where I stretched out my legs, sleek and iridescent, so no one could see the seams at the back. I had become the girls who mutely arranged their

legs in their school desks. The one consolation during these times of
self-contortion was that I lived everywhere temporarily. I would soon
be leaving again, flying back to Congo where no one wore stockings.
Dad continued stumbling on numb feet, tripping on podium
steps—concerns much weightier than my seamed nylons. He still
disagreed with the diagnosis of multiple sclerosis (MS), but the neu-
rologist was reluctant to use radioactive dye for x-rays that close to
the brain stem. Instead, the doctor said there was nothing he could
do. MS could go into remission for up to twenty-five years. Dad was
released from medical care and we prepared to return to Congo.

This time though, Dad would add "linguist" to his accomplishments and train as a Bible translator. To produce the most culturally dynamic Chokwe Bible, he would recruit a pastor and folk-
lorist to help him translate. Mom would teach a new nurse and staff
to run the clinic and leprosarium.

When it came time to say goodbye that summer, my grandmas, aunts, uncles and cousins gathered around us. I loved them
completely and didn't doubt their constancy. They would always be
there and promised to write. I could let go even though I'd miss their
fun, sorrows, sufferings, graduations and weddings.

I was good at being friends—as long as I didn't have to work
through tensions, disagreements and goodbyes. Brenda and I had
drifted apart over separate class assignments, though we still waved
and chatted in the hall or caught up at church. We could only hope
to build something with others as good as what we'd had with each
other in grade seven.

Our family winged over the Atlantic leaving a wispy conden-
sation trail in our wake.

17

AVENUE OF THE FUTURE

"Those who were dependent on us
remaining hurt craved our silence."
— NATE POSTELTHWAITE

The first thing I noticed when we landed back in Kinshasa, was how people were constantly walking—in long lean strides, passing our car stuck in traffic on Boulevard Lumumba and reappearing ahead of us when we started moving again. They balanced wood, bricks, baskets or uniforms on their heads. Many walked over 20 miles to downtown jobs where they earned a dollar a day. Ahead of us, an overloaded truck hit a pothole and rolled, flinging dozens of passengers into the ditch. People crawled out of the dust and walked away. Walking, walking.

The city had grown to one million people during our two years in Canada and the mission's theology school had moved from Kajiji to Kinshasa. Before long we'd reconnected with Jette and Leola's families who'd moved to the theology campus on the hill. To our friends' great relief, they were no longer in the Mennonite hostel, so were free to attend parties. They invited us to a school social and our parents permitted us to go, seemingly open to new levels of freedom for us girls. I was elated and proud of our parents' progress.

That night, I met so many friends old and new, my head spun. "La Bamba" cranked up on the intercom and the kids circled up for a spirited romp. In the center, lanky long-haired boys pranced their signature moves, then shimmied up to a girl in the outer ring, kissed her and she replaced him in the center, dancing her fluid moves. Toward evening's end, "Leaving on a Jet Plane" played and couples and friends danced their goodbyes for the summer or year. In our traveling tribe, some of us were always leaving and others were always returning.

Later, I sighed to Jette, "How am I going to remember all those new kids?"

She handed me her yearbook. "Here, take this to Kamayala and study it this summer. Then, when you come back, sleep over at my house on weekends so you can get away to parties!"

That seemed the perfect solution.

Back in Kamayala, there was another mission family with kids our age—our old dormmates Vangie and Steve Claassen, plus their little brother and sister who were Grace's age. Their farming dad, "Uncle" Mel, had moved to our mission to run the MCC cattle project Dad had started and their musical mom, "Aunt" Martha, would homeschool our three younger siblings. We'd pull Vangie from novels to swim, explore and picnic with us. That summer we celebrated three national holidays: Zaire's Independence, Canada Day and the Fourth of July. We handmade all three flags, sang national anthems, ran relays, grilled hamburgers and popped corn grown in the Claassen's garden.

We were also giddy to reconnect with our *ndoyis*. We ran to the river with them, carried water and clapped under palms. We'd grown taller and stronger in Canada, and could better help the orphans grind manioc chunks to flour with wooden pestles and mortars.

In the afternoon breeze, I stood across from Hélène and lifted and dropped a pestle big as my thigh in counterpoint to hers, a cadence learned from our clapping games. We grunted our rhythm in tandem—*unh-ha-unh, unh-ha-unh*—until only fine powder remained. A pot of river water boiled on a wood fire nearby and we also learned to stir in a smooth paste of manioc flour and thicken it to a dense supper mush.

Evenings in lingering twilight, I opened Jette's yearbook and, using the sketchbook and soft pencils from Gus Reimer's art class in Canada, I sketched portraits of all the new kids I'd met—MKs, military and corporate brats and diplomat kids. I even sketched Dad's portrait. Seeing my interest, Dad ordered me drawing lessons advertised in *Reader's Digest*.

The lesson manual arrived with the MAF plane along with letters from Brenda and our cousins and I felt unique and special— en-

Grace made sure her companion parrot, Kusu, was front and center in our family photo before her big sisters returned to school in September 1969. (Eidse family photo)

dorsed by Dad—and reconnected with friends. I was soon absorbed in drawing geometric shapes, figures, perspective, light and shadow, pencil sketching and water colors. But the main lesson was, "Draw at all times."

In a few months, armed with my sketchbook, I was ready to dive back in to school, get to know new friends and sketch their portraits on the walkway for a few *makuta*. I was determined, too, to slip hostel strictures and spend weekends with Jette.

At summer's end, we school kids flew to Kinshasa and were taken to the gleaming new Mennonite hostel that had replaced the old battleship on *Avenue de l'avenir*. Across the street, the relentless Zaire (Congo) River reflected a sweeping searchlight from the CIA tower in downtown Kinshasa, aimed at Communist Brazzaville. It cut across the rippled current every minute. The U.S. had put down the 1964 *Simba* revolution and vigilance continued.

In the backyard, Matadi, the sentry, whistled melodiously and coaxed a small fire to flame beneath a sheltering mango tree. We dorm kids finished supper dishes, wandered out to play with our pets or greet the sentry and sit awhile, transported to deep village nights in our upcountry homes.

A shrill whistle from the living room cut into our pet care. It was "Uncle" Hector herding twenty-four missionary kids around the upright piano. Square-jawed and muscled in casual white tee-shirt and khaki shorts, he tolerated us as though we were errant nieces and nephews. The grade school kids jumped onto vinyl sofas, punched each other's arms in a game of pass-it-on and called for the chorus, "Pass It On!" After singing every night, "That's how it is with God's love, you want to pass it on, pass it on," the high school boys couldn't resist a terse, "kick it back, kick it back."

Uncle Hector grinned at the boys a moment, then silenced them with a glance. He adjusted his glasses and opened the Bible to I Timothy 2. "In like manner also, women adorn themselves in modest apparel with shamefacedness and sobriety...Let the women learn in silence with all subjection...For Adam was not deceived but the woman, being deceived, was in transgression..."

After suffering through dress codes in Canada, I could see the irony in women having to dress modestly to prevent men's evil thoughts. But many people still agreed—women were responsible for inspiring evil thoughts. Mom's parting words to me at the airstrip were, "Don't become a cheerleader." Mom had sent us off with dresses to our knees yet demanded even more eccentricity. I couldn't even do cartwheels. Our bodies had been off limits to us, sources of shame, not pleasure—unless we were hoeing or cleaning.

Uncle Hector looked around at the gathered children, ages eight to eighteen, and asked for examples. "How can we apply this passage to our lives?" Silence reigned.

How could I speak aloud of how muted we "young ladies" were expected to be? I was fourteen and knew Mom worried I'd attract attention from boys. She didn't have to preach to Hope who voluntarily wore her blouse tucked at the waist and buttoned to the neck, her skirts long and wide so she could keep running. Charity was just twelve, growing taller not fuller, and dressed boyishly in jeans and culottes.

The high school boys lounged in shorts and tees, legs splayed, tilting their chairs back, away from the devotions circle. They didn't have to put up with any of the modest dress nonsense. Why should there be separate rules for girls?

My bare legs in running shorts permitted me to dribble down the court, jump and shoot baskets. I didn't want to be the only girl my age wearing granny clothes just to prove we were Mennonites. The week I'd arrived at the hostel, I had cut all my dresses three inches shorter. I ironed and pinned them in the sewing room across from Uncle Hector's office and then sweated and stitched in my room until they were four inches above the knee. Had Uncle Hector noticed my sewing project?

"Now with all heads bowed, all eyes closed," Uncle Hector

said in a low, commanding voice. "Raise your hands if you want to follow Christ."

I hesitated only a moment, realizing hesitancy would be suspect, then raised my hand. At first I had not seen anything sinister in his tally of who would serve and obey and who would need convincing. But afterwards the tally made me uneasy. It was as though he had just acquired a weapon against me—against all of us—one way or another.

We dispersed and I paused at the patio window where I caught the orange flicker of a supper fire at an unfinished mansion across the street on the riverbank. It lit up open concrete walls and wafted the nutty scent of hot palm oil.

Uncle Hector joined me, his muscled bulk looming over me. "It seems the Belgian owner left and his sentry moved in with his clan."

"Nice place." I moved away slightly, giving him space.

"Can you see how easy it would be to finish that blocky house? Put in windows, doors, locks—if I could just get my hands on it."

"Umhm." I wanted to stay on his good side even if I disagreed. The Congolese "squatters" on our block—whose kids we'd played with—had finally moved and their house was renovated as a mission business office. The former girls' dorm had been turned into a guest house so that the mission owned the whole block.

I turned only slightly, not looking directly at him. "What about going to Jette's for night this Friday?" I didn't want to miss the first school social.

Uncle Hector frowned. "Let me check with Aunt Clara."

The next day, I felt his scrutiny following me when I crossed the living room.

I turned at the stairs and faced him.

"I checked with Clara," he said. "There's a party this weekend."

I froze.

He scowled. "You must've known…so *no*. Besides, we have a policy. You can't spend the night unless all the girls your age are invited." He turned and walked away.

I skulked up the stairs to my room. I had walked out of several friends' lives when we'd left Canada and it seemed I would miss out on some great friendships in Zaire, too—the most carefree moments with my best friend Jette. At the hostel, instead of encouraging our uniqueness like Dad did at home, we had to all blend in. Rules and buzzers controlled our sleeping, rising, eating, social and private lives.

Charity passed me on the stairs, grinning and taking two steps at a time with her long legs, seemingly doing better than expected. She had been so distraught before returning to the regimented hostel that Dad taught her to "practice the presence." The ritual, invented by seventeenth-century friar Father Lawrence turned the monastery bells into a reminder to open his heart to the love God painted on his soul.

I went to Hope's room on the big girls' wing and found her doing sit-ups.

"We big girls are going together to ask Uncle Hector for pads and supplies tomorrow—wanna come? Need anything?"

"Hundred-fifty, fifty-one," she said aloud when I interrupted her. "I don't use those anymore…fifty-three, fifty-four…"

Did she use rags like the African women or had she lost her period again? Hope was shedding all the roundness we'd put on together in the kitchen in Canada and seemed to be pulling away from us in a cycle of running, push-ups, sit-ups and chin-ups.

"Guess not." I rose and left her to her routine. It would be me and the other high school girls—Linda, Marcia, Becky and Vangie. Our lunar cycles seemed regulated not only by the phase of the moon but our close living quarters so that we all menstruated at the same time. However, Uncle Hector controlled our toiletry purchases—ensuring that the sanitary pads were counted and locked away in a supply closet accessed only by his keys. If we asked Aunt Clara, she had to beg him for them.

The next morning, we followed Uncle Hector's thongs flip-flopping on the tile floor as we traipsed behind him. He bent over the padlock, unlocked, unhooked, creaked open the cupboard doors and retrieved his notebook. "How many for you?" He wrote each name and date in neat columns beside "24 Kotex pads."

His eyes twinkled one moment, glared the next when I brought up the rear. I winced and glanced at Marcia disappearing down the hall. "Hey, Marcia, Linda, wait for me." Marcia was a tall, "older sister" who seemed independent and composed since she'd arrived at the hostel already in junior high. She was more self-assured and confident than we knew a girl could be.

"Come on." Marcia, a year older than me, smiled back and strode on.

"A box of twenty-four." I squirmed, feeling exposed at revealing these private details.

Uncle Hector broke his gaze a moment to tally my order.

It seemed weird that he should take such interest in our cycles, should note the quantity and frequency of Kotex purchases, as though we were duty-bound to report our fertility and virginity to him.

"I need to talk with you, young lady." He held back the blue and pink box.

"Okay." I reached for it. "When?"

"Monday after school." He gave me the box and turned to lock the closet.

I marched upstairs and plunked my box in a corner of the closet. I thought of telling Hope about Uncle Hector wanting to talk to me but she had frowned silently when I'd shortened my dresses. Our family was supposed to be better than other missionaries, more modest, more obedient.

Instead I found Marcia, Linda and Becky bent over homework at the open windows overlooking the Zaire River. "Uncle Hector wants to talk to me Monday."

"Why?" Marcia looked up.

"Did you do something wrong?" Linda lifted her pencil.

Vangie, showed up from across the hall, a finger holding her place in her novel, *Exodus.*

"Like what?" I could think of nothing. Something else gnawed at me—the bedtime whiskerings from grade school. Uncle Hector was much stronger than I and his talons could hold me down while his bristles sliced my cheeks. We girls sat silently for a while, knowing what talks with Uncle Hector meant. Accusation. Control. Prayers of remorse we had to repeat after him. Kids left his talks sobbing and speechless.

"Just don't knuckle under." Marcia's eyes flashed.

"Don't cry." Becky turned and fixed me with her dark eyes. "Don't give him the satisfaction."

I felt braced that evening when I crawled into bed. I could even try to ignore the way he scowled if I crossed his gaze, the way he looked me up and down as though there were something wrong with me.

I flung my blanket off and tried to lie still under the thin cotton sheet. I never slept uncovered even on the hottest nights. It felt unsafe, as though something was out to get me. Not snakes. I wasn't afraid of them. I had once brushed a viper with my bare toes, but it had slithered away faster than I could jump. Three-inch cockroaches crawled the ceiling sometimes, waving their antennae, and one had landed in my mouth one night. But what I feared most was Uncle Hector on his nightly rounds, bursting in on girls stepping out of the shower or boys looking at magazines.

I tried to lie still in the fluid heat. Monday was school again and it would be hard enough knowing I had a talk waiting afterwards. Streetlights cast a bar pattern across my bed. Outside, mango bats screeched, releasing rancid odors as they sucked juice through soft skins.

Monday in the van after school, I received several "talk-waiting" looks from Uncle Hector. I went upstairs and laid my books on the table in my room. I sat a moment on my bed and tried to pray. It felt useless. I couldn't much hope that God would be on my side if He was already on Uncle Hector's. I descended the stairs and found Uncle Hector cracking a tray of ice into the ten-gallon water cooler. That was a good sign. He was feeling generous, taking his turn filling the cooler for kids coming in sweaty from basketball.

"Is this a good time?" I asked.

"Great." He set the tray on a long dining room table, wiped his hands on a tea towel. "Come on."

I followed him across the living room hoping he'd called me in to praise me on my jump shot. But that was wishful thinking. We passed the stairs, his back stiff and inflexible. He'd found me guilty of something I could not yet name. Perhaps it was the night he'd spied me from the bottom of the stairs. At first I didn't register him standing there, I had lifted my nightgown for a full-body turn in the hall mirror, assessing my diet and exercise routine. The foreshortened view of me, muscled thighs to pert breasts, must have been arresting because he endured several pirouettes before calling out. "Fa-aith." A deep warning tone. I dropped my nightie and fled to my room. Why, if it were an accident, would he call my name? Did he want me to know he had seen me?

We entered the hallway and it echoed with clattering ping pong balls from the rec room. Perhaps Uncle Hector would drill me about the night he'd caught me stealing cookies from the kitchen. It was stealing because I had resisted my two cookies at snack time.

Still Uncle Hector couldn't know for certain it was me because at the flip-flop of his approach, I had slipped ghostlike in my nightie behind the kitchen door. I stopped breathing as he stomped around the dining and living room in his khaki shorts. "Faith?" he'd called, a question, a guess. He looked under the piano bench. "Faith?" I pressed myself flat as a paper doll against the stucco wall not wanting to be gripped by his claws, struck by his knuckles, gouged by his whiskers. "You better get to bed," he hissed, and flip-flopped back to his suite.

Following him down the hall, I focused on Uncle Hector's purling calves chiseled on the basketball court. There he challenged us to games of four-on-one, only to erupt if we scored against him, flinging his body into us.

With me in tow, Uncle Hector checked the rec room where two grade school boys were playing ping pong and motioned me into the laundry room. I could be punished for any number of things. Tasting wine at the Mackays where I babysat. Hours after the kids were asleep, I poured a sip from each open bottle so as not to arouse suspicion. Fruity rosé, crisp chardonnay, thick red Beaujolais—a *mazout* (fuel) mix that got me through their fifties pop albums.

Uncle Hector pulled out his keys and locked the laundry door. I backed against a table, the late afternoon sun streaming through the diamond openings in the cinder block wall. It wasn't far enough because Hector approached, eyebrows drawn. He leaned close, jaw stubbled.

"Let's start with the way you dress."

My thighs cut into the wooden table. I clutched it and eased around the corner, backing blindly along its length.

"You wear those jeans so tight, you turn men on when you walk."

Was I safe locked in this room with him? Would he beat me for it?

"You do it on purpose." Uncle Hector closed in again, face flushed. "You're a whore, a slut, a prick tease."

I winced. I might be a bit rebellious, maybe. What teen wouldn't be with strict rules like ours? But these new labels were hard and unforgiving, reducing me to a scornful sexual thing.

"What were you doing at lunch on Wednesday?" He braced his arms on the table, caging me in. "You kept me waiting."

My insides congealed, my tongue shriveled. I had told Marcia I would be learning to develop photos at lunch—since we had to report our whereabouts without fail. Yet I had apparently left him waiting at the lunch van, his count incomplete without me.

"Marcia said you were in the dark room with Asher."

Asher—yes—Asher hadn't touched me. He was a flashy senior, tall and lean with sparkly eyes, luscious grin and dark hair; old enough to drive his own sports coupe, fabled for picking up girls in any language. A gold star of David chain glinted copper on his bronzed chest in the red light and his hairy legs in khaki shorts may have brushed mine while we sat on the floor waiting for the chemicals to take. My breath caught but I resisted touching him and focused instead on the chlorine-smell of the developing bath.

"I'm just flashing the red light." Uncle Hector inhaled, shoulders spread.

I cringed and wished I could slide down the drain hole in the floor.

"One of these days you're going to find yourself pregnant before you're married."

Pregnant, the final humiliation. Already, Uncle Hector had implied, he would be justified. A punch, a slap in the face would have stung a moment; this knowledge wouldn't let go.

"I think our little rap session is over." Uncle Hector unlocked and opened the door, motioning me out ahead of him, all polite now that I could barely move. My legs were two blocks of wood. I avoided looking at his smiling eyes. He had unloaded his shame like a boulder on my shoulders. I squeezed against the doorjamb, as far from him as I could, and moved down the hall feeling naked. Behind me, Uncle Hector's thongs flip-flopped.

I ached all over, from my sealed-up throat to my stiff legs. I pulled myself upstairs by the greasy metal handrail and navigated to my room. The view through the barred window was of a fenced and gated compound.

Beyond the fence, the massive Zaire River flowed steadily westward in its ancient channel. A fisherman in a canoe drifted downstream, trailed by a raft of green and purple hyacinth. Borne on a puckered current, the fisherman and his retinue crossed my barred window in seconds.

Marcia appeared at my door, tall and gentle. "How bad was it?"

"He said—" a faucet opened, hot tears splattered.

"What? What did he say?" Hope, who seldom left her room except to run laps around the hostel or do pullups on the chinning bars, appeared with three other big girls.

"He said I—I was a...a prick tease." The tears gushed, wave upon wave.

"Aw." The sound of sympathy, the feather of stroking hands. "He's nasty, low-down, mean."

"You? A prick tease?" Becky knew I woke every morning before the six o'clock buzzer to read my Bible.

The other girls had Uncle Hector stories, too. He told them crude jokes, came upstairs to the girls' wing without announcing himself.

"I was naked in my room once," Becky said, arms crossed as if hugging herself, "when suddenly there he was right in front of me. I don't know why, but I covered my navel instead of my breasts or pubis." She was a doctor's daughter, always precise in her medical terms.

"He came up to me at the chinning bars once," Hope said, hands on her jutting hips, "and told me to act more feminine."

So that's why Hope couldn't stop exercising? Uncle Hector had only uttered a phrase, a sentence at the chinning bars, but Hope never again ate a full helping at meals. If he wanted her more feminine, she would be more muscled. She whittled at her curves with her will. Mind over body, she clamped down on hunger and filled her afternoons with laps that carved a trench around the hostel, sit-ups until her protruding tail bone ulcerated and she dropped to 87 pounds.

She prowled the kitchen with a growling stomach and passed up stalks of yellow bananas, tubs of chocolate chunk cookies and ate the stale bread and leftover oatmeal set aside for the dogs.

"More feminine?" I couldn't understand. "Why, so he can call you a prick tease?"

Laughter rolled, echoing through the barred windows, until even the mango trees rustled in relief. As long as I had my sisters—my *ndoyis*—I could withstand such indignity.

Not until Ruth Keidel arrived the next year—not as a child but at age 14—did I see a girl stand up to Uncle Hector. He had again appeared on the girls' wing without calling first, "Man on the floor." In bra and panties, hands on hips, blue eyes flashing, she declared, "You're not supposed to come up here unannounced!"

He turned and left without a word.

———

I had not dared mention to the other girls the fantasies I gave Uncle Hector. I kept those to myself, mulling how I should dress and move in his presence. Perhaps I could still wear my own clothes if I just moved more rigidly. Years later a friend would ask why I walked so stiffly.

If I needed punishing for being sexual, I could do it myself. I could diet, exercise, get rid of my curves like Hope did. I was already eating the required minimum of everything served. I'd have to skip dessert, count calories, and exercise two times a day. I went to see Hope, who was doing 200 sit-ups, a folded towel cushioning her raw tailbone. We made plans to run *Avenue de l'avenir* every afternoon. She'd be my partner and together we'd face gangs of taunting *Kinnois* (Kinshasa) boys who formed roadblocks and pinched our breasts as we crashed their ranks.

At dinner I took small bites and ate slowly, counting 24 chews per bite. I had read this trick in *Seventeen* and recommended it to the other girls. I also cut out a paper doll me from the magazine with ten extra fat pads along my torso. For each pound I lost, I sliced off a piece of my torso.

Marcia and Charity, both shooting past five-eight, thought I was nuts for counting chews. They hatched a plan to stop my obsession. I scooped a spoonful of rice to my mouth and they led everyone in counting, "One, two, three,…twenty-two, twenty-three, twenty-four." I took another bite.

"Do we have to count again?" Aunt Clara asked.

"No." I grinned but told no one about my incessant calorie count—studied from Mrs. Mackays Weight Watchers charts. Each evening was turmoil for the calories I'd eaten beyond my 1,200 limit. Each morning was new for its unused calories. Sometimes I carried the overage into the next day so I could eat only 600 or 800 calories. Within months my period stopped and I learned why Hope no longer needed Kotex.

I worried that I was somehow pregnant, though I'd experienced nothing more invasive than a French kiss from a tenth grader. We'd started holding hands at a school movie. Then one night at a basketball game, he'd led me into the shadows, kissed me deeply, unbuttoned my top buttons and slid off my bra strap. Panicked, I broke free and ran back to the game. After that, according to his friend, he threw darts at a poster-sized photo of me he'd developed in the school dark room.

Purity was prized, we'd been told—and despised—I learned that day at school. Making girls its gatekeepers, blamed for guys' "uncontrollable lust," could be perilous.

Marcia and the other girls vowed "never to let Uncle Hector make you cry again." But the next lecture was delivered in his office with the door locked and the window fan turned full blast. For years I blanked on what had happened in that session until I was raising my own two young boys. Then it came back to me in full color and sharp relief.

I was conscious of my clothes, yellow shorts and thin, white tee-shirt. I arranged myself tightly in the chair across from his desk. "You've been drinking." His eyes turned steel gray.

"Me?" I was confused. I had sipped a quarter-goblet of wine now and then at the Mackay's but how could he know that? "Yeah, water," I said, chin up.

Uncle Hector didn't laugh. "You're lying!" He charged from his chair, 200 pounds of welted muscle. "We know you did it. The McKays mark their wine bottles—and we read your calendar."

I wanted to die. He had poured over my wall-calendar-diary and read every pathetic word. For the previous Saturday, I'd written cryptically, enjoying the irony of it, "Had a swig of the Christian Brothers."

I bit my quivering lip. *Don't knuckle under*, Marcia had said. "I just tasted it." But I knew that whether I'd drunk a gallon or a drop, it counted as drinking to people of his generation. My own mother had signed an abstinence pledge, promising publicly not to touch a drop.

"Alcoholism starts with the first sip. Lushes go around drinking little sips from the bottoms of glasses. Then they try to cover it up. First you drank, then you lied about it. Just like a LUSH!" He leaned in, spit flying.

The tears gushed with such force I could not stop them

"Pray after me," Uncle Hector said. "Please forgive me..."

I did, gasping and sniveling; my pre-dawn heavenly father had turned into the hulk set against me. "Please forgive me...for drinking and lying about it—"

The prayer was interrupted by tapping at the door. "Excuse me, Hector?" It was Aunt Clara's soft voice.

"What is it?" Uncle Hector's voice boomed.

"The big girls are here with a question."

When he opened the door, there were Marcia and Linda in the lead, Aunt Clara retreating behind them.

"So what's the question?" He sounded harsh, commanding.

"Are you done with her?" The stern look on Linda's face said he was. Uncle Hector let me go.

I followed my big sisters through the living room, past Carl who glanced up from *Popular Mechanics* and clenched his jaw knowingly. We girls climbed the stairs and crowded into the two-stall bathroom at the end of the hall. I splashed water on my red, swollen eyes. Up close I could see red veins, creased skin, elasticity sagging away.

Marcia leaned against the wall. "Did he make you repeat a prayer after him?"

"Yeah, how did you know?"

"Kitty told me. That's what he did to her."

"But she's from a different mission!"

"Doesn't matter. She's dating one of our guys. He sent a note for her to appear in his office. He accused her of letting her hands wander, of ruining a red-blooded American boy."

The laughter started deep, deeper than pain, and burst like a gentle rain around us. My sisters, my *ndoyis*, to the rescue.

18

DELUGE

The first squall of rainy season stopped us in our tracks. Lightning and thunder cracked so close together out our dorm windows there was barely a second between them. We'd be crossing concrete floors in bare feet and have to jump to the nearest rug or chair. We'd seen fireballs exploding from electric outlets, faucets and down toilets.

Our skin turned yellow in the greening light and palm trees creaked and groaned, brittle from a six-month thirst. Their brown tops whipped and bent nearly to the ground. The earth opened and the waters of the deep rolled through the mission compound. Cardboard walls from shanty towns floated through the streets, and the newly homeless pressed together in store fronts along the boulevard.

After daily downpours, we eased our vigilance and went back to walking barefoot across concrete, as though nature's display were a minor shower. We knew people struck by lightning but they'd been out in it. A Mukedi woman, carrying a tin bowl of water on her head, struck dead just as she reached the mission. One of our mission administrators paralyzed for weeks by a lightning strike. Dad struck unconscious one night while outside, adjusting the downspout over the rain barrel. The thunder crack that followed was so loud my mother woke, thinking a wall had fallen. Dad was not there beside her so she lit a lantern and wandered around calling for him. Half an hour later he regained consciousness and limped inside, frazzled and dazed. Under her caring, watchful eye, he made a complete recovery.

Rain marched like specters through the yard while we dug through stacks of *Newsweek* and *National Geographic* or spun the hostel-approved *Singing Nuns* album. The stereo cord was frayed and we got a warning shock whenever we plugged in the melancholy "Joy Is Like the Rain." We reported it to Aunt Clara or Uncle Hector and were told, "Unplug the stereo if there's lightning."

During one deluge, Charity and Becky were busy with their Saturday chores—dusting the living room, straightening piles of magazines, sliding records back into jackets, unable to resist spinning a few on the stereo.

The way Charity told the story, she'd stepped onto the porch in bare feet to shake a throw rug, and lightning ripped through the compound, followed by tiered thunder. She dashed inside and shouted, "Unplug the stereo!"

Becky lifted the record player arm; Charity pulled the plug. The frayed cord came apart in her hand. A 220-volt shock knocked her down and grounded her to bare tile. The current surged through her arms and legs, contracting her muscles, turning her rigid and helpless on the floor. She heard screaming, she told me later, but at a distance, as though she were hearing her own voice from somewhere in the stratosphere.

Becky—barefoot too—jumped on a couch cushion and ripped the cord from Charity's hand.

Charity's hand was charred black and dripping off the bone like candle wax. The moment Becky disconnected her, Charity jumped up, grabbed the wrist of her burned hand, and ran mad circles around the room as though her legs held a charge.

"Aunt Clara!" Becky screamed.

Hearing the call for a nurse, Hope left the biology paper she was writing on electrical burns and raced downstairs. The treatment procedure she had just written leaped off the page. She and Aunt Clara caught Charity and laid her on the sofa. They covered her with blankets and Hope talked to her soothingly while Aunt Clara called the OAU clinic at the presidential compound.

Becky rushed upstairs to the girls' wing to tell me that Charity had nearly been electrocuted. "I don't know how I thought of jumping on a cushion to break the current before ripping the cord out of her hand," Becky said. "I guess it's all that training about wearing shoes during a thunderstorm—which I wasn't."

I went downstairs to see Charity, shivering under the blanket and holding up her black hand. The three middle fingers were completely fused and I recognized immediately it was her left hand— the one she wrote with. Under the melted flesh, bone and raw skin gleamed.

Charity said she continued to hold her hand while she waited four hours to see Dr. William Close, President Mobutu's personal physician. But she didn't feel pain until he inserted an anesthetizing needle directly into the burns. With his scalpel, he separated the fingers and sliced away incinerated flesh. He said he might have to do extensive skin grafting on the bare bones and she might never use her hand again.

I waited all afternoon for Charity's return. When she did, she held a fat, gauze-wrapped hand gingerly in the air. Aunt Clara suggested she stay home and rest while the hostel attended a school carnival that night, but Charity was so elated at being alive, she couldn't help joining us on the bus. She guarded her hand against jostling from either side and retold her story several times that evening. A typical eighth-grader, she gloated that Dr. Close had excused her from written schoolwork.

The next day I heard Charity cry out. She was sitting at her desk, left hand raised, left elbow propped on a piece of paper, pencil in her right hand.

"What are you doing?" I asked. "You're not supposed to do school work."

"True, but I'm going to be wearing this bandage for four months. I'll have to learn to write with my right hand sometime."

We both knew how Charity had scrapped and fought with her

teachers since kindergarten, refusing to switch hands for any task—coloring, writing, cutting. Even Mom had tried at first to hand rattles or bananas to Charity's right hand. But Charity had resolutely taken everything with her left and Mom had defended her ever since.

"Here." Charity handed me a page scrawled in wobbly letters. "You try writing with your left hand."

I sat down, clasped the pencil in my left, the paper in my right. The pencil felt square, the paper minuscule, my writing backwards. My letters were huge and wobbly, much worse than Charity's. For a moment I felt in my fingertips what Charity's struggle meant.

The more I looked in on her, the more I learned that Charity was having a hard time at the hostel, just as she had in grade five. She didn't feel that she fit in with all the rules about staying in the compound, when all she wanted to do was live outside it. She was homesick for Kamayala; sick at not being able to speak Chokwe with anyone, play games with the Congolese, home-school under Mom's care, hold newborns at the clinic. Charity didn't mix much at the hostel, even four months later, after her bandages came off and her scarred fingers shone pink and tender. Dr. Close had put the remaining skin back so carefully, he didn't have to graft at all. Charity was able to use her left hand again, but ever after, guarded the tender scar between her middle and ring finger.

She turned her transistor to Congo Jazz, leafed through the Chokwe hymnal, and wrote letters to her *ndoyi*, Sala. Afternoons with the heat steaming through the windows, I sat on the edge of her bed, she on the floor at my feet, and I brushed her long wavy hair until it shone. The tinny descant of *soukous* rang softly around us.

She told me news from the radio—Tabu Ley's Afrisa had played the Paris Olympia and Congo Jazz was an international sensation. I brought her news from school—the Baptist kids wanted to skip the American service at Kalina and go to the Kimbanguist church a few blocks away. The Kimbanguists had an African religion more expressive than the Catholics or Protestants. They danced and sang with rattles and drums and decorated their church with flowers, palm leaves and throw rugs. I thought Charity would enjoy that. "You go." She made it clear she didn't need my rescue. "I want to go to a Chokwe service."

We had heard about a Chokwe church, but it was miles beyond the *Grand Marché* (big arts market downtown) and it would take hours to get there by bus; all afternoon to get back again.

I would go with my Baptist friends instead.

———

Meanwhile, Jette and Leola who followed the pulse of city nightlife, told us dozens of Mennonite conscientious objectors were arriving in Congo to do alternative service to the Vietnam War. The capitol filled with accomplished, free-thinking twenty-somethings—farmers and college students from across the U.S. They would train upcountry for agricultural, building and education projects.

Kamayala would be assigned two PAX volunteers whom we cloistered Eidse girls had yet to meet. Ron, a college student, and Dan, a farmer.

Dan had landed in Kinshasa and entered the nightclubs in a black wide-brimmed, Amish hat, a symbol of such mystery to my school friends they longed to uncover it. They begged to visit Kamayala but the flight was costly and the pursuit frivolous compared to the demanding work the newcomers had to tackle.

The PAX men would establish rabbit projects in surrounding villages to help reduce seasonal hunger and retain young people in agricultural service. MCC's extension work was proving so meaningful that President Kennedy had modeled the Peace Corps on it and volunteers arrived to dig fishponds at nearby, burned-out Kandale.

———

During school breaks, we sisters roamed Kamayala with a fresh need to hear and speak Chokwe. By moonlight we wended between mud and thatch huts that glowed orange in the tremor of supper fires. We breathed the sour, sharp scent of *matamba* and *pilipili* (greens and red pepper). We searched courtyards for the most animated storytellers and watched for fires that drew the most listeners.

We had learned over the years never to walk, white skin exposed, into the village at this time of night. It was a magical time when *chingandangalis* (monsters) and ancestor spirits hovered, and children startled easily at the sight of us. They took off screaming, *"Mukishi!"* (Ancestor spirits.) Instead we tied *divunga* (cloth wraps), around our waists to cover our legs and tented them over our blonde hair and white faces.

A soft breeze licked at our *divunga* as we took the worn path to the village. Sand flowed through our sandals and crickets trilled and crescendoed beneath a haloed, rainy-season moon. We took the road to the clinic and turned onto the wide path that led to the Kabule house. It was a good first bet. If there wasn't an outright storytelling, there would be animated talk about Congo's future. Congo jazz was trending, President Mobutu had spoken at the U.N. and Congo was a leader among African nations.

At Kamayala, though, seasonal hunger continued between planting and harvest—just when the children started a new school year. Weva Kabule, the young secondary school director, often spoke of how hard it was for children to sit in a classroom and think about numbers with empty stomachs. My parents would one day sponsor his education in Canada and he would present to the U.N. his PhD dissertation on teaching malnourished children. He would become a tenured professor in Canada and implement his policies as Congo's Permanent Secretary on the Permanent Commission for Education. Wenyi, his brother-in-law, would run the MCC agricultural extension program for decades and establish enough rabbit hutches among hunter-gatherer villages to end sea-sonal hunger pangs.

On another night seeking out the best storytellers we start-ed past the tuberculosis ward, where a faint keening rose above the cricket chorus. Imagining ourselves incognito in our dark cloths, we checked stealthily and saw three rail-thin women crouched around banked embers, one of them holding a newborn baby.

A soft gust flipped at my head covering and the new mother called, *"Ufudielo, tweya kuno."* (Faith, come here.)

We didn't know the forty patients who rotated through the ward from distant villages, but they knew one or two of our names, since we sometimes made rounds with Mom, or helped wash basins and sterilize needles at the clinic. Mom had men-tioned that you could catch TB from infected droplets sneezed into a hand and had advised us not to shake hands with tuber-culoid patients. It was just as polite to clap when greeting them, she said.

This I did, from the path, a four-syllable clap and greeting. *"Moyoenu Mamans."*

But the woman called again, urgently, *"Tweya 'Fudielo. Mwa-nami kanafu."* (Come Faith. My child is dying.)

"You go ahead to the village," I told Charity and Hope. "I'll go sit with her awhile." I crouched with them around the fire. Mom had said that TB was once linked to genius. Many famous nineteenth-century writers had it—Robert Louis Stevenson, Elizabeth Barrette Browning, Henry David Thoreau and the Bronte sisters.

Through smoky tendrils I gazed at the infant cradled by the skeletal mother. *"Kuchi Mama?"* (What is it Mama?)

Tears streaked her cheeks, her collarbones jutted above sagging breasts and her neck glands were swollen by TB.

"Here." She thrust the baby at me. "Hold my baby. It's dying. You can save it with your white person powers."

I felt awkward taking the baby, as though I had agreed that my touch were somehow magical. The tiny, naked girl felt like a small sack of sticks in my arms, her eyelids were closed but she seemed to be taking every third breath, barely hanging on. I breathed a prayer over her and tried to pass her back, but the mother wouldn't take her. I tried to hand the baby to the other thin woman at the fire, but she too said that I must hold her. I held the baby close, wrapped her in my *divunga,* and felt the mother's sorrow.

"She's still breathing," I told the mother.

"A little," the mother said, and returned to her wailing. "Oh child of mine, I'm knocking on your coffin but you don't answer me..."

How must it feel to be suspended between worlds and hear the wailing before you're gone? Was it a comfort or burden? Did it help you go or make you want to stay? Did it rush you away before you were ready or help you leave feeling loved and embraced?

When I checked again, my ear close to the baby's mouth, the girl had stopped breathing. There was no sign of life in her limp body. "Look Mama." I held the baby for her to see. "I think she's gone."

The woman screamed and picked up a stone. "You killed my baby! She was alive when I gave her to you. Now she's dead."

I thrust the girl at the woman next to me and ran.

A stone hit the path at my heels, another hit the grass beside me. I ducked and ran on, the mother's voice harsh in my ears. "Your white person powers killed my baby."

Through the schoolyard, past the volleyball net and bougain-villea bush I ran. At a safe distance, I stopped to rub my hands on my skirt. Tainted, inept hands. Wavering, useless prayer. Mom was known for bringing people back to life; I would be known for killing them. Mom had even revived the boy I "killed" in a bike accident when I was just eight and learning to ride.

I ran on until I reached our sheltering cement porch.

"Mom!" I called through the screen door. "They say I killed a baby at the TB ward."

Mom opened the screen door wearing two pairs of bifocals. "What happened? Where are your sisters?"

"Hope and Charity went to the village. I was holding a baby, and it died in my arms."

"A baby girl, tiny?" Mom's tone was calm and understanding, her hand warm on my back, pulling me inside.

"Yes. The mother thought I could save it—the way you always do."

"Not always."

I followed her to the lamp-lit dining table where she'd been sorting through a box of eyeglasses sent from mortuaries in America. "I'm surprised that baby lasted until tonight." She shoved aside a medical journal and took off a pair of glasses. "I told that lady this morning her child wouldn't live through today. She started wailing this afternoon already." Mom often fretted about people wailing while family members were still alive. Wasn't this a time to fill the room with hope? Finally, she'd relented, realizing it might help release the patient.

Mom looked at me fully with her warm hazel eyes. "I often wish I could do more. I keep thinking about the woman who sells us bananas."

The banana seller from the leprosarium had only a stump for a right hand, a knuckle for a thumb, her Hansen's disease had been arrested but the after-effects continued. She walked miles on numb feet, 10-kilo banana bunches balanced on her head. When she came to our house, Mom sat on the front porch with her and talked, offering cold water, *chindu*, beans. The woman ate, a spoon gripped between thumb and hand stump.

I wished too I could do more than help bathe her patients or sit with them while a baby died. I was grateful for Mom's experience over years of treating malaria, burns, bullet wounds and TB. Her faith was science and her science faith.

Mom loved her two-mile walk home from the leprosarium, buoyed by her purpose in caring for the "people no one else would sit with," as Kafiy Sidonie Nzeya-Weva said. (Hope Wiebe photo)

19

MELTED HANDS

"That multitude of molded hands
Holding out flowers to the azure skies
... a hidden source
Wells from their untainted palms."
— Jean-Joseph Rabéarivelo

I stepped up to a stone and tin roof house at the leprosarium near Kamayala, Congo, carrying a wash basin and bar of soap in gloved hands.

"*Koko?*" A verbal knock, a pause before I entered the dim room. A woman moved on a bamboo cot, her bony frame draped in crusty cloth wraps.

"*Ayy?*" Her thin voice trembled.

"*Yami, Ufudielo.*" (It's me, Faith.)

I had not seen this patient before, or if I had, she had not looked this low. She may have arrived an advanced case while I was completing grade nine at the American school in the capital, which was newly named Kinshasa. I was home for summer vacation, helping Mom with her nursing rounds.

I set down the basin and soap and shuffled blindly along the floor, feeling with my shoes for uneven patches, sticks of firewood, small animals.

"*Moyo Mama.*" Hello, Mama. I pulled off my rubber gloves not wanting her to notice this barrier between us. In a shaft of white-hot mid-morning sun, she raised an arm to shield her eyes against searing light. The leprosy bacillus that grew in the cool extremities—fingers, toes, knees, elbows, ears, nose, eyes—would not dull her shooting cortical pain until she went blind.

She lay on a bare woven mat and reached a contracted, molded hand, pushing uncertainly at my knee. Hers was a numb hand, so long dead to sensation that its muscles and tendons were paralyzed. Her bones, damaged by bumps and bangs, were being reabsorbed by the body, so that her fingernails grew on her knuckles.

I wanted to touch her reaching hand, grip its stiff form. The medical term Mom used was *mains-en-griffe* (claw-hand). Mom was right behind me with more water and soap, and I knew she would say—heard her say—"Faith, put those gloves on."

My breath caught and my pulse skipped a beat. My skin was blemished with nothing worse than acne and I felt immortal, even marble. But I slipped the gloves back on.

"Start on her feet." Mom often took one of her four daughters to work, to help us feel involved and to keep us near her. I set the basin down at the foot of the woman's cot and soaped my wash rag. Mom cradled the woman's hand, finding her pulse. "Have you eaten?"

"No, how can I eat if I can't get up?"

The woman's toes were shredded, brown tattered skin revealing jagged pink beneath. I gently held one foot at the heel and rubbed each toe with the soaped rag. Yellow, sulfurous pus oozed from several of the chewed-up stumps. I had never seen toes in such a state. The woman did not flinch. This was no accidental run-in with sharp stones.

Mom shifted her gaze from the woman's face and stared at the toes. "Who did this to you?"

The woman folded both arms over her face and mumbled something.

"Pardon?" Mom asked. "Did a person do this to you?" From pregnancy to planting and harvesting, to pounding manioc into flour, women were this region's heavy labor. Was Mom asking whether someone had beaten her for her disability?

"*Kaaaa*." The woman wailed. "Rats do this."

Mom turned gray under her generous freckles.

The woman struggled to grasp a stout stick beside her. "I have this stick, but I don't know where they are until their teeth sink into good flesh."

Mom tried to lift the corners of the woman's wrap to check the bites, but the cloth stuck. "Do you have another cloth?" she asked.

"There. It's dirty." The woman pointed with her chin to a corner of the hut.

Mom sent me outside with my bowl and soap to wash the wrap and told the woman the rats would not bother her again. They

Patients sit in the shade of their houses built by Dad and the men of Kamayala in 1953, funded by the World Health Organization. (Ben Eidse photo)

would put down rat poison. I set the bowl on a stout chair and dipped a section of black crusted cloth into the water. I rubbed it with soap and scrubbed it to a lather between gloved knuckles.

From beneath the dirt, a gold and green pattern appeared. The worn cotton blurred under my eyes. A solid despair rose from the pit of my stomach. If infecting myself with leprosy would have eased the woman's suffering, I would have done it. Perhaps that's why I ignored the dousing I was getting through my gloves, the brown, mucous-laden water bathing an open cut on my hand.

This infection impulse was not unusual among survivors, especially in the days when Hansen's disease (leprosy) patients were separated from society, and families were divided. But immunity to the bacillus increases with age, and transmission is mainly by mucus, or through active lesions. Teenagers, due to cooler temperatures of extremities in puberty, are the most susceptible.

Mom emerged from the woman's hut, her jaw set, lips pursed.

"Can you buy rat poison?" I gave the wrapper one last rinse and wring out.

"Yes, we have some. We'll put it in the corners so people won't track through it."

"Hey, look at this." I came to my senses. "There's a hole in my glove."

Mom was typically cool and rational, so when she leaped to examine my hand, I jumped.

"Why didn't you tell me the gloves were leaking?" Then she saw the open sore. "Why didn't you tell me about the cut? I would never have let you help if I had known."

If there had been a spigot nearby, she would have doused my hand on the spot. But as it was, we would have to return to the clinic where rain barrels were hooked to indoor-outdoor taps.

Mom fell silent as we passed the spreading mango trees where a man and young boy sat in the shade. We walked up the steps into the tin-roofed, fieldstone clinic. There the nurse, Izamo, bent over a microscope checking sample slides. He turned to greet us brushing his hands on his white lab coat.

Mom nodded and rushed me to a stainless steel sink. She turned on a faucet and handed me a bar of soap. "Wash your hands and soap them good—for a full minute."

Sparkling water poured out splashing my cut. I sudsed my hands and washed between my fingers, under my nails and up over my wrists the way she'd taught me. Mom found a large brown bottle of disinfectant among the sulfone drug, DDS (diaminodiphenyl sulfone), which arrested Hansen's disease in six months. Still many patients stayed on near the clinic for wound treatment.

The disinfectant fizzed in my open cut, and Mom dabbed it with a sterile cotton ball. Then we told Izamo, "*Sala kabema*" (stay well), and walked our bikes through sand to the packed dirt road across the savanna.

"You know I'll have to put you on medicine," Mom said. "You mustn't breathe a word of this."

In the 1960s and '70s, Mom dispensed medicine and clean bills of health at the leprosarium clinic. (Ron Goertzen photo)

I nodded. I had no words anyway and no voice with which to say them. I would be a hidden leper, crouched in elephant grass not breathing a word. The marble had cracked. I, too, could be watching my hands grow numb. How would I hold my pens and pencils? How would I write and draw? The banana grower no longer had fingers for tearing chunks of mush from a ball of *chindu*. Just stumps and an opposing half-thumb to grip it with.

Behind us a tire iron clanged on an old tire hub, Chief Dominque calling his people to a meeting in the chapel. Over time he had gone from walking with a cane on numb, flapping feet, to crawling on his knees, his feet turned to toeless clubs, his walking muscles lost to the dead peroneal nerves of his inner thigh. Mom had made him rubber knee pads.

In nearby fields, women paused from hoeing the beans Mom had brought to improve their diets and give them a market crop. A sweetly sorrowful melody rose behind us, *Kuwakungu nyonga*. "Amid the trials that I meet, amid the thorns that pierce my feet, one thought remains supremely sweet, thou thinkest Lord of me."

We were many and we were one, sitting on our beds each night checking fingers and toes for nicks or burns, watching for lesions near elbows or knees, patches of pinkish-white, insensitive skin.

Deep into the night, while the moon rose over the savanna, Mom and Dad's low voices rose and fell behind their closed bedroom door. How could I have been so careless? It was as reckless as jumping off the cliff at the falls. If I had done something deliberately to get Mom's attention, it wouldn't have been more effective than this unthinking act. Yet I fell asleep knowing the woman I'd bathed was safe and wrapped in a clean cloth that night.

During the next six months, I guarded a pill bottle full of Dapsone, the tablet form of DDS. It was a large, white pill the size of a nickel. Its only measurable side effect was the stuttering gulp required to swallow it, and the gag reflex that followed. Mom had warned me, "There is still a lot of stigma about leprosy. You mustn't tell anyone, not even your sisters."

Hope would have been interested in my case, medically. Charity, whose scarred hands were still sensitive from her electrical burn, would have felt along with the insecurity I felt. Either of them would have made great confidantes. But I believed Mom's warning and kept silent.

The solitary nature of my cure drove me to a secret obsession with leprosy. I counted myself a hidden patient checking to see if my toes had curled into hammertoes as nerves fought off bacillus attacks and tendons shrank. I checked knees and elbows for numb, white patches, and felt my big nose to see if it had caved yet.

Perhaps it was in the hostel library downstairs, I found *Who Walk Alone,* Perry Burgess's novel of a serviceman living in exile with leprosy. After his diagnosis in the U.S., he returned to the "sanctuary of sorrow," a leprosarium in the Philippines and married his beloved Carita, also a patient. There was a lonely romance in the life of an exile, an added dimension to the everyday, an existence beyond the ordinary. Perhaps there was even a heightened awareness of other realities, a sense of living in another sphere, in tension with the world around you.

Later, I was gripped by a science fantasy character, Thomas Covenant the Unbeliever of *Lord Foul's Bain.* Thomas was created by a missionary kid like me whose father worked with patients in India. Covenant was so cruelly shunned on the street for his leprosy that he slipped into a metaphysical state. He became one of the living dead, transported to a spiritual plane, though he was still living and breathing in the modern world. He called himself the Unbeliever because he dared not believe in this alternate world where he possessed a mystical power, white gold, against Lord Foul the Despiser.

It was the lepers' resilience in struggle that inspired Jean-Joseph Rabéarivelo, the great poet of Madagascar. He compared their hands to flowering cacti. "They say a secret spring rises in their leathery palms. An inner spring, they say, to slake the thirst of hordes of oxen and the thirst of many tribes, lost tribes, in the country to the South." (Rabéarivelo)

I discovered the "leper mass" conducted in the Middle Ages. It was a ceremony of symbolic burial, to comfort the lepers being ritually segregated from society. It reminded me of Dad's story that widows of our tribe were once expected to throw themselves into their husband's graves to show their grief. The medieval church required the patient, in rags, to follow in procession a cross-bearer and priests in ceremonial robes. From the cathedral to the cemetery, where a new trench had been dug, the leper went in a death march with her wailing family. There she stood at the lip of her own grave, taking part in her own funeral, hearing the final prayers for her soul, and the list of prohibitions that she must live under. She was to remain outside the city, ring a bell to warn oncomers and hold out a pail on a stick to receive handouts.

On school mornings, I joined the procession of the living on the hostel bus, chatted on the walkway and shared cokes from the school store. I blanched a moment when the fizzy liquid burst on my tongue. How could I just hand the bottle on without a pang, or confession? Did I not care if my friends got leprosy? If I rubbed the bottle hard on my skirt would they guess? And would that be enough? There was so much I feared if I told—friends turning their backs, walking away. There was so much I didn't know. Was my treatment just a precaution or was I actually infected and contagious until I completed the therapy?

I lingered to talk with the teacher after biology class. Could I write an extra credit paper on Hansen's disease? Could I visit leprosariums and talk to doctors? My teacher grinned at first as though I were joking but I persisted. He asked a dozen questions but finally consented.

Mom had flown to the city and taken me to visit a hospital administrator at his home one evening. They discussed my case in soft tones under diffused lamplight. Mr. Robert Watalet, from Belgium, in white shirt and glasses, nodded. Yes, I must complete a full six-month course of Dapsone.

He ran the national leprosarium in Kinshasa, *L'Hopital de la Rive*. It stretched along an abandoned rail bed overlooking the lush Zaire River. Here, Mr. Watalet dispensed sulfone drugs, provided occupational therapy and pioneered small industries to promote independence. His patients worked long hours, pushing numb fingers to perform exacting work like shoe stitching and basket weaving.

I was transfixed by the setting and the patients who seemed committed beyond their ability. Sometimes their hands were so numb, they used their teeth to grip and pull thin rattan fibers or raffia threads. Sweat beaded their hairlines, and ran around raised bumps on brow bones, noses and lips. *Lepromatous nodules*, I had read. Would I be willing to sit on the ground, sweating and forcing numb fingers to work just to prove I could be industrious and independent? Or did they receive some satisfaction, recognition and value from this work?

Over Thanksgiving break, I hitched a ride home with my classmate, Amy, whose father, Dr. Wayne Meyers, was a microbiologist at a hospital known as Kivuvu, "place of hope," at Kimpese, "place of cockroaches." I followed Dr. Meyers through the cinder block building, while he chatted with patients and checked their faces and toes. He rebuilt sunken noses using a piece of the patient's rib. This was important for a person's dignity, he said, to walk in the market again and not be shunned. He introduced me to an orthopedic surgeon who restored tendons in feet and hands.

He examined the bumps that grew on the faces, ears and hands of patients with lepromatus leprosy, and the flat, pinkish-white lesions of patients with tuberculoid leprosy. Some had a mix, flat lesions with bumpy borders, or borderline leprosy. Kimpese was a half-day drive from Kinshasa, but Dr. Meyers' patients got there any way they could.

Dr. Meyers took me to a large laboratory banked with microscopes, beakers and petri dishes. He showed me slides of the three types of leprosy bacilli swimming in suspension and gave me time to draw and color the images.

The Sunday night of our return to school, I examined my prominent nose gratefully and swallowed my Dapsone tablet without gagging.

———————

Decades later I was hired by the Department of Health, Office of Minority Health and Health Equity in Tallahassee, Florida. Near our home, on early mornings, nine-banded armadillos scuttled into holes alongside roads and ditches. Clunky, prehistoric critters with an endemic leprosy rate of ten to twenty percent, they had become an immunology agent in the campaign against leprosy. At the end of 2018, there were 208,000 cases globally, down from 5.2 million in the 1980s. Worldwide, 16 million people have been cured of leprosy (WHO). Because of the rate of leprosy among native-born Texans, Louisianans and Alabamans, researchers continue to ponder the armadillo-to-human link. Was leprosy first transmitted to humans from armadillos, or the other way around?

My classmate Amy would one day move to Houston, Texas, and dutifully brake for armadillo roadkill. Her father had requested the animals' hands and feet and she donned plastic gloves and cut them off to send to his research lab at the University of Hawaii.

Today the Kamayala leprosarium has been converted into the Mennonite Agricultural Village, a 2019 grassroots vision of ten local leaders and their seed money, with a match from Dayspring Ministries (founded by Ron Goertzen, Henderson, NE) and a grant from Schowalter Foundation into sustainable development projects. Patients' fields that once produced "Mama Eidse Beans" were overgrown. But the land was again cleared and planted, this time with

improved varieties of disease-resistant manioc that are lower in naturally occurring cyanide, which if not properly soaked results in a
crippling disease called *konzo*.

The walls of the dispensary, chapel and several patients' houses
were sound enough to be refurbished with new roofs. The fields grow
lush with manioc, soybeans, corn, pineapples, onions and bananas,
as well as greens to feed livestock such as pigs, chickens, cattle and
honey bees. The new varieties of manioc are widely distributed and
training is offered to introduce more productive farming methods
to young people who anticipate a new future in farming and market
gardening.

I received countless gifts from my mother, but perhaps the
best was the opportunity to feel along with the suffering of others, to
identify with rejected outsiders.

For the half year that I had crossed over into the Hansen's
disease camp, I was infected with a consciousness of displacement,
amplified by adolescence, womanhood, and my traveling childhood.
It became an inner spring of heightened awareness and sympathy.

From that multitude of molded hands swells a secret river, a
hidden source rising from untainted palms, "an inner spring...to
slake the thirst of hordes of oxen and the thirst of many tribes, lost
tribes, in the country to the South."

20

FOURTEEN LASHES

The moon over Kamayala during Christmas break 1969 waxed into a giant, visible in the eastern sky by mid-afternoon and high in the sky by sunset. The week of Christmas was lit with it and we planned a New Year's Eve sleepover on our balcony with Vangie Claassen.

Ruth, James, Charity, Grace, Vangie and I gathered on our balcony around a cassette recorder learning new folk tunes. (Hope Wiebe photo)

We found it hard to sleep inside anyway on nights lit by such a cosmic radiance. This would be one of our last holidays with American kids on the station before the Claassens left the next summer.

On Christmas Eve my sisters and I pulled ourselves in from playing with the orphans to roll, cut, bake and ice sugar cookies. The toffee smell of fresh-baked cookies mingled with the turpentine-scent of the pitch pine branch we'd cut and decorated the week before.

Some unspoken need to be praised for my creativity drove me even to hanging and displaying the dainty treats on the tree.

"Faithee," Hope frowned. "There's gonna be ants."

"Maybe," I admitted but went on icing and stringing up cookies anyway. Some were a tad burned and those I layered with extra icing. "But we can just brush 'em off before eating."

Dad looked on grinning at our disagreement. "Well, I hope so."

He showed us tables he'd created of 14 different Chokwe verb tenses and 12 noun classes and their corresponding adjective changes. These included separate tenses for storytelling. "It's a complicated language but I believe Ron and Dan will make good progress with language study. I hope that having two agricultural workers at Kamayala will reverse the loss of young people to the cities."

"That sounds great!" I cleaned up my icing mess, proud of his language smarts.

I rose Christmas morning with high hopes for my cookie ornaments. But when I peered through the early morning grey, black shapes hung in place of the green and pink cookies we'd iced the night before.

"Look." Hope's tone had a ring of told-you-so. "Your cookies."

"It must be the burned sides turned out." I crossed the cool concrete floor to turn them but the moment my hand touched them, it tingled with excited sugar ants. The glimpse before bedtime, green and pink cookies gleaming in yellow lantern light, was the last tantalizing sight we'd had of our Christmas treats. They had to all be tossed into the wood-burning stove.

We salvaged the holiday by attending the Christmas pageant at church, complete with goats herded down the center aisle and angels appearing in white cotton slips. The school choirs transported us to heavenly realms, accompanied by multilayered rhythms on bottles, and Mrs. Claassen on the pump organ. Drums would not be far behind.

That New Year's Eve, Vangie's rippling laughter filled the night from our balcony sleepover. Her easy glee melted anxiety. We ate a panful of fresh roasted peanuts and I forgot to count calories.

———————

Back at school for grade 9, we met at our gym teacher's house and spun Carol King's "Tapestry" for creative movement and group discussions. From the danceable, "I Feel the Earth Move" to "You've Got a Friend" and "So Far Away," it became the soundtrack of our global nomad lives. King had forever answered James Taylor's "Fire and Rain." From her curtained Laurel Canyon windowsill with grey cat, she'd opened us up to the grief of our traveling lives but tried to assure us that somewhere we'd have a friend.

In full vagabond mode, I pencil-crayoned notecards of hippy teens in blue jeans carrying hobo stick satchels, labeled, *So Far Away* and *You've Got a Friend.* I sold dozens on the walkway and took orders for more. The school announced a poster contest and I won prizes and sales with shaggy blue dogs lifting doleful eyes as though asking, "Leaving again?" or "Be my friend?"

In Western Civ, I wrote an essay on T. S. Eliot's "The Hollow Men." I noted his travels, how he'd soaked up cultures in urban centers and declared that he did not want to get rooted in one place for fear it would make him narrow-minded. Our teacher, Garry Schmidt, who had grown up in India and Canada, asked in the margin who I was quoting. Must have been me adding my own interpretation.

———————

That year, books from America's budding counterculture circulated in single copies. Students gathered along the walkway for group reads, scanning over each other's shoulders, breathing down each other's necks, turning pages together. One week it was *The Electric Kool-Aid Acid Test,* the next, *Les Girls.* The blue paperback smuggled to school in someone's backpack became community property. Kids skipped class to read it, and I followed its progress down the walkway from seniors to juniors as first one gaggle of students and then another huddled over it. It was, apparently a light read, skimmed in an hour. Not since *The Harrad Experiment* had a book generated so much interest.

Among the reading students one afternoon, Gavin stood out. He was Art Garfunkel but younger—more hair, bigger eyes—and he played jazz on the piano as though it were instinct. A sophomore from my typing class, he was such an error-free speedster that he finished early and typed me notes instead. While the rest of us stumbled over "A quick brown fox," he typed, "Whisper a little prayer for me." Gavin had a southern drawl, freckles and big, soft curls. When my last class let out, he was reading *Les Girls,* surrounded by dormmates. They excused themselves when I approached, as though they knew about the typing class notes.

"Sure is taking you long enough," I ribbed, conscious of my light tone, followed by nervous laughter.

"You want to read it?" He held up the book.

I hesitated, considered the title—did it refer to French prostitutes? Still, I didn't want to miss out on new ideas going around school. "Sure." I reached for it. "Shouldn't take too long."

"Sit here." He patted the wall beside him. "Look at this." He pointed to a paragraph describing a close, intimate hug between girls—not prostitutes—but women in love. So this was what Aunt Nettie had warned about when we were nine years old rolling on the floor laughing.

"I don't like reading over shoulders." I made a grab for the book. Girlfriend love might seem new to Americans. But in Congo, girls often held hands, hugged in the streets, or stood talking, hands on each other's breasts.

Gavin dodged. "You'll have to come home with me."

Home for him was the wild Methodist-Presbyterian Hostel (MPH), a five-minute walk from school through the jungle. MPH kids spun the Rolling Stones and threw dance parties. It was off-limits to us Mennonites.

"Hang on. I'll have to tell someone." I knew there was no one left but the varsity basketball players and they hated intrusions. A small knot tightened in my gut. Even if I did tell them, it didn't count as getting permission from Uncle Hector. I raced to the intramural field. At the basketball fence, I waited for a throw-in by Tom just feet away. "I'm going to MPH."

"No you're not." Until then I hadn't noticed how much he sounded like a dorm parent. Could he really tell me what to do? He was my hostel "brother," older by two years, but still one of us kids. I didn't know boys could make rules for girls just because they were boys. I had thought women's submission was a marriage thing and, when the time came, I'd want to. I hadn't agreed to this unspoken rule that any girl could be over-ruled by any boy.

Tom threw in the ball, his long hair trapped under a headband, his muscles pouring sweat. Except for his ongoing row with Uncle Hector over haircuts, he seemed to think like Hector did. Tom pounded down the court, dribbled and shot as though exercise would save him from sexual passion.

"Goodbye!" My voice was firm. Clear.

He scowled over his shoulder and I knew I had not gained an ally. The knot twisted tighter in my gut as I raced back to Gavin. "Come on." I could still get back for the last bus if we hurried.

Gavin's soft tread in tire sandals along the forest path was too slow for me. I wanted to get to his hostel, skim a few more chapters and then catch my ride home.

"Slow dow-un," he drawled. "He-ere." He reached for my

hand and laced his long fingers through mine. The brush of his curls as he ducked a branch, the quiet pause as he bent towards me pulling me in, his pink lips touching, lingering on mine, melted anxiety. We swung around curving lianas, stepped over fallen logs and passed so soundlessly, the birds continued their calling in the jungle canopy. A second and third kiss set my lips ablaze.

At MPH, a dorm parent appeared from the kitchen and I shrank back.

"Aw, don't be scared," Gavin said. "Hey there, sir. This is Faith, from the Mennonite hostel. We're just gonna do some reading."

"Ok, welcome." The man disappeared down the hall.

Gavin led me to a sofa overlooking a backyard jungle. We snuggled close and paged through *Les Girls*, with Gavin pointing out highlights, opening my eyes to surprising possibilities of girls in love.

Finally, I felt an internal scowl as square-jawed as Uncle Hector's. I straightened. "I have to run back for our bus."

But Gavin pulled me in again. "Time is relative. We're having a relatively good time, why wreck it? My hostel parents can drive you home later."

Gavin, at least, was beyond our dorm's control. There was freedom in his thinking, ease in his movement. He guided me upstairs to the music practice rooms and asked me to play piano. All I knew were hymns from the book. "How Great Thou Art," "A Mighty Fortress Is Our God." Gavin was encouraging. "You actually played a hymn with four sharps? Why didn't you just switch it to one flat, like this?" His improvisations looked smooth and graceful. He added descants and trills, took the tune out of church, loose and easy and launched into raucous ragtime. "You're so wooden." He nudged me beside him on the piano bench. "Why don't you get up and move a little?"

"You know me." I rose gingerly and swayed slightly to his beat. "I would've danced all night, but I'm a Mennonite."

"But dancing is such a simple pleasure!" He shook his shoulders and cranked the tempo. These were the outside views—the reality checks—I'd been guarded from.

I saw that Gavin was trying to rescue me from a stiff and rigid life. If only. *Please let it be so,* I pleaded inwardly.

Yet at that moment, the dinner buzzer was sounding at the Mennonite hostel—and I wasn't there.

My stomach twisted so tight as the MPH van trundled downhill past the President's park with its grazing okapi, that I thought I would throw up. At the wheel, Gavin's hostel parent, who had been dragged from a shortwave radio set upstairs, scowled silently. He could charge me for this extra trip, gas was so scarce and costly in this city.

The railroad rolled past and the river below it. The lingering tingle from Gavin's lips, his easy freedom was a moment past, a place out of time. I knew he could be snatched from me in a Hector tirade and I promised myself to hang on no matter how bruising the punishment.

When I unlatched the Mennonite compound gate and crept into the dining room, the picture was all wrong. Dinner was over, and my mother was sitting in the living room, her brown eyes serious, her freckled face drawn, white hair showing among the auburn. She'd been called from upcountry to corral me. My sister Hope would later find the letter from Uncle Hector that had compelled Mom's trip. It read, in part, "We're worried about Faith. She is getting in trouble with boys."

"Getting in trouble," to my parents, was the same as getting pregnant. Mom had come to the city and, sure enough, I had disappeared without permission and reappeared late for dinner. The rumors were confirmed. Over some boy at school, some wild Methodist, I had turned rebel, disobeyed the hostel rules, flown out of control.

There were times when I had longed for my mother's presence; to hug me goodnight my first nights at the hostel, to watch my triumph in a school play, to shield me from Uncle Hector's wrath. This was not one of them. I would rather face his anger and take my punishment without dragging her into it. It was more painful with her here, enforcing Uncle Hector's codes. Her punishment would be worse because it was coming from my last ally, my mother.

Mom didn't say much. She didn't seem to know where to start. The dresses in my closet were too short. Why had I ruined them that way? By week's end, she had called in help. I didn't know it until I got off the bus Friday afternoon.

Hope met me and took my books, her tone urgent. "Dad is here. He's waiting for you at the guest house." I would have preferred a public welcome, a bear hug for all to see, as though I were still Dad's favorite artistic, reading daughter.

The ground was slippery with sticky fig tree droppings when I picked my way to the guest house that had once been the girls' dorm before we all moved into the sprawling new dorm together. The fat silver baobab had dropped a watermelon-sized breadfruit pod, a green velvet skull cracked open, its spongy pink insides lolling out. Along the compound fence mango trees let go the overripe fruit of their upper branches. The air was heavy with the saccharine stench of ripeness and decay.

I passed the basketball court and kicked a flat ball out of the way. Thud. It lurched and wobbled. Whatever sense of proportion I had leading up to my fifteenth birthday, whatever sense I had of seeing through new eyes and gaining control of my life, was rapidly getting kicked out of me. How had I imagined I could escape the compound and mission dorm controls? How had I hoped to hang out with Methodists who danced and lived without rules? How had I thought I could read about lesbian love and not get punished for it?

I reached the "torn heart hedge," my name for it since my early years. The leaves were hand-sized green valentines, and I had taken some pleasure in tearing them apart. Shred, shred. My heart longing for Mom and Dad's hugs. Tear it up, stuff it down. Then try to piece it back together again.

My parents whom I had not seen in a month had arrived to punish me. I had no advocate in the world but myself.

Shred, shred. Why was Dad only called in to punish me? Surely Dad could see through this. He would be fair, ask me for my side of the story. I would tell him that the night Mom arrived was the first time I'd missed the bus. I'd tell him how considerate Gavin was, how free-thinking. I'd tell Dad how stagnant a person could get in here, not being permitted to read, explore, venture out, find out how other people lived—something he'd devoted his life to.

I passed the garage storage unit and paused on the red steps of the guest house under its concrete rain lip, anticipating the game. Scold me, pray with me, fine. Just let me keep Gavin and let me keep reading. The fence, the dorms, the overripe trees were too constraining and overshadowing. How was I going to experience anything outside the dorm when every time I launched out there was another barrier? Even Tom seemed threatened by the small outward steps I was taking. "Gay Gavin," he'd teased when I squeezed past him at the hostel water cooler. I blanched a moment—how could he know what we were reading—then recovered and filled my glass, realizing he couldn't possibly. He was only referring to Gavin's obvious lack of interest in sports or rigorous exercise.

At the guest house, I banged through the tight-sprung screen door. "Da-aad." I tried to sound cheery. I passed the cupboard where I had folded the dust rag five times when I'd first arrived, the dining room where I'd permitted the typewriter to be stolen with my engrossed reading and the piano where a groping teacher had reduced me to tears.

"Dad?" He was not rising to meet me in any of the common rooms. My back stiffened and I turned into the back hallway. My shoulders tightened in the pervading gloom. In a back bedroom, Dad sat at a desk, dark head bowed, over 1 Timothy 3.

It was a passage I knew well about special standards for church leaders. Dad had taught it to us as though it were his burden, but I had always heard it as mine. "He must be able to manage his own family well and make his children obey him with all respect. For if a man does not know how to manage his own family, how can he take care of the church of God?"

A lump filled my throat, hard as a mango pit. I raised my arms, palms out, a trial gesture, half-hoping for a welcoming hug. I dropped them again and waited. The time tunnel I raced through to shore up my faltering hope was filled with the smell of oil. Oil of the generator Dad cranked so we could keep reading after dark, oil creased into his knuckles on the throttle of a new dirt bike, with Dad instructing me to open up slowly. He stood back helplessly as I raced off toward the village, cranked the throttle, and popped a wheelie. My reputation as a kamikaze biker was instant and Dad got a new nickname, *Shafulafula* (father of a fast-fast, crazy driver).

"Sit down." He barely looked up. The only other chair was behind him, near a twin bed. Mom sat on the opposite bed, and this added to my distress. The room felt small for three people, especially since one of them was Mom. If Dad punished me I wanted to run to Mom for comfort. If they were together, I had nowhere to go but myself.

"You've disappointed us." Dad's back was still turned. He stared at the wall, took off his glasses and rubbed his eyes.

I swallowed against the mango pit. When he turned, his large blue eyes were gray and watery.

I had once nuzzled the deep vibration in his drum-like chest while he practiced Chokwe phrases. But that was before gesture had turned wooden between us. My only hope was to win Mom back. Her presence said the only way to do that was by submitting.

Not now, I wanted to say. *Don't make me submit now.* I want to loosen up, dance, keep reading, keep Gavin. Please don't make me give it all up.

"Your mother and I have prayed about this. We've decided to punish you, so you will remember it."

I had once been the daughter he called out to the car pit to help change the oil. He'd said nostalgically, "We did this on the farm in Canada, wedged in mud to our eyeballs." That was the drudging life he'd rejected to trek the remote villages of Africa with a tape recorder, capturing the purest language of the Lunda-Chokwe, tribes descended from the ancient kingdoms of the Kongo. They'd held off Leo's forces for twenty years, inflicting heavy tolls (Hochschild, p. 124).

Yet Mom was here, on his side. Wasn't she supposed to plead for me, she who was my first love? Instead she was sacrificing me to Dad's rule—or was it Uncle Hector's? Silence was all that came from her and all that was invited from me. During Christmas vacation Mom had discovered that I'd lost my virginity to tampons—bought, not from the dorm supply closet, but at the stores with my allowance. Too late to warn against them, she'd settled for quizzing me. Did inserting them give me pleasure? I could only look at her in disbelief. Inserting them had given me great pain since I did not know the slant of my own body. I had poked wrong and burst my hymen so that it burned like a scorpion pinch. I had gone back to wearing pads until the hurt healed. Then, with the damage done, I could explore with less pain.

How distant she'd seemed then, how out-of-touch with my growing independence. Her wide pale lips narrowed. She shifted on the bed, straightened, squared her shoulders, allied with Dad, looming against me. Loss of father and mother love. Love withdrawn.

"...so we decided to spank you," Dad said.

I reeled inside. *I'm practically grown already.* I've been on my own since I was nine years old. But I had never talked to my father that way, I who had tried to be his son-substitute. Our relationship was pieced together from road trips, riverside picnics and intensive chess duels during school vacations. Usually it was I who conceded checkmate, laying down my king.

"Lie down on the bed." Dad gestured. "Face down."

This seemed too exposed for a daughter and a dad. But the bed was firm, the Amish-star quilt rough against my cheek. I closed my eyes. No sound, no slap, no pain. Was he having second thoughts? I opened one eye.

Dad was unbuckling his belt, taking it off—way too exposed. He had always used his hand before—back in my grade school days. I must've talked in church when my parents were at the podium. But all I remembered was the high purple of his descending face. In the years that followed, it had never come to his using a weapon on me. Gavin was costing me a great deal. Perhaps more than I could afford, especially since I would have my family all my life. My back stiffened again. I shut my eyes, anticipating the belt.

"How many shall it be?"

None. If I spoke would I betray myself? Would I give in, give up Gavin to recover Dad's love? "Forty." I pronounced it as though I were some kind of martyr. Could I ever again be the innocent girl my parents wanted? Was it possible to grow up and stop knowing? If they beat the sin out of me, would I forget what I'd already learned?

"Fourteen," Dad said. "Because you're fourteen."

"Thank you," I remembered to say. Did fourteen mean that the older I got—the closer to independence—the more drastically I would be punished for declaring my own position? The process of becoming a woman was the process of submission.

The belt when it bit, left a searing burn. *Mommy,* I had cried into the pillow on those first hollow nights at the hostel and had not distinguished between her and Mommy-God. *Mommy-Daddy,* I had added the night of my first toothache and had not separated them from Mommy-Daddy-God. Ever since, I'd carried comforting images of them in my head.

When the strap hit again, I clutched my fading parent-gods. I had summoned them on my darkest nights, their voices soft and low, their shoulders absorbent as a pillow for a child to sniffle into.

Four...five...six... I glimpsed Dad's shadow on the wall bent to his task, felt Mom's presence backing him up. Hadn't they been there when Uncle Hector pinned and whiskered me? Hadn't they felt the agony of Uncle Hector branding me as a *whore* in the laundry room? How could that father and mother now be set against me? Ten...eleven...twelve.... This father was some robot following orders. He was under Uncle Hector's spell. Otherwise, how could he be so separate from me?

"Fourteen." He looped his belt back on.

I slowly turned and sat, stung. The mango pit had swollen and closed my throat. I could not speak, could not hide my flowing tears or my running nose. He stood with his arms extended. It was like Uncle Hector holding the door after calling me *prick tease*. Mom sat, her eyes liquid, her mouth set in a thin line. Perhaps they thought they had saved me from myself. I let Dad pat my back, my arms folded against my body, and brushed past him to the bathroom. They were not the hearing, feeling parents I carried in my head. I bent to wash away the sticky, overripe oozing of my rage.

The summer of 1970, the whole mission met for a week-long conference upcountry at Nyanga secondary school. Dozens of PAX men and women filled the dining hall and gathered for sessions in classrooms. I was 15 and entering grade 10 but felt wise beyond my years knowing that a strongly held belief against war could be turned by visionaries into development programs to benefit Congo.

The first night we young people, MKs and PAX, piled into a truck bed and bumped along narrow roads to fabled Lake Madimape where many of my dorm mates had summered and played. I jumped

The Eidse and Claassen families with Ron Goertzen (back left) and Dan Yoder (back center right) attended a mission conference at Nyanga in summer 1970.

off the tailgate but noticed that my girlfriends held back. Leola, Jette and Linda were offered sturdy arms and hands to help them down gracefully. Having failed to read the moment, I plunged ahead and waded into warm black waters lit by headlights. By finally touching these magical waters I was closing the gap between us MKs from remote Kamayala and those from the mission center.

Other nights we filled dorm verandahs and sitting rooms to read novels (for me, the tragic sinking of the *Titanic*), play cards and listen to cassette recordings of Bob Dylan, Simon and Garfunkel and Peter, Paul and Mary. As the week evolved, we built an evening fire in the yard, strummed guitar and sang, "If I Had a Hammer," "Where Have All the Flowers Gone?" and "Bridge Over Troubled Water." Henry from B.C. taught us his original high school grad anthem and we sang along making it our own, "Here am I on the brink of my life." He was a long way from the cool mountains of home and he noticed Hope's ease with singing and guitar. He later asked her to dinner in Kinshasa—her first date.

The teens played pranks on the grown-ups, and I stood watch while Linda and Leola raided bras from dorm rooms and froze them in the kitchen freezer. Another evening the teens sneaked to the MAF plane and threw cutlery inside, laughing at the alarm it would raise at takeoff.

It was on a tour of the nearby training-demonstration farm, while admiring Fremont Regier's pillowy pink pigs, that I noticed a tall, dimpled, black-bearded farm boy. His eyes twinkled when they met mine and his grin revealed cute buck teeth—a familiar trait in my Reimer clan. He was from Goessel, Kansas, he said, and knew Elda Hiebert, the nurse-midwife who'd fled Mukedi with us when I was eight.

He wanted to know all about Zaire, and I all about the States. So we roamed the farm and traded stories of wheatfields and waterfalls. He tried to make me sit but his hairy, muscled arms made me shiver and I was soon up walking the sandy roads again.

"Don't you ever stop walking?" He tried to pull me down again.

Snarky dude. I was afraid if we sat I'd get swept away by his caresses.

Finally, in the descending darkness, he pulled me close and gave me my first full-bearded kiss. Until that moment, I thought I hated prickly beards but his was soft and full and I responded to his moist lips.

For years we traded teasing letters and a few times saw each other again. But distance was hell on relationships.

21

RAT HUNT

Dense smoke clouds billowed, shutting out the summer sunrise at Kamayala. Cinders settled on my window sill and the smell of burned underbrush hung in the air. From mud-and-grass huts, villagers ran evenly and with purpose, as if setting out on a marathon. Women carried hoes, men carried homemade rifles, and children jogged alongside with sticks.

They loped past my window with the grace of kids accustomed to using their feet as wheels. They carried sharpened sticks, a hoe, a club. The seasonal grass fires on the other side of the river flushed out grasshoppers, long-tailed kite birds, Thompson's gazelles and field rats.

"Come on, *'Fudielo* and *Zango*," Hope whispered from the doorway using our African names.

I stirred against tired muscles and longed for a few more winks. We had returned late the night before from the village where Hope had led us, cloaked in African cloths, to join the drumming and dancing under a full moon. She had left the hostel early to take Canadian grade 12 by correspondence and prepare for nurse's training. But studying alone in an empty house had fueled an urge for daring escapes and tiny transgressions. At the moonlight party, she'd insisted that we not let our cloths fall to reveal our white faces but I had blown it and created a ruckus.

Her voice from the hallway was stern, "Try not to wake Grace." Hope was already dressed in light denim culottes that left her plenty of room for running. We couldn't wear shorts in this mission village or we'd get laughed back into the house.

Hope's calves were flexed for take-off, her ash hair pulled into a tight braid. A water canteen was strapped across one shoulder, a large cloth tied over the other and she carried a stick as thick as her braid.

After months back in Kamayala, she was well ahead of us in sensing the action in this village. She was often right at Mom's elbow at the clinic, dispensing drugs or giving injections. She was the first to jump on a bike to deliver a message to the village chauffeur about a hemorrhaging mother to be rushed to the Kahemba hospital.

Hope must have planned ahead, lying awake in a swatch of moonlight, recalling *Tata* Michel's preparations the day before, sharpening his knife, cutting tin cans to strips, and rolling them into shot. Otherwise how had she known to leap from bed before dawn and get an early start for the big hunt?

We had trailed as stragglers to hunts before, but this time Hope planned to catch something. I could tell by the heft of her weapon. She was getting better at Africa her last year before college, better at all the survival traits—running, carrying water, planning for the hunt.

Charity and I scrambled into skirts and sneakers, careful not to wake eight-year-old Grace, and slid out the screen door after Hope. She was already attached to a group of women showing off her stout stick.

We followed her down a gullied path to the river keeping an eye on her bobbing braid. Charity closed the gap with her long-legged stride, I ran double-time to keep up. When at last we caught Hope it was at a flat, worn log that crossed the Kamayala River. This was where she had been baptized in 1967 into the Congo Mennonite Church. It was not our usual swimming spot where we dipped and dove from swinging vines into fresh springs. This was the highway to the remote Lunda villages on the eastern plateau. Women from both sides soaked manioc here to rid them of deadly cyanide. They waited a week to retrieve the starchy tuber, somehow knowing which underwater mound was theirs. I had not come this way since last summer, and the river was shallow, clogged with manioc skins, peeled before hauling uphill for drying and pounding into flour.

I ran recklessly downhill and caught my canvas shoe on the glistening crossing log. My arms flew up, my legs shot out, and I hit the dark water with a splash. Whoops and laughter closed over me. Silent, weightless, in the dark green, sour-woodsy water, I groped for solid footing amid shifty, gelatinous manioc peels. I stood thigh-high in tannin-stained water and scowled. The procession shouted and laughed some more. I climbed the bank, wrung out my skirt, and shook peels and brown water from my shoes.

Charity waited, hands on hips, but Hope had no time for sideshows. "We've got to keep up!"

In this too, Hope was more serious than I. She had surveyed the women going to the hunt and determined that Mama Beya's group was the most skilled. Mama Beya was a legend of hunting prowess. She wiped her feet on an otter skin beside her bed, a serpentine sharp-clawed attacker she'd grabbed and killed with her bare hands while swimming one day. There would be no falling back with jokers, no slacking off. We would be right in the thick of things with the best hunters.

We trudged up the opposite ridge and I wanted to pause for a drink from Hope's canteen. It was water as clean as we could get it, boiled and strained of insects, sloshing with ice at Hope's razor hip.

"May I have some water please?"

"Later. We have to save it."

I knew she was right but I felt a familiar rebellion, a silent retort. Her ramrod back, her trim waist, her sunken cheeks all shouted control. She was all control; I was all impulse. It was a defense, a defiance on my part.

She had said at the hostel the year before—stopping me on my way to the cookie tub—"If we both lose five pounds, we can take an extra ten-pound sack of flour home." Flour broke the monotony of *chindu,* goat meat and bananas. It meant Mom and Dad could eat fresh bread and cookies. Controlling ourselves had a way of benefitting others. But beyond the nobility, was the obsession that sometimes gripped us. It came from trying to "be perfect even as your Father in heaven is perfect." Mom washed her hands repeatedly in her clinic work. Dad repeated Greek and Hebrew verbs incessantly and advised us to divide the day into five-minute blocks and fill each with purpose.

Perhaps because of our family's compulsions, I resisted guilt-tripping. Would the pilot really deny us a ten-pound sack of flour that we'd scoured from the stores and stood in long lines to buy—especially since we weighed so little? Even if we had to hold it in our laps and the plane needed an extra twenty yards to take off?

"See?" Hope had stepped on the scales she'd dragged from the hostel store room. "I weigh ninety-five pounds. How much do you weigh?"

I had started eating again, 1,500 calories a day, to get my period back. I felt only slightly superior as I stepped on the hostel scales. At fifteen my skin was nut brown, my hair held a natural wave, and I was dressed in a white shirt and short, tight skirt I'd sewn myself.

"A-hundred-and-five! If you don't eat any dessert for a week, you can make it to one hundred."

I had marched to the kitchen and selected two of the biggest cookies in the tub.

On the uphill climb to the grass fire, my mouth watered for one of those cookies. We had left home without breakfast and the day stretched foodless before us.

Up ahead, a young girl of about five held a shish kabob of fresh grasshoppers, skewered through the thorax, brown and neon jumpers—spring green, yellow, fire orange.

"*Moyo.*" (Hello.) I nodded at her collection. "*Kabema?*" (Are they good?)

"*Ewa.*" (Yes.) She grinned and popped a brown one in her mouth.

"*Ni yami?*" (Me too?) I held out my hand.

In a flash, the girl selected the brightest green and red critter on her stick.

I caught the girl's grin and knew she was laughing at the way we white girls collected the brightest hoppers when brown were the tastiest.

"Faith!" Hope turned onto a new path. "You have to watch."

"We're cutting off up here to the left." Charity disappeared in the grassland. She had once joined a hunt for forest caterpillars, stripped the leaves of the worms and fed us all.

I trotted uphill, slipping the grasshopper in my pocket, and turned left at the fork. We emerged from the valley under a roar like waterfalls. Drifting cinders rained down on us and the overcast day turned hot as an oven. Mama Beya jogged through a small collection of huts in a sandy clearing. The village was deserted. Behind it, the savanna was charred and brittle.

We cut along a path at the edge of the new burn, keeping off the loose ash. Around us, orange flames leaped and translucent heat waves shimmered. Thick dark smoke rose from snarled undergrowth and green trees fighting off the flame.

A writhing life churned near the fire. The orphans—Hélène and Sala among them—grabbed insects out of the air or chased a stream of rodents, snakes and beetles.

Charity caught a large brown grasshopper, roasted it on a smoldering stump, pulled off its stick legs and popped it in her mouth.

Gunshots rang out behind a wall of fire, followed by shouting and crashing of underbrush. Out of the flame a deer leaped, clearing grass, coals, fire. Its long pointed ears laid back, eyes wild. It came in long leaps, its hooves thudding and lifting, raising ash and soot, scattering our friends.

I shrank back behind Hope without meaning to. But she was

ready on the front line, stick raised, a stance so familiar from our pre-school days when Mom was sick and she had to fight for me. Around us on the blackened plateau, the women crouched with hoes ready, waiting for the right moment. And when it came—when Mama Beya cried "*Shaha!*" (Kill it!)—the hoes arched and dove, bouncing off the deer's hide, making him twist wildly. And as he rose, his long throat bared, Mama Beya's hoe lodged true, deep in the deer's neck.

The animal veered and toppled in the dirt, raising a cloud of ash. Mama Beya's hoe in its jugular gathered a dark wetness. There was a shout, hands raised, a cheer, ululating. Behind the deer, men with guns came running. Several knelt and pulled hand-wrought knives from their belts to finish bleeding the deer. Women chopped down a small, straight tree, cut raffia strips and tied the deer to the pole. Later, it would be cut into pieces enough to feed the whole village.

Mama Beya was just getting started. She fetched her hoe and led the women into the burned field, lunging at a hole in the ground, hacking with her hoe, cleaning the bloody blade as she worked. An-other woman ran to the exit hole and the digging continued. The rest of us, Hélène, Sala, Hope, Charity and I, got down on our knees and dug with stout sticks to unearth long deep tunnels. Finally we trapped a family of huddled field rats as big as toy poodles. The rats faced us with two long, yellow front teeth bared, bodies hunched, fur standing on end.

"*Kwata!*" (Catch!) Mama Beya shouted again as she poked with a long stick and sent them scurrying across the charred earth. I chased the one that hurtled past me, but I lunged and pinned it so awkwardly, my hand two inches from its fang-like teeth, that when it lurched, I let it go. What if it had ripped my fingers to shreds? I waited for the next dig.

Hope seemed to clamp down on fear as she singled out the fat-test rat and chased it to ground. "*Nakwata!*" (Caught it!) She yelled, pinning it beneath her stick to a still smoldering patch of ash. The rat shrieked at the scalding.

She bent resolutely over the yellow-toothed rat, her jaw set, her eyes narrowed, her arm muscles taut as she held the thick stick against the writhing, clawing rat. Mama Beya trotted over with her hoe and delivered a single whack to the rat's head, crushing its skull. Its claws spasmed and it lay still.

When at last I held down a rat of my own, it was Hope who came and crunched its skull for me.

The sky deepened to fuchsia and I joined the procession home—Mama Beya's deer in the lead carried by several men. Then came Mama Beya and the other mamas, their heads piled with firewood and field rats, then the rest of us—Hélène, Charity, Sala and me. We each carried limp rats the size of squirrels; our mouths watering for roasted flesh at the end of a marathon day. Hope was just ahead of me, her carrying cloth wrapped around a few choice sticks of firewood and a ten-pound rat. I carried the empty water canteen.

The procession moved steadily towards its cooking fires on the other side of the river. The men, heaving against the weight of the deer, raised a rhythmic song, praising Mama Beya for killing the deer with her hoe, and named the other hunters as well. Something like this:

> Mama Beya killed a doe,
> Struck it with her garden hoe.
> Can she be matched?
> No she can't
> What match is a deer,
> For the elephant?
> Threw her hoe, now hear us tell it,
> Cut its neck, that's how she fell it.
> Added rats—this big—a dozen,
> What match is a rat
> For the elephant's cousin?

And Hopie, and Hélène,
And *Zango*, and Sala
And *Fudielo*.
Can they be matched?
No they can't
What match is a rat
For the elephant?

Hope's feet on the path ahead were black to her knees with soot. Her culottes, once a sky blue, were smudged and gray. Even her neck and face were creased with sweat-soaked dirt. What she would have to cut from herself when she flew home for college—what we would all have to carve away one day—went deeper than African soil. It shot through our blood and marrow on savanna-laced river-jungle-runs and plunges; the village-rhythm life-toil-beat of hunting, gathering and water carrying with our *ndoyis*.

"*Oyé Hopie*," I reached forward and thumped her back, my own nails caked with dirt, my knuckles encased with it.

"*Oyé*," Hope answered, a lilt in her voice. Her silhouette, as she swayed beneath her load, cut an angular wedge against the orchid sky.

Africa would linger even when we opened college textbooks, wrote term papers, chemistry and teaching exams; when we practiced nursing, journalism or education; fell in love, married and raised kids. Grace returned to Congo to teach English and welcome her first child. Charity raised hers for several years in Burkina Faso before returning to Congo with husband John as election observers, then as Congo rainforest preservers.

But over time the village beat fades when we no longer have *ndoyi* lifting water pails to our heads, pestles falling into mortars, *unh-huh-unh*. The chant and clapping game Mom begged from us whenever we sisters met again, the rest of our lives: *Mande, Mande, ndoyi, Mande, Mande.*

22

COMFORT MY PEOPLE

At a dusty storefront in Kinshasa II, Charity and I waited for a bus. The sooty blue and white buses were famous for drivers flooring the pedal, speeding through straightaways, screeching around corners, throwing off shotgun riders. Or, off-balance due to hangers-on, they lost control on hairpin turns and tumbled into ravines, throwing off passengers as they rolled.

Hope had sent word from Kamayala that her *ndoyi*, Marie—married for just a year to a rough man from Kamayala—had escaped to Kinshasa with a soldier. Marie was living with the soldier in the army barracks at *Ndolo* (little insect airport). We were going to see how she was doing and to let her know that someone from Kamayala still cared.

The last time we'd visited Marie at Kamayala, we heard her woodsman husband shouting at her long before we reached their windowless mud hut at the edge of the village. Marie didn't appear right away when we called, "*Koko!*" And when she did, her face was puffy, her eyelids lowered. We hoped to find her life improved.

Congo jazz rumbaed into the street from every doorway, and Charity and I rubbed bus fare *makuta* together in sweaty palms. We had seen passengers flung into the wind and knew the risks we were taking. This foray, ten miles through the *cité*, was not sponsored by either the hostel nor the mission. We hadn't exactly asked permission, though I'd looked around nervously for Uncle Hector.

"Forget it," Charity said. "Let's just sign out and go."

We wrote *"Ndolo"* in the sign-out book and I laughed nervously when we'd slipped out the gate. "They'll never believe we've gone to the little airport! They'll think it's a joke."

Charity smiled faintly and picked up the pace. She'd been operating in the margins as an invisible all the time I'd been operating at the center of attention. That's when I understood that her experience was opposite mine. She'd had none of the confrontation, accusations and prayer sessions I'd endured. Where I felt constantly watched and censured, she felt overlooked and forgotten.

At the bus stop, a bus braked in front of us and the sulfurous stink of diesel fuel chuffed around us. Enough passengers stumbled out to allow us standing room in the aisles. But as we pressed into the crush of bodies, gentlemen stood and offered their seats. We thanked them profusely knowing better than to refuse such gifts. The vinyl seats were cracked and stained, but it was better than being pushed to the doorstep and hanging by our fingernails. We sat gratefully, and crowded together on one seat, to allow for the usual four-to-a-bench. It seemed like a much too easy ride on the maligned bus system of Kinshasa.

Small cinder block shops in pastel blues, pinks and yellows wafted smells of briny dried fish, sharp red pepper, dense roasted peanuts, nutty palm oil. Between the shops, one-room houses supported tin and cardboard lean-tos, their packed dirt yards swept clean of debris. These were set around with stout thorn bush fences. Men in wooden chairs lounged on tiny verandahs. Over all this poured the multi-layered rhythms and ringing descant of Congo rumba, a sound so well-honed by Franco and Tabu Ley Rochereau that it was becoming Zaire's chief cultural export.

The bus stopped in a black cloud of diesel exhaust at the *Ndolo* army barracks, and we walked to the guard house. The compound sprawled like a small village beyond. Would the guard know our Marie from Kamayala? A man in uniform and smart white gloves came to the window and asked our names and destination. Then he called to a small boy playing under mango trees and told him where to take us. We followed the flitting, skipping child through rows of block buildings, hoping to find the old Marie, the one who'd disappeared after her first marriage. We just wanted to hear again her rolling laughter, see her bulging cheeks, her head flung back in merriment.

We stepped inside the gray cement apartment the child led us to and at first saw only a short, round woman in a sparse kitchen, bent over a tub of dishes.

"*Moyo!*" Our eyes adjusted to the dim light and we realized this large woman was Marie. "*Kutohwa!*" (Fat, beautiful.)

She wiped her hands on a crisp new *divunga* shot through with rich reds and golds. And just for a moment, she tipped her head back and flashed her old smile.

She sat and stretched out her wide feet, kicking off worn sandals. Children came and went, some were hers and she stroked their

Marie Milonga (right), nearly blind, with her youngest daughter Nadine and granddaughter Grace at Kimia (Peace) Parish in Kinshasa. (John and Charity Schellenberg 2017 photo)

heads and spoke softly with them, gazing into their upturned, luminous eyes. Others weren't and she let them roam. There were other wives, she said. There were other children, his, theirs, all crammed into a two-bedroom apartment. True, there were no fields to hoe, but life was busy—and costly. There were endless feedings, cleanings, scrubbings and trips to market. Few here spoke Chokwe or knew our old clapping games. There was no bubbling, spring-fed river to run to. Yet the orphanage had taught her to raise children and hers stayed close even in later years when she gradually lost her eyesight.

The afternoon faded and Marie rose to her supper tasks. We lingered over goodbyes and caught a bus home. The visit reminded us of a childhood, not perfect, but easier than anything we'd face as hard-working women separated from childhood friends. *Ndoyi.*

At the hostel I was conscious always of Uncle Hector's presence and critical gaze. I tried to avoid him and, one Sunday, slipped even further beyond his control. I asked Aunt Clara if I could join my Baptist friends from Kikongo who often walked past to the Kimbanguist hall in Kinshasa II. She agreed to it without even consulting Uncle Hector.

Bibles and offering money in hand, we crossed the boulevard and wended back behind the stores, their barred windows and doors shuttered for Sunday.

Beside the soccer stadium was a huge cement block building, lemon light slanting through high windows, crepe-petaled bougainvillea and glossy palm branches nodding along the walls. Faded throw rugs and carpets covered bare cement floor, and seats rose theater-style from an altar festooned with printed cotton, frangipani petals, a wooden cross, pots of water, offering baskets.

Musicians with drums and rattles, laid down bass, tenor and descant rhythms, people rose and proceeded to the altar with small coins, manioc tubers, baguettes, oranges and bananas. This was all familiar from our first fruits offering upcountry. But the music was different, livelier. "*Suka zi suka, suka zisuka*," they sang. "*Mbongo twasalaka zi Tata Diangenda a a a.*" (We are seeking Father Diangenda.)

Tata (father) Diangenda was the second son—Jesus reincarnated—of founder Kimbangu. So threatening to colonial labor systems were Kimbangu's Baptist-style services preaching freedom from toil that the Belgians imprisoned him until his death in 1951.

I asked my friends what it all meant. "They're waiting for the return of the black Messiah." And when a robed priest spoke they added, "He's preaching from Isaiah." Isaiah, I knew, was the poetic prophet who inspired Handel's *Messiah*.

I understood some words, but the gist my friends had to translate for me. "Small and weak though you are, people of Zaire, don't be afraid; I have the life force, I will give you *strength!*"

That was what I needed, strength to live my life to the fullest despite all the criticisms and restrictions.

"*Ah-may,*" (amen), I chorused with the audience of children kneeling on rugs, adults crowded into seats.

"The prophet Simon Kimbangu has spoken.... He proclaims the black messiah who will throw off the burden of *mundele* (white man). The black messiah says: 'I have prepared a feast to give you strength. I have wiped every tear from your eye and removed the cloud of sorrow that hangs over our nation.'"

"*Ah-may.*"

"Comfort my people, comfort them. Encourage the people of Zaire, tell them they have suffered long enough and their sins are forgiven. Clear a road in the *cité*, fill in the potholes, prepare the way for our black messiah!"

"*Ah-may.*"

"Don't be afraid when you pass through deep waters, I will be with you; when you pass through fire, you will not burn. You are my chosen people. I will give you *ngolo* (strength)."

I walked home feeling a surge for the weak and forgotten. There was a time and place for them, a strength to borrow from the future that would change their lives and free them from rule makers and fear.

So unifying was the message of a black messiah among Kimbangu's 22 million followers, said my friends, that President Mobutu was creating a single national church—the Church of Christ in Zaire—to mute its political power.

———————

I went another Sunday with Charity to the Chokwe chapel beyond the *Grand Marché*. To avoid the two-hour bus ride and arrive on time, we begged a ride with Mennonite missionaries who visited outlying churches. Set among one-room huts on barren ground, the chapel was an open-air block building under a roof with half walls that filled to the sills with Chokwe speakers. We had never seen so many of our tribe in Kinshasa at one time, and the sheer familiarity of language was like diving through soft bubbles into the Kamayala River. Charity had brought a Chokwe hymnal and Bible, and we sang until our lungs burst, "*Kuwakungunyonga.*" (Thou thinkest Lord of me.)

The people around us were barefoot and simply dressed, but they begged us to stay for dinner. Charity would have given up her ride home and might have stayed forever had I not excused us and pulled her back to meet the car for the trip home. I didn't want to get her in trouble at the dorm though she preferred our special acceptance in this familiar community—free of fear. She looked back at listing houses, razor grass hillocks, tiny home shops. She was still craned around when we reached tarmac and trundled downhill to the hostel.

We got braver after that, riding the bus to visit Chokwe friends we were getting to know beyond the *Grand Marché* (Grand Market).

The families we visited, set us at small tables in tiny courtyards and served us brimful glasses of orange soda. They hovered and topped off our glasses before they were half empty. When they ran out of soda, they sent a child for more from home-front stores. The families never accepted our cash and never stopped filling our glasses. Finally we learned to sip slowly off the top and never drain the glass half full.

Charity and I went home to our natal village of Kamayala in 1971 to spend a last summer with Hope. We four sisters together again, lapsed into easy banter. Grace was ready to join Charity and me in the land of chocolate bars and swimming pools. She had taken a combined year of grades 2 and 3 with James and Ruthie Claassen taught by their mom. She then graduated from grade 4, home-schooled by Mom, and from the Kamayala grade school in a shower of talcum powder. The mothers of the village had formed a choking reception line and sprinkled them white with baby powder.

We were together again in our familiar village, as a complete family. We pretended none of us were hurting, congratulated ourselves that Hope was eating again, however sporadically. Sometimes we joined in her binges—devouring a batch of fresh-baked jam cookies—then ran and swam it off in the welcoming spring-fed Kamayala River.

We joined the afternoon river run with our *ndoyis* and in the evening built a fire in the front yard. There, we sang protest songs to Hope's smooth chordings, "Love is but the song we sing."

Often Kamayala's PAX guys, Ron and Dan materialized through the palm tunnel from the house at the end of the station. They had bicycled to distant villages and delivered rabbits in an agricultural extension project that helped bring self-sufficiency to southwestern Congo. It would give our hunter-gatherer tribe livelihoods during lean months and keep our young people occupied. Ron and

Dan were among 1,200 young Americans and Canadians who served in 40 countries from the Korean War until the Vietnam War ended.

Though Kamayala's PAX men were from the wheat fields of Kansas and Oklahoma, they had never lived anywhere so remote. We were eight kilometers from the nearest stores, ninety kilometers from the nearest post-secondary school and days from any industrial center. Ron called it "a pinprick in the universe." They spent days cycling dirt trails, crossing rivers on fallen logs, sleeping in villages and building rabbit hutches. Back in Kamayala, they killed time with ping pong in our garage. They leaped and lunged and smashed little white balls as though their sanity depended on it.

What could be worth so much sweat and strain? We learned they were playing for Primus, Zaire's dark honey beer. These Mennonite farm boys were rebelling without constraints. In them it seemed a healthy sign of independence. Was I accepting a double standard for myself while Ron and Dan drove to the state post at Kahemba and drank their winnings in a soukous-soaked bar? Would I remain sheltered and ignorant while they gained experience and knowledge? After Ron and Dan each won several rounds, we joined them for ping pong doubles. But there was no mention of beer winnings for us.

Ron was tall and serious and, after ping pong, invited us home for anti-war songs strummed under pale moths on their front porch, "Where have all the flowers gone?" He brought out books and magazines and loaned me one on Marxism, how it compared to a communal faith like the Mennonites'. Dan strummed his guitar or handed it to Hope. His teasing smile, the way he curled his generous lips, was almost scornful I thought, and recognized in him another rebel.

Afterward, tossing in dusty lamplight in our attic bedroom, we sisters chose our favorites. Grace, who was eight, liked them both because "they play with me." She chipped a front tooth, while swinging around a porch column with one of them, permanently marked by their playfulness. They took photos of her playing with our *Kusu* (parrot), *Jaku* (in Kikongo). He would sit on Grace's shoulder, nibble her lobe and whisper his names in her ear, "*Kusu, Jaku.*"

She put him on the back carrier and pedaled like the wind while he hung on with his beak—ripping her skirts—practically flying despite his clipped pin feathers. Once when Grace let him out of his cage, a dog chased him. *Kusu* waddled fast as he could to the nearest fence, squelching an alarm sound in his throat. Yet, as soon as he'd climbed out of the dog's reach, he turned, fluffed his neck feathers and laughed a demonic, "Hahaha." He sounded just like an evil Scarface from one of Dad's bedtime stories.

Charity, who was passing five-eight and hated anything so fake as flirting, liked Ron for his height and sincerity. Hope, who was painfully shy, liked Dan for his attention to her. I liked Ron for his Bethel College books, journals and ideas—critiques of T. S. Eliot, Marx and communal living—Dan for his knowing wink, his scorn-

Kusu *had a strange way of begging Grace for neck rubs. (Eidse family photo)*

ful grin. Had he noticed my wild speed on Dad's Puch motorcycle, my willful smashing of ping pong balls, my daring words in any language? Or did he wink that way at all the girls?

My TASOK girlfriends had begged to come home with me on vacation, the way Charity's classmate Linda Morrin had the year before. Linda's visit, however, had focused on playing with our orphan friends, worshipping together and spiritual awakening.

When my friends found the $150 plane fare too steep, they loaded me with letters and gifts for Dan—45's of "Lay, Lady, Lay," 35 millimeter film so I could snap pictures of him in his Amish hat.

Even my *ndoyi*, Hélène, flirted with Dan, tilted her face up, swayed her hips, teased him about his new Chokwe. She seemed unusually bubbly that summer, a woman in love. One day she leaned close to me, the way Chokwe women do, placing a hand on my breast—a neutral spot, or an intimate one—and said, "Dan is your man."

I pulled back. "No, I don't have a man."

She laughed at my denial, stroked my arm, and caught my hand in hers. "I meet Rafael at night."

I was surprised that she had made a mating choice so early. At 16, she was suddenly mature and I had years to go. At least she had chosen for herself, unlike Marie, who lasted only a year in her arranged marriage. Hélène had selected Rafael, Pastor Shambuyuyu's son, the diligent boy I had admired years ago, laying out his school clothes at the river. He sometimes read the Bible or led singing in church. Confident in his schooling, he lifted his broad, pleasant face and spoke with a sure, quiet cadence. Theirs seemed a modern romance, one in which Hélène's lack of family and wealth didn't matter compared to their love for each other.

Charity glimmered that summer, too, and I was surprised that someone so quiet and hermetic at the hostel, could come alive overnight. She strolled the paths past the school to the village and chatted away in Chokwe with a group of secondary school students she seemed to know immediately. What I didn't realize was that there was one student, especially, for whom she shone. Since I had made no such distinctions, I followed her into things, like afternoon soccer games at school. She seemed effervescent, fired on adrenaline, all her senses live. She covered ground with her long legs, hair flying, accepted passes from me and booted goals by reflex. "Pelé!" bystanders shouted, and she laughed as though her accuracy were a fluke.

However, everyone knew we were second string compared to Kamayala's travel team. After we cleared the field—and sometimes before—shouts for "Jean Kapunda" and "*Kuchola*"—his nickname—rent the air. *Kuchola* was a dried, strong-smelling fish, rubbery when chewed but delicate when soaked in gravy. A small, sinewy acrobat, he bounced onto the field, trapped the ball, kicked it straight up, leaped, twisted, headed it halfway 'cross the field, or double-kicked it overhead.

Finally Charity came right out and told me what had been firing her all summer.

It was after soccer while I sat reading one of Hope's Canadian correspondence grade twelve novels on a log in the front yard.

Her eyebrow arched in triumph, "Kalema asked me to go for a walk with him."

"Okay." I abandoned Somerset Maugham's *Of Human Bondage*—club-footed Philip Carey and waitress Mildred in Paris. "I'll get my shoes on."

"No, I mean alone." She seemed irked at my lack of awareness. "I'm going for a walk *alone* with Kalema."

Kalema was Lunda royalty, tall, slim, hair trimmed in a close, high crown. His uncle was a wealthy merchant with dozens of trucks plying the stores between Kahemba, Kikwit and Kinshasa. Kalema's big brother Wenyi, was in charge of the MCC cattle project whose wife was the deer-slayer, Mama Beya. Kalema's older sister, Kafiy had married Weva, the secondary school director who was headed for a tenured professorship in Canada, his Ph.D. presentation at the U.N. and appointment as Congo's Permanent Secretary on the Permanent Commission of Education.

I looked up at Charity's deep blue eyes, pert nose, flushed cheeks, and wondered why I hadn't thought of Kalema for her. She walked off toward the village and it was evident that I had missed something momentous in her life. Perhaps I hadn't realized she would grow up so soon, become independent and surpass me in selecting the most princely man in the village.

My suitor, as it turned out, was wiry, witty Jean Kapenda. At first he tagged along with my *ndoyi* Hélène and her fiancé Rafael and teased me gently out of my novels. Whenever he visited he wore a long-sleeved navy shirt—his best—even in the scorching heat. He was Chokwe-short, barely five feet, and funny—his satirical chortle alone cut me up.

"Why do you sit in the sun?" he asked one day. "The shade is cooler."

I pulled my nose out of *Tess of the D'Urbervilles*.

"I like the sun," I said simply. "It makes my skin dark."

"*Ah.*" He rolled up his navy sleeve. "You want to be beautiful like me!" He flexed his dark, ropy arm against my pale smooth one.

Charity's walks with Kalema concerned Mom and Dad. They talked for hours behind closed bedroom doors and finally called her in. She had found one of the most eligible men in the village, they said, and they could not stop her if one day she wanted to marry him. However, she should consider how her life would always be divided between two cultures if she did. Either she would have to settle into Chokwe life in Zaire, or she would have to take Kalema from his people and culture and force him to adjust to life in Canada. His culture or hers, it would always be a struggle.

The question of taking Kalema from his culture troubled Charity. He shone among his people. How could she remove him to a country where he'd have marginal status, if any? He would be an immigrant, all his survivalist talents on the savanna wasted and unrecognized. Charity was spinning away from me in a vortex of problems I'd never considered. Would the two of them be able to balance their unequal worlds? Charity continued to meet Kalema for long walks across the savanna, where he taught her which leaves drew viper poison, which soothed wasp bites, which slaked thirst. I'd glimpse them again as the sky purpled, sitting under palms, his lithe black arms propped on the lawn, her wavy blonde hair blowing over them.

Altogether at home in Kamayala in 1971, we sang Gospel, pop, folk, rock and protest songs, Hope confident on the guitar. (Ben Eidse photo)

23

PLACE OF COCKROACHES

The summer of 1971, Ron and Dan spent their evenings around our after-supper fire at the reading log. Dad brought out his slide steel guitar and we sang lusty four-part harmony, "How Great Thou Art."

Our parents were usually the first to bed after long days of Bible translating or drug dispensing. "We'll leave you young people to it."

That was our signal to switch to folk tunes. Ron played early Peter, Paul and Mary, "Lemon Tree," "If I Had a Hammer." We girls mixed it up with, "Que sera, sera."

Then Ron yawned. "I'm turning in." He unfolded his lanky legs and waded home through darkness.

"Me too." Grace left and Hope and Charity followed her inside. Alone at the fire with Dan I realized this was the ultimate in arrangements—my sisters scheming on my behalf.

"Are you going to be free this summer?"

Would I be free? Or would I be entangled? I was sixteen and freedom was exactly what I wanted. "Yes."

Dan grinned, put on his Amish hat, and melted into the night his whistle fading under a dark tunnel of palms.

During the weeks that followed I became impatient with sunset, eager for nightfall. Hélène's primal suggestion, perhaps, or my rebel spirit made me climb down the stone chimney from the attic balcony and sneak through a wall of trilling cicadas. The night offered pools of hot humid air to wade through; palms swayed overhead. My heart beat a rhythm in my throat. I slowed. What was I thinking? Just a kiss? How much innocence was I willing to sacrifice for knowledge?

Dan had a proper girlfriend back in the States, a girl whose soft-focus picture he kept on his desk. Smooth, pale skin, delicate nose and mouth, dark somber eyes. Her dark hair was pulled up under a white net covering, her shoulders and bodice covered by a cape. These were Old Mennonite modesty shields to keep men's thoughts pure, women blind to their own beauty. She seemed angelic, removed, beyond reach. The complete opposite of my loose blonde hair, tanned skin, blue eyes, large expressive mouth and prominent nose.

I should leave him alone. Quit fooling around. But I was just playing and I sensed Dan was, too. He did not seem desperate for a girlfriend, had not responded to my mini-skirted friends in Kinshasa. He had not thanked them for the Bob Dylan record, though he played it often. He had not consented to photos though I told him I had film to fill. So I knew that if we met after dark it would be just for fun. And experience.

I crouched between onion-scented dahlias under Dan's bedroom window and listened for stirrings. Dylan crooned, Gordon Lightfoot strummed, "That's what you get for loving me." Was Dan awake, or did he just play his records or tapes like lullabies all night long? Would I call and wake him, or let my head cool?

My head cooled. I ran home, climbed the quarried stone chimney to the balcony, crawled into my cot and cursed my heavy breathing. A smirking moon rose over the balcony rail.

———————

Next morning, under stirring palms, I stopped Dan as he pedaled past to the village. "Do you play Gordon Lightfoot all night long?"

A playful grin spread across his face. "Next time, wake me."

Dang that wicked, mustached grin, that wind-tousled dark hair.

The next night, bare feet on vapors, I glided beneath a waxing moon to the dahlia bed again. This time I called softly through Dan's screen window, so as not to wake Ron in the next room. Dan met me on the front porch, lifted me off my feet, covered my mouth with his, soft mustache dusting my protruding nose.

I had worried about deep-kissing with a nose like mine, but the problem vanished with a tilt of his head. The knee-length gingham dress Grandma had sewed me was cotton thin. The colors in my mind were a kaleidoscope of bright scarlet, soft lavender, deep purple. I agonized over wanting the washed silk of his hands and having to push them away.

How devastating sex could be for me. Pregnancy. The Clap. Loss of virginity, a state Uncle Hector had implied I deserved. Could I do this just for fun or did I have to take it seriously? Unlike Hélène's midnight meetings, mine were not about proving my fertility for marriage. Still, I understood Hélène nudging me towards Dan, if only for the taste of his cinnamon tongue, moist lips, and yes, those traveling hands. Just, not too far. I collected his midnight kisses until the mission sentry reported me to my parents.

Mom never mentioned what she thought I was doing with Dan. She preferred spirit over flesh every day. But apparently chasing a Mennonite was approved over dating a Methodist, especially a Mennonite devoted to pacifism and alternative service in Africa. Or perhaps—and this I dared not speak aloud to any of my sisters—he had charmed my mother, too.

All Mom said was, "The sentry says you've been running across the station at night." End of conversation. And a little later, "You know in my day, girls got married at your age."

"Forget it, Mom." Perhaps she wanted to suggest options in case I was pregnant but marriage seemed like the fastest way to untrack my life and all that I still wanted to do.

From my pop art sales at school, I had acquired a set of oil paints and started painting portraits of children who gathered around

Ron Goertzen with little children, me, Hope, Grace (in car), Charity, Dad, Mom and friends seeing us off on Hope's farewell trip out of Congo. (Eidse family photo)

the reading log. I loved capturing their rich brown skin, tight black curls and sparkly eyes. I hoped to keep learning new techniques.

Dad spent his evenings reviewing cultural anthropology books and notes on animism, origin stories and cultural values. He had taped and transcribed interviews with the Lunda-Chokwe chiefs and villagers. They themselves had said that witchcraft tore their families and clans apart. He would not have put words in their mouths. The objectivity of the anthropologist was vital in entering a culture. He was pioneering a new approach to missions and preparing to speak at an MCC conference at IPE, the theology school in Kimpese; then to teach a college semester SEA course for PAX workers at the theology university in Kinshasa. His coworkers had taught him that it was critical for success to enter a culture through the heart language, stories and values of the people.

For Hope's road trip out of Africa, we loaded our 1960s Chevy Carryall with luggage, supplies and eight people, and headed north along the Kwilu River. We bounced over open savanna, descended into deep jungles, hair-pinned over red clay hills and climbed steep, sandy grades. It lasted two days and one eternal night at the ferry over the Kwilu River to Kikwit. There, merchants had to unload their over-burdened trucks before crossing. In the back seat, pressed against my sleeping sisters on one side, Dan on the other, he and I kissed secretly.

I should have guessed it would be our last. Dan had only asked me to be "free" for the summer. At Kimpese, he turned away without explanation. We were suddenly surrounded by dozens of new or seasoned service workers—some from his home area. In that setting, I was a youngster, 16 to his 22. It never occurred to me that someone—Dad, Mom or me with my deflecting hands—had warned him off. I was too young for lasting commitments anyway.

The Bangu hills rose over us and dozens of MCCers hiked the foothills or gathered in the large brick church, education buildings, dorms and dining room.

Hope, age 18, said Dan had joined her while climbing a hill at Kimpese and said his goodbyes, that he'd enjoyed their time together at Kamayala. "He never said much. He was a man of few words. Besides, I wasn't like my sisters, 'Kiss sera sera.'" I laughed outright.

When, in the darkened IPE conference hall, with Congo's volcanoes boiling on screen, I stood beside Dan, he looked pointedly the other way. The shun was so obvious that a PAX guy on the other side, whom I had never seen before, said hello and shook my hand to save my face. He said he'd prayed for my picture on the fridge since he was a boy in Kansas. Must be what saved me.

After the MCC conference, our family moved to campus housing at the Ecole de Théologie Évangélique du Kinshasa (ETEK, now l'Université Chrétienne de Kinshasa) and participated in the university's grand humanitarian vision. Hope enrolled in Dad's SEA course for college credit since she had qualified by completing high school by correspondence. Charity hung out with Grace and I found a fulltime babysitting job.

The Mackays hired me to swim, romp and play with their two darling preschoolers. I tried not to mind Walt Mackay pinching me at first. He seemed harmless, even boyish. I let it slide. But then he started lingering after his wife left for work and tackled me while I fetched food from the pantry or made the children's beds. I couldn't escape except by calling the kids in. Then Mr. Mackay pretended it was all a game of keep away. I told no one, thinking it was my fault.

It was a relief to gather in the evenings at the theology school with my sisters and the SEA students. One was a college art major and I pulled out my sketch pad for tips on shading, perspective, cross-hatching.

With other students we discussed cultural anthropology—or practiced it—learning card games from rural America and pop tunes on guitar. "How can you mend a broken heart?"

I mended mine by discussing literature with Dad's brightest student, Nate. For more on anthropology, he challenged me to read James Michener's *Hawaii.* I dug in and finished in a week.

"How did you get through it so fast?" Nate arched an eyebrow at me.

"I skipped the sex scenes." I grinned at him sitting on the steps of one of the campus houses.

"Sure, sure." He laughed. "I thought you might slow down for those, read 'em twice."

"Ha." I hoped I wasn't blushing.

"So what is your assessment? Did you think Michener's portrayals of Polynesians, Japanese, Chinese and missionaries were good and fair?"

"Sure—maybe." I wanted to sound balanced. "I've met tone-deaf missionaries who don't know the local language. But they're not our family or other dedicated service workers—like you."

He nodded and smiled ear to ear.

When August 1971 rolled around, the Falks and Bullers returned to ETEK campus from vacations and Hope prepared to travel
to North America with her PAX friend Suzette Graber. Leola had
become a gifted seamstress and sewed Hope an African print dress
to match Suzette's.

Nate invited me to a classical piano concert at the Palace Garden amphitheater in the presidential compound. "It's a dress affair."
He grinned as though challenging me, an MK who dressed in worn
cotton shifts.

I considered which of Grandma's handsewn dresses I should
wear. Instead, my true friend, Jette, handed me her catalogue-or-
dered, tailored dress—still in plastic. It was a pink, double-knit, zip-
front, drop waist dress. She had shot up to 5-foot-10 and said it fit
my more petite 5-foot-4 frame perfectly. Besides she was heading
back to the States where stores were full of options. I sewed up the
drop waist so the skirt wouldn't be too long and felt the best-dressed
I'd ever been.

*Mom, Grace, Hope, Suzette Graber, Charity and myself at N'Djili Airport in August
1971. Hope and Suzette flew via Mali and France in matching African print dresses.
(Ben Eidse photo)*

The night of the concert under open skies, I shivered with delight at the virtuoso performance. The pianist's flawless swelling chords and white-hot energetic phrasings looked effortless. She was so fine in her elegant black dress, long black hair bouncing, that I rued my own uneven progress in music lessons.

However, Nate was lost in a deeper grief for his pianist sister who had died of Hodgkin's lymphoma at Christmas. Before her diagnosis, she was the first MCC volunteer to Yugoslavia and Nate was sorry he had not been able to leave his MCC work in Congo to attend her funeral in the U.S. We were both swallowed up in memories but lifted by the transcendent performance.

At summer's end, our family took Hope and Suzette to N'Djili airport for their flight to North America via Mali to visit our McNeill cousins and France to visit Suzette's friends. Hope was bound for college in Canada and seemed prepared to go—hair down, relaxed, ready to fly. In our parting photo, I look sullen at her leaving. Yet I'm wearing a dress with handkerchief sleeves that I designed and sewed myself. Grace, age eight, hugs herself guardedly in a dress Charity sewed her in Home Economics. It would be Grace's first year at the hostel.

Our parents returned to their work upcountry and we three younger sisters settled back into the hostel. Someone had propped the old battleship ladder against the baobab. Unknown to me, Grace would climb up to escape a pestering freshman until he followed, pinched and assailed her. None of us older girls liked the way he treated us but we did not see what he was doing to the younger girls.

Nate came to see me again before returning up north to build a school for refugees. We kicked off our sandals, climbed the old battleship ladder and perched high up under the spinning Milky Way. He covered my bare foot with his. "Bright people hold feet." His face lit up with a dimpled, mischievous grin.

I laughed but heard it as affirmation. He considered me bright and that gave me new confidence. So I told him how I struggled with Mr. Mackay's ambushes.

He sobered and gave me a warning look. "Watch out for Mr. Mackay. It's always the babysitter's fault."

I realized what an easy target and scapegoat I made when not surrounded by people invested in me. It was up to me to stop Mr. Mackay's advances. Period.

He tapped my barefoot with his. "Hey, you don't have to cut off your foot to know it hurts."

At the gate, when he turned to leave, the little boys shouted instructions from their second-floor window. "You can kiss her." And when he hesitated. "Now." He may have kissed me but all I remember was my own embarrassment. He drove away but continued to write from upcountry and affirm my evolving ideas. He was on a global journey for peace and justice himself—exploring gender issues, sexual orientation—and would one day marry a Liberian refugee, raise a multi-ethnic family and become a voice for inclusivity in the Mennonite Church.

I continued babysitting on weekends. But one Saturday morning Mrs. Mackay blocked me at the door—before her kids could rush me and jump into my arms—before we could twirl, sing, read and color again. "I'm letting you go. I'm quitting my job, taking our girls, going back to the States. Walt didn't come home last night. He's carrying on with another embassy wife. I'm leaving the *lech*."

The following Sunday night, Uncle Hector plucked me from the after-church crowd gathered under frangipani trees. "Get in the bus, I want to talk to you." Uncle Hector sat in the driver's seat, muscled arm slung over the steering wheel. I crouched across from him in the jump seat.

"You're a homewrecker."

I was mute, my tongue wrapped in cotton. Was he crazy? What did he know that I didn't? Beetles droned and pinged against the yard light.

From the corner of my eye, I saw Carl approach the bus, his shoulders stooped in a perpetual crouch, a defensive stance honed at the hostel where he, too, had been shamed and nearly smothered in building sand. He leaned against the bus door, pretending happenstance but I felt his protective presence like a cool cloth against hot eyes.

"The Mackays are getting a divorce because of you." Uncle Hector faced me full-on.

My tongue fossilized. How could that be? Mr. Mackay was nowhere in sight. He'd taken up with a grown embassy woman, someone I didn't know and couldn't name.

"Mrs. Mackay said it was your fault."

What could I say? She'd fired me, and now she was spreading stories out of church. With all the evidence against Mr. Mackay and his new woman, could it still be my fault?

The step creaked and the bus tilted slightly as Carl entered and selected a window seat. He said nothing, only stared steadily out at the pinging beetles. The deck was stacked two against one, but Uncle Hector held his posture. Did he expect Carl to cower and leave?

In a minute, two more high school boys entered and planted themselves in window seats. Then came Marcia, Linda and the other girls. Uncle Hector started the engine. He steered the bus through the after-church crowd and rolled silently along Kinshasa's cracked boulevards. At a bend in the River Road, the bus shuddered, lurched and groaned. With Carl's help, I had held my own against Hector. Out the window, the searchlight bounced off rippled waves and the Zaire River flowed steadily westward.

———————

At the Little Falls, in a river valley beyond Djelo Binza and Lovanium University, the hostel kids invented new levels of risk. It was as though we didn't care about hurting ourselves, or as though we didn't think anyone else did. I followed Carl, across the slick rocks on top of the falls. If I slipped, there was nothing to do but give myself to the water and shoot the falls. When enough of us had gone over the falls by accident, we went over on purpose, a roller coaster ride around slippery rocks that dropped us six feet into a deep pool, just clearing edge rock.

When shooting the falls stopped thrilling us, we continued across the falls to the twelve-foot cliff on the other side. From there we'd take a running start through razor grass and launch ourselves over rocks and shallows into the pool below the falls. One afternoon, as I flew off the cliff, I heard a shout. I hadn't launched myself far enough. I flailed, pitched forward and sailed on adrenaline. When the water reached me, it was with a sand-paper hand along my back. I had landed just millimeters inside the deep, water-cut pool. I surfaced, feeling the burn on my backside and gasping, gasping for air.

24

NATION OF TRAVELERS

*"When we come together we form our own nation of travelers...
we meet our own again and know each other—this one understands,
we speak the same memories."* – Beth Rambo

The year 1971 was a landmark for women—and for me in Grade
11 at TASOK. The Equal Rights Amendment (ERA), first proposed in 1923, was ratified in October by the U.S. House and headed to Congress. It still had to be ratified by the various states but
I vowed to fight for equal rights and justice and vote for the most
qualified woman whenever possible.

In American History, lanky Don Fast paced the room and
wrote digits and labels on the board—political power and weakness
by the numbers. The lower education of minorities meant lower involvement in voting and leadership. And lower involvement meant
less minority representation and power in the laws, courts and judi-
cial outcomes. Nevermind that government itself often took the side
of the wealthy powerful against the poor and weak.

Also, the U.S. had fewer women and people of color in leadership than less powerful nations. Mr. Fast raised, as examples, the
prime ministers of India and Israel and the queen of England. We

discussed how U.S. women still did not receive equal pay for equal work. At the time, we could not yet see how a right wing "Christian" backlash to the ERA would push us all back into the kitchen. Many of our teachers were conscientious objectors doing alternative Christian service for the Mennonite Brethren Church and I clung to a new vision of social justice and political empowerment. We were all committed to advancing women and minorities in leadership.

I ran for student council and was elected secretary alongside Nancy Woodcock and presidents Paul Derksen and Bill Burgess. I also continued reporting for the student paper, *The Condor Chronicle*. I wanted to serve and learn all I could to fill my knowledge gaps and became eager for college and life in a wider world.

On the Girls Athletic League (GAL), I played soccer, ran track and learned that calories gave me strength to hit the volleyball over the net. In spring 1971, the girls in my class had won school track records that would stand for years—Hassina in the 880, Jette in high jump, I in the mile (6:21). In 1972, Charity with her class relay teams would topple the 440 and 880 relay records. Together, we planned a GAL campout for April 1972 at Kimpese where we hiked the steep Bangu, swam and slept on sun-warmed lava rocks around the upper falls—our remote, sublime Shangri-la.

Back at the hostel, I ran the canopied *Avenue de l'avenir* along the river. We had a new, free-spirited dorm parent on the girls' wing. A chestnut-haired social worker with Liza Minelli eyes, she lived with us and joined us during fetid afternoon gab sessions when it was too hot to move or study. Shirl lay on her back and propped her skinny legs on the wall beside ours and never enforced rules like, "Feet off the walls!"

She lay in our rooms, or we lay in hers, and listened to her records, fresh from stores in the U.S. "He ain't heavy, he's my brother." That was her philosophy in a nutshell and it troubled her that the hostel did not operate that way. Our first clue was when she showed

Chutes de Vampa (Vampa River Falls) on the Bangu. (Laurie Bowers-Connolly Braun photo)

Charity elated after our campout at Bangu's upper falls near Kimpese. (Faith Eidse photo)

up with bruises on her upper arms and cringed when Uncle Hector called her "Wifey."

Our feudalistic system at the dorm was reflected in America's callused support of Mobutu. Missionaries had at first excused Mobutu's arbitrary arrests, detentions, public hangings, co-opting of opposition, saying "at least we have stability." At the American school we learned that Mobutu was a personal friend of the U.S. and that ambassador Sheldon Vance wanted no criticism of him. We got free t-shirts with Mobutu's mug in black-rimmed glasses, leopard print fez, and tunic-style *abacost*—a collarless "authenticity" suit named for "down with the western costume."

Add to that Shirl's training with Christian fundamentalist Bill Gothard, and we were surrounded by hierarchy models. Gothard's training manual portrayed male headship as God the hammer, man the chisel, woman the diamond. But the way we were being chiseled didn't gleam at all like diamonds.

Some pre-Christian personality flared and gave Shirl a power we'd never seen in a woman. Perhaps it was that she'd grown up a Brewmeister's daughter and toured Europe as a concert pianist. Perhaps it was that she hadn't been raised Mennonite and didn't automatically submit, couldn't forget what she knew, and accept what she was told. Whatever it was, she took Hector on, knowing she was defying "God-ordained authority," she said, and "silently asking forgiveness for every anti-headship move I make."

"Hands off the girls and me," she told Hector. "I'm in charge of them now." But she couldn't ignore the boys either. The grade school boys sometimes came from Hector's office crying openly. One later confided that his big brother waited outside to intervene in case he punched Hector.

Another "little brother," Paul Zook, reminded me decades later that I wrote him encouraging notes after seeing him in tears. In 2021, he gathered several of us dormmates around for emotional support in daily emails written from Pueblo, CO. Despite our ef-

forts, he took his own life in early March 2022. He did not want to
return to prison over violating a neighbor's restraining order for kicking garbage cans in the street.

Carl, who had once been so muted, had put away his pocket
knife and opened up to Shirl. They spent hours talking on the front
patio, back patio and under the baobab.

With Shirl buffering us from Hector, the girls experienced
new freedoms. He no longer dictated our dress ("more feminine"),
our walk ("less sexy"), our associations (none outside the hostel unless approved). There was no longer a record in the sign-out book of
where we went. Instead we signed out leaving a blank for our desti-
nations and scooted down the block to the Baptist hostel, strolled the
neighborhood or plied the riverbank.

Mel Tari's, *Like a Mighty Wind*, had fallen into our hands and
we explored new spiritual freedoms. Transported by the 1965 char-
ismatic awakening on the Island of Timor, I spent several sunny Saturday mornings on a grassy bank above the river—far from hostel
controls. I stripped to my underwear to tan in the tall grass and feel
the river breeze on my skin while I absorbed Galatians and Ephesians
and basked in promises of spiritual gifts and blessings.

However, when I returned to the hostel, Aunt Edna Gerber
was visiting her children and had found a pamphlet on the coffee
table declaring that speaking in tongues was of the devil. She, too,
had read *Mighty Wind* and found it uplifting. Yet I, who had once
numbed myself to my own feelings and distrusted my emotions, assured her she could trust her spiritual experience.

Shirl took us camping at the Little Falls, or out to restaurants
for girls' nights over beef fondue. She celebrated our spiritual growth
and didn't criticize us for our exploration outside prescribed beliefs,
or me for my friends among the Methodists, Presbyterians, diplo-
matic corps or business kids.

Some afternoons I even invited my girlfriends to the hostel
with me. I loved it when Pat Ricardo came for the night, showed

us the bus stop dance and how to fold a silk scarf over a choker for a simple halter top. Once we big girls even held a sleepover with friends on the basketball court, sang Barbra Streisand and danced to our cassette tapes.

The hostel was becoming a safer, freer, more caring place, especially for those who wanted to consult Shirl about problems too weighty for them. Pregnancy. Abortion. Shirl didn't think young teen girls should bear the burden over pregnancies they couldn't have acquired alone. Girls of fifteen and sixteen—sheltered kids who'd been taught only to abstain—should not have to pay with their futures or, potentially, their lives while their boyfriends walked free.

Our meetings with Shirl became a growing awareness of ourselves as women, separate from men whose wishes we'd been taught to anticipate and obey. Instead of allegiance ("do what he says"), she taught us to trust our instincts ("do what you think is right").

That's just what I did after Thanksgiving at a school retreat at *Nsele,* a posh presidential resort beyond the international airport. Dozens of us upper classmates had read Alvin Tofler's *Future Shock* and helped plan the conference. Our speakers were MAF pilot Marv Bowers, Surgeon Roger Youmans (Chief of Staff at Mama Yemo Hospital) and college graduate Judy Ericson. They encouraged us to be leaders in a rapidly changing, more nomadic world.

Student panels representing some of TASOK's 37 nationalities discussed a future led by increasing diversity and acceptance of differences. The world we would enter after graduation would be filled with people like ourselves who had become more nomadic with jobs that were more transient. We buzzed with these ideas all weekend in large and small groups. In a faster, more stressful but exciting world, information would evolve quickly and we'd have to evolve to keep pace with it.

Over our catered meals, Seniors, like Hans, pointed out how scary this was. Others, like Nazir, grimaced at magots in the rice. His family would be forced to emigrate before Mobutu nationalized their businesses and that stress would affect them for life.

Under a spinning disco ball made from broken mirrors, our TASOK rock band Bella Nzengo performed—Dave Rumohr, Marvin Falk, Fred Dirks and Roger Ericson on drums, guitars, bells and rattles. Our myriad reflections glinted and pulsed in rainbow hues.

At a poolside lounge, Bill stretched his lanky limbs, brushed back his long blonde hair and challenged my thinking. He was a Canadian MK from Angola whose Marxist views were similar yet different from my communal Mennonite ideals. It was defiance just to listen to him. "Religion is an opiate, don't you see? It keeps people submissive." His dark-rimmed glasses reflected jets descending toward N'Djili International Airport over a shimmering Zaire River. "Whose backs do you suppose Mobutu built this on?"

Later, after further reflection, he found a deeper, more humanitarian meaning in Karl Marx's words, one that might motivate service workers like our parents to raise up leaders and help alleviate the suffering of the poor. "Religion is the sigh of the oppressed creature, the heart of a heartless world, and the soul of soulless conditions. It is the *opium* of the people."

Mobutu's gold-framed portrait glowed on the walls. He wore a leopard print fez and held a carved chief's scepter. The brass plaque read, "*Mobutu Sese Seko Kuku Gbendu Wa Za Banga*," an old saying that meant roughly, the cock that lets no chicken get away and never loses a fight.

The year before, the entire Lovanium University community had voted "red," against Mobutu, in his single party "*Votez Vert*" election. Mobutu had closed the university and jailed its leaders without trial. That didn't prevent our new principal, Lee Sanders, a former Olympic diver, from securing use of Mobutu's resort and regulation-size Olympic pool.

Mr. Sanders jack-knifed and triple-flipped off the high dive to our applause.

Below us, under a setting sun, rusted boats lolled at anchor, waiting for fuel. On the loudspeakers over grass-roofed cabanas, recordings of rumba star Tabu Ley Rochereau feted the president in Lingala. "Let us, folks, gather around Mobutu; the new program is Objectif '80 and clean-up work."

But many of us were no longer optimistic about the future of Zaire. We believed that even Tabu Ley's loyalty was paid out of Mobutu's largesse.

Given the disaster of Mobutu's imperialism, Bill saw Marxism as the only course for Africa. He'd grown up in Angola where socialist ideals would eventually win out over Henry Kissinger's secret guerilla war on communism. Socialism was the original economy of the village, he said. "From each according to his ability, to each according to his need."

The 1964 revolution had promised this and required fighters to respect the people. But the *Jeunesse* had warped it with violence, tribal favoritism and theft.

Yet I also knew that villagers would kill their last rooster to feed a visitor. Women exchanged childcare to hoe their fields and sell their produce. A man with a raffia belt climbed palm trees and traded oil-rich nuts for charcoal—each one supporting local industry.

Socialism barely entered Mobutu's policies except as the "clean-up work" ethic in his *Objectif '80*. In a 1965 stadium rally, he had rolled up his sleeves and asked everyone to get to work for the nation's prosperity (Close, p. 178).

Yet six years later, distrust of his administration ran deep among my school friends. Mobutu had called for "Zairianization" of businesses in two years, a call that echoed Uganda's nationalization and set their economy back by half a century.

The international business kids talked about their parents spending lifetimes building up factories that produced soft drinks, shoes and other exports. Their families had employed, trained and promoted Zairians and paid taxes. My friends worried that these businesses would be stripped and they'd have to leave with nothing.

That November, I joined a committee from Garry Schmidt's Political Behavior class to run a mock U.S. presidential election. Our goals were to give students a chance to openly participate in political affairs, to teach the basics of how elections were run in the U.S. and to evaluate the political awareness of our students. Our committee would use the results to make a statistical record of political behavior at TASOK. Registration was held the week before November 7 to spark interest in studying the process and candidates, President Nixon and Senator McGovern. The experience was real but the results and records are lost to memory.

Instead, during my last two years in Zaire, the land and people immersed us. We held a walkathon fundraiser for a cause I can't remember to *Les Petites Chutes*. It was over 20 kilometers, a three-hour pilgrimage over hills, past Lovanium University, through valleys and past mud-and-thatch houses. Bill and I kept pace with each other, enjoying the open sky, the green savanna and woodlands.

Back at school, a new presidential decree reached us. No one with white skin could become a citizen of Zaire even if they'd been born and raised here. That meant half my class, on reaching their eighteenth birthday, would have to carry passports of countries they barely knew. This seemed like another effort to dispossess us of our identities and deny our rich heritage. I was not prepared for the dismay I felt at being excluded for my skin color. When the hostel bus came to take us home, I declined the air-conditioned ride and walked downhill in sweltering humidity instead. I strode along white-hot concrete, past the OAU compound. Yes, I recognized the brutal history of my race in Zaire, the privilege of my skin color. I often rode while my friends walked. I flew to boarding school, while they struggled to get into secondary school. Global political systems had betrayed us.

Yet our families had worked together with Congolese colleagues to build medical, church and education centers; had trained and funded doctors, nurses, teachers, chauffeurs, builders and carpenters. Together we were helping to recover local economies after revolution. Dad had even offered to bank Kamayala leaders' money in Canada where they could make 12 percent interest per year. Our students had become school directors, hospital administrators and government officials.

At the OAU compound entrance, I nearly walked into a chauffeured BMW and stopped short to let it pass. Unknown to me at the time, one of our own village friends would be trained for the presidential chauffeur pool—an exceptional driver with an accident-free record. A select few Congolese had filled the places of departing whites, and Mobutu kept circulating his critics into well-paid ambassadorships and government appointments to keep his hold on power.

Behind the wrought-iron fence of the presidential compound, an okapi grazed in a manicured park, far from her home in the upper Congo basin. Her coat varied from reddish brown, to mahogany, to jet black. Her leg bands were dark chocolate and creamy white—a layered contrast of colors—ancient as the Miocene and Pliocene ages. This camouflage in the filtered light of equatorial forests had hidden her, helped her survive undiscovered by science until 1900.

I swung downhill above the river rapids rushing around Mimosa and Macaques Islands to the Atlantic. Africa's roiling rivers ran through my veins, the vast savannas knew my footfall, its rich jungles offered up treasures like our bush babies from Kamayala's river forest. Large-eared, saucer-eyed, wooly fur babies with little fingers, they slept all day and woke at dusk to jump and cuddle around our necks, near our voice boxes. I was woven like a raffia mat with this place, its creatures and people—Hélène, Rafael, Jean, Ufulielo. How could I just pretend all this was nothing?

At the hostel, though, our bush babies suffered in bare wire cages that attracted maggots and mine would not survive. Charity sold hers to Pam Weaver who sneaked it to California under her long

Pam Weaver sneaked Charity's bush baby to California and back again. (Charity Schellenberg photo)

blonde hair. Over the summer, it thrived—and escaped—but was returned by a zoo. By then it had grown so large, she smuggled it back under a maternity top, determined to set it free in its jungle home.

The Atlantic stretched between me and Canada. Letters had slowed to a trickle from my friends in Canada—until only Brenda wrote—our decision to steer clear of boyfriends briefly forgotten. Hers drove a blue Camaro and sold cars in a small Canadian prairie town; mine collected African soil in his bare toes and dreamed of socialist revolution. Both Brenda and I had a long way to go in discovering who we were and what we would become. She however, auditioned and was juried into the famous Steinbach Treble Teens choir and toured all across Canada.

I had promised myself detachment, but at a special youth meeting in Sims chapel one evening, while blending our voices to *Kumbaya*, Bill's fingers enfolded mine beneath the chapel's high ebony altar. Under amber-flowed windows, tissue-thin on top, an inch thick on the bottom, I jumped right back into deep water.

Bill was another off-limits resident of the lawless Methodist-Presbyterian Hostel and he hated propaganda—religious or political. We both experienced mission life with awe when it was sung and danced authentically. But Bill displayed a low tolerance for empty platitudes. If the preacher promised riches in heaven for some burden of compliance, Bill scribbled on his Kalina church bulletin, *BS!*

For all Bill's rebel talk he was my most unthreatening boy-friend. To encourage my curiosity and exploration, he loved to say, "Nothing ever hurt you, you didn't do." This was opposite Nate's, "You don't have to cut off your foot to know it hurts." But I was opening up to more complex thinking and welcomed the weight of Bill's philosophies. It seemed the evils of runaway capitalism—might makes right and all that—trumped any of my trivial concerns.

From our traveling lives we took the promise to live in the moment, to be self-contained apart. This helped during weekends at separate hostels and school vacations in different countries. Letters filled the gaps—but empty promises—never.

I had found a critical-thinker and a good time to be challenged by one. With Uncle Hector at arm's length and Shirl buffering me, my motives were not questioned. I was learning how I would relate with intellectuals and how they would relate with me. I had not chosen the most bronzed or athletic. I had not adopted hostel standards of extreme physical rigor for boys. Bill was more likely to cross campus in an army surplus shirt with an armload of books than in a sports jersey kicking a ball.

Bill and I met most often on the walkway at school, once on a real date when he and a friend borrowed their hostel's van—a freedom not granted at our hostel. They took my classmate and me far away from rules and bells for a day out of time. At secluded *Ngombe* beach, ornamented by jungle and volcanic boulders, we waded the refreshing Zaire River, checking for water vipers and crocodiles. We'd heard of an American GI who'd stroked to the river's swift center until his buddies called, "Crocodile!" The GI could not outrun the reptile and his buddies discharged grenades, killing crocs until they found one containing his arm.

We splashed along the edges of the river, air-dried on the sand and black lava rocks and lingered while the sky turned orange-pink, bright orchid, indigo.

Some evenings Bill hitched a ride or pedaled his bike to our hostel—a freedom our own hostel did not permit. No bikes, no mo- torbikes. Bill rarely came inside. We talked on the patio outside, side- stepping soldier ants and swatting at flying termites.

One of our last evenings together, under yellow streetlights, we sprawled in thick grass beyond the patio and watched the sentry's fire across the street flicker off the open walls of the abandoned river mansion.

A buzzer sounded from our hostel for evening snacks.

"Your hostel is spooky with all its buzzers." Bill pulled a grass stalk and sucked its moist stem end.

"Want me to get you a chocolate chunk cookie?"

He grinned hugely, long hair flopping into his eyes, creases lining his lean cheeks.

"We're allowed two each."

"Naw, it's not normal." He spit out the grass and pulled me closer.

"Well, I've lived and coped here for almost ten years now." I grinned back but felt the knot in my gut that I was passing up snacks and would not get another chance.

I carried my poetry notebook everywhere, here at the school office (likely waiting to interview the principal) with stylish Munira Premji, class of '75. I'm wearing Char- ity's Belgian kilt, which she outgrew when she shot past me to 5-foot-9.

Overhead in the boys' wing, a Beatles album spun. "Will you still need me, will you still feed me when I'm sixty-four?"

"Who knows?" Bill rolled on his back and tugged me to his chest. "I'll keep writing you from Angola and South America. Maybe we can meet up in Toronto next year." He and Angola MK Gerry Knight were planning a Che Guevara pilgrimage after they graduated, backpacking where Guevara was hunted with CIA assistance and executed by the Bolivian army in 1967.

"Sounds good," I said and meant it. That was a date I planned to keep. I would miss Bill and his revolutionary ideals, but he'd opened my eyes to the boundaries that limited me.

On the walkway, Beth waited for me outside the *Condor Chronical* office after we'd put our last newspaper of 1972 to bed. She and Cathy, senior co-editors, were passing the editing to me for my senior year and Beth and I had been sharing our poetry journals.

"You can't put all your hopes into one person." She adjusted thick glasses and brushed curly tendrils from her face. "With our traveling lives, you just can't risk it."

"What're you thinking of risking exactly?" I peered into her eyes, noting how thin she'd grown despite her curves.

"A long-term relationship. It won't work. I can't just give up college to travel, kick around Europe—" Beth was headed for St. Andrews Presbyterian College in North Carolina, but captivated by a classmate headed for university in Germany and England.

"Yeah, all for one guy—what future is there in that?" I was only slightly sarcastic.

"Exactly. I'm afraid of getting involved yet I can't resist." She opened her journal and passed it over so I could absorb her wistful words.

"Me too." I passed her mine so she could read every pathetic sigh.

"Don't I know it?" She gazed at the clouds. "I'm on the brink of throwing everything over for love, yet…"

"I have to get a grip and follow my own course." I sounded surer than I felt.

We sat in the lengthening shade of the walkway, sketched mazes in the sand at our feet and inked storm clouds in our notebooks. For me, "Draw at all times" had become "Write at all times." Or "Draw and write at all times."

Beth's motif was a waifish girl caught in a downpour without cover. The girl leaned into the wind, hair and skirt blown the other way. You could land at a new college and find yourself in a gale without a banana leaf.

Beth would study medieval literature and become a popular professor of monster literature, focused on the transcultural "Buffy the Vampire Slayer."

Our class designed invitations to the junior-senior banquet and hand-lettered the notes inside.

My classmates, Peanut, Evelyn, Libby, Pat and I designed a calligraphy card and hand-wrote invitations to the junior-senior banquet to be held at the elegant Mandarin Restaurant on May 19, 1972. We would be embracing and releasing 43 seniors, some of the best friends of our lives.

"It'll be so hard to let them go." I had selected some of my best friends from the list of names.

"Don't worry, we'll all see each other again." Libby reached for another card to fill. That seemed easy for her to say since the state department flew her family around at its will. As a child she had seen "seven dead bodies" on the streets of Vietnam though her mom said it was many more. Her parents had permitted her to stay at MPH her senior year so she wouldn't be uprooted by their next assignment.

The Falks hosted a reception for TASOK class of '72 graduates, such as Vangie Claassen (left) whose parents would be our next dorm parents. My commitment to short skirts is evident (center) next to Becky Gerber's more modest leather skirt. (Peter Falk photo)

"Maybe." I concentrated on my calligraphy. "I hope so."

"And if you don't keep in touch, I will." Libby's determination seemed more than wishful thinking. For years, she would write letters and emails, keep traveling among nomads, even when life had moved on for the rest of us.

The night of the junior-senior banquet, we dressed in tuxedoes and gowns and sat down to linen and china at the mirrored Mandarin banquet room above the city. We passed platters brimming with rice and stir-fried beef, chicken and veggies. I had practiced at the hostel picking up morsels one-handed with two knives so chopsticks were a breeze. Ice clinked in our water glasses. Curtis and Elijah got up to play guitar and conversation ran high.

Someone at my table slipped some silverware into his dress boots, someone else a plate into his cummerbund until the winner had hidden a whole place setting in his formal wear. We laughed about possibly walking out with tea cups and glasses bulging from tux jackets. Were we deliberately acting childish, resisting growing up the month before many would graduate and launch out on their own? Apparently some seniors did leave with place settings and our sponsors had to deal with it the next day.

Still it had been a night spent with my nation, my tribe, some of my closest friends in the world—Bill, Beth, Hans, Ragui, Curtis—and so many others. We had lived our global nomadism, and the senior class would once again fold up their lives and carry them around like luggage. We usually traveled light and clung to memories of people and surroundings instead of artifacts. The problem with memories is we do not recall the same things and end up grasping at mist that slips through our fingers.

The all-night junior-senior party following graduation was held at a spacious marine house with pool that Shirl fought Hector to let us attend. Credence Clearwater Revival played over loudspeakers, "Have you ever seen the rain?" We gave ourselves to the etched sorrow of parting. An airplane crash movie played onscreen—perhaps "Skyjacked"?—just before many seniors boarded flights out of Africa. Some of us, like Leola and others, skipped it and sat around the pool. People came out to linger and share last words and goodbyes. Bill and I hung out there for a while in the humid night air, the calm before the storm of him actually leaving.

The night dwindled and Bill led me upstairs to a hallway lined with seven doors. Which would we choose? The first and second were locked. The third opened onto a large double bed.

Completely clothed, we fell into it, Bill's mouth like fresh mango on my tongue. "I wish...," he said.

I did, too. Our last night should be momentous, but we were MKs, schooled in the consequences of using up the marriage act. It was bound to turn out all wrong and ruin us for life. No matter that the sexual revolution was in full swing all around us—and I'd been targeted as both a prude and tease—I still believed that virginity was my only gift, purity my only prize. The line we would cross could not be redrawn and only regrets would follow.

I pulled away and sat listlessly on the edge of the bed until the door opened and Pam walked in. "You're not—" She stopped.

"No. Come in."

She sat beside me. "You wouldn't, would you?" She'd just broken up with her boyfriend, Gerry Knight, who would tour South America with Bill.

"No." I thought she might like to talk with Bill about his best friend but when I glanced over, Bill's eyes were closed.

"Well, good. I can't find a single bed not in use around here." She stretched out beside Bill. "Goodnight."

I turned out the lights and closed the door. While she and Bill dozed, I drifted through the vine-bowered patio and exchanged last words, lingering hugs and kisses with the senior class. I stayed in the moment, all senses present, smelled the musty night in their hair, tasted the sweet acrid weed on their lips. One of our TASOK bands played and I mingled with Ashif, Nazir, David, Roger, Perry, Bob, Loren and Cathy, among so many others.

Hans hung out in a corner on the other side of the leafy patio with Beth and could not bear to leave any of us—all of us—at once. He hugged Beth and me by turn, groaning. "The walls are crumbling. How do you have the strength to go on? Who broke the bed?"

Our years together, like a multi-colored *batik* dye would begin to bleed away by daybreak. Beth would tour Europe with a backpack, stay in noisy youth hostels, and perhaps see Hans one more time before crossing the wide Atlantic.

As a junior, I would continue on the next year at TASOK, yet I was parting with some of the people I admired and delighted in most. The Class of '72 would be the farewell I remembered best because I did not quick-release or jump ahead. I would remember it because it was not my leaving, but theirs.

25

DOWN SO LONG

"We have no homeland but our faith."
— MIRIAM TOEWS

Early one Saturday morning during my senior year, I sat beneath sheltering mango trees on the rough cement grave slab behind Sims Chapel overlooking Bay Ngaliema. An American Baptist teacher had died here suddenly in 1893 after the area was abandoned due to King Leo's taxes ("Kinshasa Then and Now"). Yet for me, the future had just opened as wide as the river basin stretching to fuzzy green Congo, Brazzaville.

Sims Chapel, the oldest building in Kinshasa, overlooks the Congo River and became a sacred place for me. ("Kinshasa Then and Now" photo)

306

I had received a note from an author on our mission, Levi Keidel. I didn't normally dream big, but he had noticed my critical editorials in the school paper and encouraged me to pursue journalism at Northwestern University, Minneapolis. I doubted myself a little. Perhaps he was responding more to my potential than my gift. But his note changed the way I viewed myself and my future. Instead of worrying about making the wrong choice in men, I could hope to make the right choice in a career.

No more jumping aboard someone else's dreams. Time to focus on my visions, make my own path in the world. I wanted more than accomplishments—painting, poetry, athletics. Every morning I tuned into the 4:30 a.m. BBC broadcast on my transistor and often read *Time* or *Newsweek*. Dad had been a radio broadcaster and I, too, wanted a career in journalism, writing or teaching.

In that sacred place overlooking the ancient river, I whispered, *Please Lord, make it happen.* When I could not see a way forward, I had learned to lean into prayer, even if it was only a wordless moan.

The ancient river flowed persistently into river jungle and I headed back up the block to the hostel assured that Mr. Keidel had given me permission to consider my writing goals a priority. He was writing *Caught in the Crossfire,* a journalistic novel of the Kwilu rebellion, narrating how the revolution had resulted in deep suffering, yet widespread communal reconciliation. Was it possible that writing might be as great a calling as Mom and Dad serving God, family and community? That it was, in fact, serving?

That September we had a new grade 12 English teacher from Elizabeth, New Jersey. Sal Manetta wore his wavy brown hair over his collar, his shirt open with chest hair curling out. A jolt shot through me at such a racy display. I averted my eyes and found a seat in a semicircle of desks, which he'd rearranged from the usual orderly rows.

My classmates filed in and our teacher twisted a thick mustache, sized us up and whistled, *Down to here, down to there, long as I can grow it—my hair.*

We had not seen "Hair" with its profanity, drugs, nudity and irreverence for the flag, though we had bootlegged the soundtrack on cassette. Still, this was not the usual way to open a first class. My friends and I looked at each other curiously.

Sal didn't know half our pluck. All he knew was that those entering English class barefoot were MKs, easily assimilating a culture beyond the American compound. Was he implying we were still too sheltered and narrow-minded?

He raised a dark brow at us with a sneering twist in his grin, a flicker in his eye. Without saying a word, he went to the board and wrote the "f" word.

I winced. My friends looked away.

This was a new kind of teaching; I'd read about it. "Teaching as subversion," *Newsweek* called it. And, though I was willing to see where he was going with this shock treatment, I knew that for half the class, Sal had just spelled his own doom.

"Can anyone read this?" He asked it as though we were illiterate.

Most of the MKs shifted their gaze to the mango trees and hibiscus along the circle drive. Few had ever uttered the word aloud.

Sal flipped his long hair out of dark eyes and stroked his mustache. He raised his voice. "You can't read?" He broke off a piece of chalk and tossed it out the open door onto the walkway.

Reckless waste. Schools upcountry could've use it.

"Well then, someone tell me what it means."

More silence.

"Okay, let's talk about why you're all so uptight." He sat on his desk and slung a frayed blue-jean knee over the corner. The desk was stacked with several new novels, not the worn Shakespeare textbooks I was expecting.

"You're supposed to study 'Julius Caesar' this year. But I've ordered some contemporary American fiction."

He held up Robert Penn Warren's *All the King's Men*. "The rise to power of Governor Willie Stark. He was a crooked populist and messianic figure in the Depression-era Deep South. It's a study in human foibles."

"Sounds interesting?" I scribbled in my notebook and showed it to Evelyn and Peanut.

"Richard Farina's *Been Down So Long it Looks Like Up to Me*. Funny, sexy, profound, 1960s counterculture. An anarchist college student smokes dope, pursues women, travels to the Cuban revolution, leads a campus revolt against banning girls from guys' apartments. Should open your eyes to what's happening on university campuses in the States."

Students shifted at their desks. Distant thunder rolled, the sky darkened.

"And one more. *Bob and Carol and Ted and Alice*. Based on a movie of couples seeking complete oneness and acceptance of open marriages. Questions?"

A hand shot up. "So you're in favor of wife swapping?"

"Free love, dope smoking?" A pro-dope-smoking MK grinned.

"I'm not saying anything. You have to read the books," Sal dodged.

"What about the curriculum?" A straight-A student scowled.

"Hey, if you'd rather read Shakespeare you don't have to take this class."

Half the class dropped English, but I stayed on cautiously.

When the first rains came barreling out of a purple sky and pounded our tin-roofed classes like apentema drums, Sal tried to shout above them. Half a lecture on Robert Penn Warren was lost before he realized he'd been silenced. He sat and glowered out the window where the road flowed by, a river of brown mud. Lightning flared and cracked at the same moment. His eyes bulged. "Close!"

We all knew someone who'd been hit, had seen lightning fire-balls zip along cement floors, yellow-orange blurs headed straight for bare toes. We tucked up our feet and doodled or passed notes, waiting for the power outage.

Sal broke off chunks of yellow chalk and tossed them out the open door at the downpour.

"He's nuts." Evelyn scribbled.

"But cute and funny." I responded to her note and passed it back.

"Cute as in ugly, funny as in weird." Peanut wrote and grinned. She was our newspaper typist as well as Evelyn's Baptist dorm roommate.

I considered that a moment. We had never seen so much new fiction at once. Sal might not have the first clue about these rainstorms, but he got us thinking about sleazy presidential races, open marriage, radical college life. Ideas were no longer a sticky mass of religious platitudes.

Within weeks I had Sal nearly to myself, not just because class members kept dropping out in protest, but because he was newspaper advisor. I bent over paste-up with my razor knife and he asked, "Why do you think marriage is so sacred?"

The class had again opposed him on open marriage and I wasn't budging.

"Wife swapping." I met his honeyed gaze. "How's that love?" If he was defending multiple partners I could tell him that even polygamous Africans kept their wives in separate huts.

"Put down your knife." Sal touched my hand with chalk-yellow fingers, his thick gold wedding band dull under a dusting of fine ochre. "I have someone special for you to meet."

I followed him to the teachers' lounge. There, the fine-boned, red-haired, special ed teacher, Jane, rose to meet us. I watched the way Sal went to her side and touched her arm. He held the small of her back when he introduced us.

"They almost didn't hire us," Sal said. "Told us to get married. After we'd lived together for three years they wouldn't recognize us as a couple." Sal got three cokes from the machine. "They threatened to only pay my passage unless we got hitched."

"They forced you?"

"Yes, thank goodness or we'd still be living in sin." Jane had a mischievous, pixy grin. She was a competitive equestrian who'd flouted convention only to give in to a government order to promise to serve and obey.

Sal put a thick, chalky index finger to his full lips. "Shh, we're not supposed to tell."

"Right." Jane tilted her chin up at me. "We've been sworn to keep our nasty secrets from the kids."

I whipped out my pen. "Nothing's safe with me."

Back at newspaper layout, Sal asked, "Do you think we were living in sin?"

I ducked. "You two are about as monogamous as it gets." He wasn't getting any concessions from me.

"F--" His lip twisted in a sneer-grin. "Do you think I'll go to hell for saying that?"

I picked up an off-sized photo. "Shucks—" I said.

"Rhymes with?"

"—hand me the sizing wheel."

"Do you think you will?"

Sal proposed an editorial discussion on what people believe. We had all views plying the walkway, Mormon to Hindu, atheist to Ba'hai, agnostic to Jewish. "Jesus Christ Super Star" had made it to Broadway—a hero who had received Mary Magdelene—and for that, I embraced him.

"Why do you think people believe what they do? Why do you?" Sal gestured towards Hassina, sitting on the walkway, her smile gracious as she turned down sips of Coke, offers of fresh baguette. It was Ramadan. "If you were raised like Hassina you would be fasting now, too."

"I pray," I said simply. "My prayers are answered." I had joined Hassina on the bleachers at lunch—to pray far from the munching crowd.

"Coincidence," Sal said. "You've been behavior-modified to pray. You've been told you'll burn in hell if you don't."

"Naw, it's not like that. It gives me strength, calms me down under deadline."

"Are you saying you never get angry, upset, rattled?"

"Well, I don't throw chalk at the rain." I smirked.

"Aw come on now. I dare you to stop praying for two weeks. I bet you can't do it."

"Why would I want to? I like talking to God."

"Try it, see what happens. Do you think you'll get punished?"

"No, it's not like that. It's a loving relationship."

"Okay, so why not then? You think He can't take it?"

The more Sal quizzed me, the more pat my answers sounded, as though someone else were speaking for me—Dad or Mom or the pastor upcountry.

Like a person giving up chocolate, I set a date for quitting. I would stop praying the following Monday and gradually take back only the faith I could call my own. One last dose of Sunday worship at Kalina and then no more for two weeks. I would go to church, of course—I had no choice in that—but I would view it all critically, question every word, every cliché.

The first morning without devotions was the worst. Not addressing God the moment I opened my eyes, not consulting Him about the day, who to pray for, what to wear, to be with me at school. I had to monitor myself closely, tell myself to quit when I felt an interior dialogue start up.

What I had given up was a presence, a constant reassuring friendship. The wrap-around emotional comfort, I now had to fill with reason. I told myself I could face any tension at school with my wits—a crisis on the newspaper, an algebra test, an argument on the walkway—because I had faced it all before. I had know-how, smarts, flexibility. Was I being proud? Would I fall? No, this was poise.

I went down to breakfast, crossed the tile and pulled out a chair at the table. "Let's pray," Shirl said. Becky bowed her head, Charity, Carl. I was the only one who didn't bow my head or close my eyes. Everyone else looked like lemmings.

During after-dinner devotions I didn't utter a word when Shirl closed with "conversational prayer." Each of us was supposed to add a sentence, as though we were conversing with God. It seemed that during the gaps between sentences everyone was waiting for me to speak, including God.

Becky Gerber stopped me on the way upstairs. "Is something wrong?" she asked.

"No," I said, though overnight God had become a black ceiling instead of a tunneled light. "I just decided to stop praying."

She touched my arm. "Do you want us to pray for you?"

Outside my window the squeak-croak of mango bats started up in the darkened boughs and I stilled my automatic evening prayers.

How much all of us had accepted without question. I had written a geometry paper on *trompes l'oeil*, my fine arts feint towards math. How our eyes deceive us. How much we accepted as it was presented, as if every dogma existed by divine decree. A gargoyle painted in relief was a gargoyle and we were not invited to touch and discover it was only a brick wall.

"A circle appears smaller inside a square," I had written, "than a circle of the same size surrounding a square." Uncle Hector's square fist, myself curled inside his command.

Hector had told the mission either Shirl went or he would. The mission had called them in separately and Shirl reported how, after a year of listening to us kids, she felt we had enough problems to last our entire lives. The mission kept Shirl and replaced Hector with Mel and Martha Claassen. But the mission had only moved Hector next door to the business office. He could still come over on business, could come from behind while I stood on the porch and land a blow to my arm. How long would it take to break his remote control of me?

After I'd survived two weeks without prayer, I couldn't mouth the same old phrases without hearing their simplicity. I couldn't say, "Save Sal and Jane," when it was I who needed saving from excessive control, judgment and prejudice.

My response to controlling authorities was still sweaty palms. It was like the first time I went out to dinner and returned to the hostel drunk.

"Have you been drinking?" Aunt Martha asked gently. She seemed uncertain.

"No, it was just the people I was with." I hoped she'd believe that yeast smell wafted over you like smoke. My date, former MCC worker, Nate, had become Assistant U.N. High Commissioner for Refugees. We had gone out with his French friends who had filled and refilled my wine glass, saying it improved my French. They then left the table not realizing I couldn't walk. Instead of coming to my rescue, they'd stood on the far side of the polished parquet and laughed while I tottered across the pitching floor.

"Goodnight," I said to Aunt Martha and fell into bed, flattened by a histamine headache and stomach cramps. *Lush. You drink and then lie about it.* Surely this aching gut was the predicted punishment. I went back downstairs to confess and get something for my headache.

"How about prayer?" Aunt Martha asked.

I accepted her gently-offered hand, her curly bowed head and sincere request for help. Relief came at four in the morning when I threw up the U.N.-sponsored dinner—like a refugee who's eaten grass and bugs so long I couldn't stomach a rich meal.

We had been rigidly controlled and had no advocate until Shirl arrived. Who was to say how much power was Caesar's? Caesar? We understood, we'd been told. We were all making sacrifices for God's work. For that we should feel glad, and for feeling anything else we should feel guilty. Glad and guilty were the only emotions allowed.

"Streak a wheel with all the primary colors," I had written, "spin it. The colors will blend a solid white." If I kept my emotions always at the right tilt, if I didn't give in to despair or anger, I could be purely Christian—and purely numb.

———————————

Letters from Hope at the college dorm said she felt alone, cut off from us. I could only remind her of our sister bond—our runs to the river, swimming, hunting, singing—and our homecoming the following summer.

She had called cousin Penny Reimer to pick her up from the airport and caught a ride to Steinbach with Penny's mom's parents. Hope had arrived in Steinbach, planning to surprise Grandma Reimer but Grandma was out of town that week. Hope stashed her suitcase in the lilac hedge and hurried down Hanover, ringing the bell of first one old girlfriend and then another. Everyone she knew was either gone on holidays or had moved away.

When darkness descended and Grandma still wasn't home, Hope ran back across town, sneaked through an open door at the Bible School and crept into an empty classroom in the basement. To drive off the cold, she rolled herself in a corner of the musty area rug.

The next morning, with her last dollar, Hope bought a sack of week-old bread from Don's Bakery and sorted through it for buns and cinnamon rolls soft enough to eat. She collected job applications from the businesses along Main Street, took them to Kindale Park along Steinbach's Stony Brook, and sat at a picnic table to fill them out.

Later she would tell us she kept her head that week by thinking of it as an adventure, the way we had survived as refugees. She had become a refugee in her own hometown and we were too far away to reach her. It might take weeks, even months to talk her off the edge of that abyss.

I might not attend journalism school at Northwestern after all, I realized. I could be flexible and settle for second choices. There were more urgent needs—our family's wholeness, Hope's mental health and survival.

Rafael, Hélène, me and Jean in Kamayala, 1973. (Charity Schellenberg photo)

Christmas 1972 was ten days away. We'd be flying to Kamayala for vacation in a few days. I grabbed a basketball and headed to the hostel court. Charity ran out from the dining room. "Our house burned down!"

"Our house in Kamayala?" We had lived in so many—twenty at least over the years.

"Yes, the Claassens just told me—they heard it on the radio."

"Is everyone okay?"

"Yes but get this! I dreamt it burned last night. Dad went back to rescue someone and fell into the fire and I tried to pull him out. Then I woke up."

"Really?" I gaped, then hugged her.

Tears sprang to her eyes. Charity and I packed without knowing what to expect. Was everything gone? We had bought a few gifts but had no idea what was needed. When the three of us sisters landed at the Kahemba airstrip, Mom and Dad hugged us extra long and hard and we hugged them back in kind.

We greeted our friends and *ndoyis* and piled into the car.

"We are so grateful everyone's alive." Dad turned the ignition and headed down the sandy roads the few kilometers to Kamayala.

"Was anyone injured?" I had so many questions.

"Yes, Glenn sustained some third-degree burns." Mom turned her soft hazel eyes toward us in the middle seat, and brushed auburn curls from her furrowed forehead. Glenn was the new MCC PAX volunteer assigned to replace Ron and Dan when their term ended. "He was throwing sand on the fire, trying to put it out, when the medicine boxes exploded and burned his hands and arms."

"How did it happen?" I wanted all the details.

"*Tata* Michel was filling the fridge with kerosene and trying to regulate the pilot flame," Mom said. "Then he and I were called outside. The flame burned out of control, followed a trail of dripped kerosene, then raced towards cardboard boxes full of medicine. *Tata* Michel and I shoved the boxes away but the flames raced up the drapes and shot into the plywood ceiling." She shook her head and wiped her eyes and nose, still a bit shaken.

Dad gripped Mom's hand. "The fire caught the rafters and of-fice wall, desk and papers. We're so grateful the Chokwe Gospel of Mark was saved. Khege and I had just completed four years of work on it and I usually kept it in my home office. But for some reason, I had brought it to the church office the day before."

"Villagers rushed into the far end bedrooms, rescuing clothes, beds and linens." Mom adjusted her bifocals. "We also saved the ra-dio transmitter and some books and magazines."

Dad turned and smiled at me. "The last thing I rescued was the typewriter and portrait you drew of me. I treasure that."

I felt our bond tighten with those words. We were back on solid footing, after the punishment three years before, our connec-tion solidified, too, through 76 chess matches played in Kamayala the summer of 1972 during the Fischer-Spassky tournament in Ice-land. I had only won 7.

Dad slowed and waved when we entered the village and peo-ple shouted, jumped and waved back with extra intensity, it seemed. They had helped us survive a life-threatening crisis.

Still, I gaped when we pulled in at the burned-out house to look around. Its doors and windows were gone, its distinctive quar-ried stone entrance was smudged black and its tin roof was half burned away. Only the cement shell remained.

"As you know," Dad said, "the house is almost twenty years old. I finished it for the Miller sisters before we built the church."

Glenn had invited my parents to stay in his spare bedroom until the end of their term in June 1973 and we girls slept on cots in the office.

That Christmas Eve we sat around Glenn's fireplace and opened the small gifts Charity and I had purchased. But our focus was on spared lives, and our carols flowed with new meaning. "Joy to the World." "Oh Come Let Us Adore Him."

The nativity pageant at church that evening put on by Kamayala's high school students drew hundreds—perhaps a thousand. Some had walked from villages fifty miles away. The church filled to capacity with people sitting in windowsills and aisles. Several choirs raised the rafters with their intricate harmonies, drums, bells and whistles. Readers delivered resounding Christmas passages and, finally, actors took the stage.

A census was called, candidates lined up and fistfights broke out.

"I was here first!"

"So what? I'm more important than you!"

The wisemen traveled in from outside and lost sight of the star.

"It was your turn to watch."

"No yours!"

Mary and Joseph arrived in Bethlehem where they were greeted by an innkeeper already drunk from celebrating Christmas.

The play lasted two hours and Dad slipped out ahead of us. We sisters and Mom followed beneath a moon lighting up white sand and gleaming off our perforated tin roof. We couldn't help singing, "I'm Dreaming of a White Christmas."

But as we neared the burned-out hulk, Mom quieted us. "Shh, listen."

From the ruins came Dad's melodious bass voice accompanied by guitar. "I've got a mansion just over the hilltop." We joined him, "Don't think me poor or deserted or lonely."

Christmas morning was usually busy with requests at our door—people needing clothes, eyeglasses, tin cans, milk, pictures, paper or pens. But in 1972 the first knock was a woman bringing us a bowl of roasted peanuts, saying, "*Joyeux Noël!*" The next brought a stalk of bananas and a neighbor delivered hot *chindu* and caterpillar gravy. All day visitors came bearing gifts. A pineapple, greens, tomatoes, potatoes. We hardly felt worthy of their generosity. Our material wealth, which had created such a wall, was gone.

When the MAF plane arrived to take us girls back to school,

Missionaries sent fresh linens and clothing and Cornie Loewen paid to repair our burned-out house and replace the valuables we'd lost. (Hope Wiebe 2010 photo)

the pilot off-loaded boxes of new towels, sheets, blankets and clothing collected and sent by fellow missionaries.

One observer said, "No wonder you didn't weep when your house burned."

Later Mom's cousin, Cornie Loewen, paid to replace all the valuables we had lost.

Back at the hostel, one Saturday afternoon Shirl took us hostel kids picnicking to the Zaire River rapids. We parked on the bank and walked across a cracked concrete bridge to Mimosa Island, a fishermen's island below Ngaliema Bay. Dugout pirogues and handmade rafts lined the shore, and, at the southern tip of the island, the river rapids bucked and roiled. They crashed over volcanic rock in a tumult so formidable that, it was rumored, no person in this century had set foot on the next island. Macaques who had crossed on an old land bridge had lived and bred there, undisturbed for 100 years. So thick was the island with monkeys, that on a still day you could see the branches shake and hear the air ring with their shrill cries above the rapids.

The legend of the monkeys fascinated Carl who had owned pet monkeys and played Tarzan since boyhood. While the rest of us dug into *paté de fois* sandwiches, Carl called John over, and they wandered to the edge of fishermen's island. Over the deep roar of the rapids came the shrill chatter of monkeys. The boys had leaped from high cliffs into dark rivers and camped naked in the wilderness of *Lac Vert*. It was in Carl and John's nature to take on the wilds of Zaire. Almost as one, they waded into the thrashing current. John had a tin can in hand and scooped a green water snake from the current—a true gem.

Somewhere at mid-rapids, trying to spare his snake, John slipped and was pulled under, pounded and pummeled by white water. Carl rushed to shore and charged across the bridge and along the other bank of unbroken shoreline. Shirl screamed and we all rushed after Carl, back across the cracked bridge to try and reach John. We ran along the shoreline village and Shirl asked everyone in sight, "Have you seen my boys?" She gestured, hand at eye-level "This big?"

She put a thin hand heavily on my shoulder and groaned. Often she'd worried that she'd cared for us too lightly, given us too much freedom, too soon. Now she was certain she had—and had lost one of us.

I couldn't accept that notion. We had survived shooting the falls long before Shirl came to the hostel. We knew the tummy-tingling terror of getting swept up in currents, hurled against boulders, and dropped in free fall. We led with our feet, followed with our heads. We'd been pushing the limits for as long as we'd lived at the hostel. With Shirl here we had started feeling more truly cared for, less risk-prone. But we hadn't forgotten the thrill of free fall. She and I rushed on, scanning the rapids, bare feet skidding on seaweed.

At last we saw Carl staggering through the village carrying a limp body over his shoulders. He seemed bowed under the weight, his legs trembling, his head bent. I felt a momentary joy at seeing Carl again—my fellow inmate through a whole decade at the hostel—but a deep pang at seeing John immobile. Was he alive? Could he be revived?

I rushed ahead of Shirl. But when I neared Carl, he and John were grinning. Carl winked. "Shh, we're giving Shirl a scare."

I hesitated. I should shout to Shirl, "John's fine!" Yet, for a few minutes, I played along.

Shirl cried out and ran to Carl, arms wide, but before she could touch him, Carl set John on his feet in front of her. John's arms, legs and trunk were cut and bruised, but his stance was steady. He jumped up and down a few times, grinning. He was fine.

We all laughed except Shirl. She gasped, then darkened, her brown eyebrows drawn. "That's not funny! You just about got yourself killed and you're joking about it!"

Years later one of our schoolmates, Phil Braun, would rescue another schoolmate struggling against current in the rain-swollen river and get swept away himself. A helicopter searched for days, low over the tumultuous flow but his body was never found.

Our risk-taking continued to worry Shirl. She said we acted deliberately self-destructive. Carl collected poisonous snakes and had no trouble finding catchers among us. One day the little kids swam at *Ngombe* beach along the edge of the Zaire River and I waded in with them. A deadly water viper rippled among them and came within arm's reach of me. I didn't yell, "Snake!" It would be much easier not to scare the grade-school kids. Instead, I grabbed the snake behind the head—only to find I'd given it two inches of strike room. It brushed its flicking fangs against my wrist and reared back for a strike. I flung it on shore—right into a group of high school boys.

They scattered and screamed. "Faith! Are you trying to kill us?"

I hadn't intended to hurt or scare anyone else. I just wanted to save the little kids.

A few years later, one of our dorm girls, Laurie Bowers, was bitten by a water viper at that same spot, went comatose all night and was finally released from hospital two days later.

In our adult lives, we hostel kids bungee jumped, parachuted and toured the highest roller coasters. Some of us would smoke, toke and drink despite our religious upbringing. Or because of it. We'd run to the church or from it, alternately seeking sanctuary or freedom.

We'd seek intimacy and then not be able to attach. We'd hurt the ones we loved and then not be able to deal with the conflict. We'd separate and reunite, divorce and remarry.

We had practiced detaching from our own parents and would need lessons in re-attaching and parenting our own children. Each hug or kiss we gave was one we'd missed.

We'd spend hours in therapy, graduate from twelve-step programs and take them into women's prisons. We'd swear off step programs, pour whiskey in our coffee and end up in psych wards or prison. We were optimists, pessimists, obsessive-compulsive, moody, bi-polar. At least one of us would take his own life.

We bought houses and never moved again. Or traveled, got entangled or raped—prime targets. We avoided rape with clever tricks learned in transit.

We had no homeland but our faith and sometimes no faith at all. Yet we were born to justice-seeking parents who were some of the best models in the universe. In Congo, Mom begged medicines from pharmaceuticals and expanded her service to 24 clinics. In Canada, she noticed so much good food trashed behind the Bible institute kitchen that she asked the cooks to leave leftovers for her to pick up. In this way, she was able to open her home to the homeless and feed them excellent meals. Dad, the president, was also able to give his salary as a donation match to expand the institute, retire its debt and win college accreditation.

Our parents felt called to their work and faced revolution, disease, disability and death. We children felt alternately involved, inspired, distanced, neglected, deprived or privileged.

Our moving among countries, continents and cultures created complexities in who we became. We were third culture kids (TCKs), borrowing from home and host cultures to create a unique third culture. We shared experiences with other MKs and TCKs but responded differently to our circumstances. We pursued missions and service or felt we'd given enough already. We found a median course of serving when we could, escaping when we couldn't.

———————————

Our final days in Zaire concerned me, especially for Charity who longed to stay.

One Sunday evening, Charity did not appear for dinner. I had let her go on her own—without someone (Grace or me) along, as the hostel required—to the Chokwe chapel beyond the *Grand Marché.*

It was almost sundown and she wasn't back yet. Anything could have happened to her on the two-hour bus ride out there— or back. She could have been flung into a ravine, pushed off at the wrong stop, beaten, robbed, raped or killed.

But my biggest fear was that she had decided to stowaway in the Chokwe community; she had been so distraught about leaving Congo and Kalema. Also, since we were leaving after my graduation—the year before hers—she would have to adjust to a new school in Canada. She begged to stay in Congo with friends and, when that was denied, felt her life was stolen from her.

I paced the living room, then clattered out the screen door and sat on the porch where we'd once caught a monitor lizard the size of a small crocodile. I opened the gates, checked the streets, wandered to the corner, wandered back, waited at the gate.

Finally I saw her treading wearily down the street, the red sunset caught in her blonde hair. I rushed to her side. "What happened—you okay?"

"I'm fine." A tired smile flickered across her flushed cheeks. "Just taking my time, saying goodbye."

———————————

My final days on the continent were full of firsts, lasts, blanks and misfires.

Our senior "sneak" to the Atlantic Ocean was not stealthy. We piled body-to-body in the Baptist's five-ton truck, still laughing about making it halfway to the coast before school started, when the truck pulled over just outside the city. Our mechanic, classmate David Polley, turned back to the city in the convoy van "to get a gasket for the oil filter." When he walked into the Baptist hostel at breakfast everyone was laughing but the seniors.

While waiting, we slayed several hours with a card game Carol Ericson called "Killer!" and tossed frisbee before getting rumbling again along Matadi Road to Vista, near Moanda, 550-kilometer (280 miles) away. About noon, near Kisantu, the truck skidded and swerved on wet pavement and nearly tossed several classmates off the truck's high bars. Shaken, we pulled off to inspect brakes and gather our wits. Our class president Glen Chapman sensed our fear and prayed for safety and peace for the journey.

A cholera epidemic had nearly thwarted our trip and we'd been cautioned not to eat from roadside vendors. But by our noon rest stop at Kivuvu, several classmates clambered down for fried dough *mikate* (*beignets*). Outside Matadi, our health cards were required at a medical checkpoint where men in white lab coats stood ready with cholera injections. At least one classmate hid when he realized he had his father's health card instead of his own.

We piled out at the shipping lanes in Matadi to wait in a vehicle line-up for a ferry. Here at the deep ship port, twenty years earlier in 1953 my parents had disembarked when they first arrived in Congo, to drive hundreds of kilometers inland to Kamayala. They were among triple the number of Protestant missionaries of any other African nation, per capita, invited by nationals before independence to help build education, medical and church centers.

North of us was the newly inaugurated Inga-Shaba hydroelectric dam, the world's largest direct current line, one of Mobutu's extravagances that would employ several of my classmates well beyond high school. An effort to harness the power of the Zaire River rapids and transmit it 1,000 miles to secession-prone Shaba, Mobutu was counting on the control the power lines would give him over Shaba. But cost overruns pushed the $230 million project to over $1 billion.

Back on the road, our hopes of reaching the ocean before sunset vanished. Darkness descended and the roads turned narrow, dusty and rugged. We pulled into a cinderblock, tin-roof bungalow owned by Christian and Missionary Alliance mission on Friday about 1 a.m., 22 hours after we'd left Kinshasa. We grabbed our bed rolls and found rooms or space on the floor or beach and were soon asleep.

Morning dawned on the heaving blue Atlantic, the start of a four-day dream. We ran along seven kilometers of open beach to Le Beviour Hotel in Moanda or body-surfed, buoyed and pummeled in the tannin-stained swell. We played frisbee football, buried classmates in sand or played water tag with our sponsors, yelling, "Get Sal!"

Charity and John walk Moanda beach on the Atlantic Ocean. (Hope Wiebe 2010 photo)

On the edge of the continent, and our lives in it—the Atlantic and our dreams across it—the week became an intensive nostalgia, even as we lived it. Joni Mitchell's "Both Sides Now" played on the turntable. At the close of each sun-soaked day kids strolled the beach or ate on the cliffs, the sunset glinting off the ocean clear to the horizon. Our brain waves slowed to match the hypnotic roll of the sea, meditative and relaxed.

One evening we roasted hot dogs on the beach and sang around the campfire with our drama and Lingala teacher Ted Ericson strumming guitar. He had taught me to die onstage and was teaching us to live spontaneously in real time. That weekend was also Sandy's birthday and we drank hot chocolate and played the hokey pokey—moves even Mennonites could "get." Another night we went to the Mangrove Hotel in Moanda for a fancy dinner and at 1 a.m. walked to an old lighthouse high on a cliff. Sunday morning we held a worship service on the rocks and dipped our toes in the tide.

We lived the days as if in memory, carved our names and class year deep into red clay cliffs, waves crashing below us—remembered and forgotten, here and gone. Before leaving the coast on our all-night return to Kinshasa, we stopped at the Le Beviour bar and some of us 18 year olds ordered or shared our first legal Primus beer. Its fizzy bubbles exploded and faded on our tongues.

We were intensely aware of this being our final spree, our last chance to drop all barriers and confirm hopeless entanglement with a nation, a continent and its people. Hopeless because we would be flung so far and wide—Antwerp, Bujumbura, Puu Waawaa, Dar es Salaam, Istanbul, Hong Kong, London, Houston, Abidjan, Winnipeg, San Diego, Cambridge, Omaha, Toronto. Few of us would meet again.

Our return was punctuated by Wendy Golden's jokes.

"Knock, Knock."

"Who's there?"

"Stain."

"Stain who?"

"Doesn't anyone stay-in one place anymore?"

We approached Kinshasa in the dead of night and were stopped at a roadblock by uniformed men with long guns. "What are you doing sneaking around at night? You're spies. Come with us!" They selected several boys to interrogate and the rest of us waited anxiously until their release.

Back at school during our final weeks, we learned that our Pakistani classmates—Hassina, Zahir, Asifa—born and raised in Africa, were being kicked out of the country. Two thousand businesses would be stolen for Mobutu, his relatives and friends in a disastrous Zairianization that resulted in stripped assets. The Bank of Zaire estimated that fifty companies (several claimed by Mobutu) secreted $300 million illegally overseas (French). Thousands of Zairians lost jobs and the tax base crumbled.

Hassina spent the last few days of school head in hands on the walkway, her dark hair pulled back in a low pony-tail, her sparkly eyes somber, her dimples gone. Her family would lose everything but what they could cash in. She asked me about Canada, which was accepting Pakistanis. Congo/Zaire, the country we'd grown up with, was crashing around us, as if sensing our flight.

Our junior-senior banquet was held on May 18 at the new Intercontinental Hotel ballroom under a 10-by-15-foot mural of two castles, one old and worn, the other with sunlit turrets among pink and blue clouds painted by school artist Willy Klassen. Our theme from the Moody Blues, "On the Threshold of a Dream," was played by TASOK rock band Bella Nzengo.

Jeff Stormant's junior choir serenaded us with "Bye-Bye TASOK" and "When You Walk Through a Storm" and teachers Karl Benson and Harold Ens showed slides of our years together illustrating that "memories are a form of meeting." And letting go.

I attended with longtime classmate Dan Chapman, a fellow mile record-holder, whose outdoor adventures with his brother Glen and friend David Rumohr rivaled mine and my sisters'. They had canoed during windy-rainy August for 12 days from the Wamba, Kwango, Kwilu, Kasai and Kwa to the Congo/Zaire River—chased by a hippo, pursued by air force, suspected as spies and sleeping on sandbars, rocks and in fishermen villages.

We would leave Zaire with its rivers and jungles, its broad savannas dropping into valley floors, its mineral wealth, its falls plunging 200 feet to coastal plains, its flickering supper fires suspended in blackness.

So attached was I, the pain of leaving so great, that my last night in that country became a black hole, not one glimpse of it retrievable. It was blocked from memory. Vanished like the sun swallowed by the equator.

I was class vice president and helped plan graduation. A copy of the program in my scrapbook says several senior girls performed, "Desiderata." "You are a child of the universe, no less than the trees and the stars...." The southern cross was etched on our nights, baobab bark caught under our nails, yet our right to own it seemed to be slipping away. The girls' chorus sang out, "You have a right to be here!" We were accompanied by Bella Nzengo on tiered drums, guitars, bells and rattles.

Dad delivered the invocation and benediction in his low, resonant timbre. "The Lord bless you and keep you, the Lord make his face shine upon you and be gracious to you. The Lord lift up his countenance upon you and give you peace."

Outside the auditorium we stood in a receiving line of multi-colored African print gowns and abacost shirts—hugged and squeezed by caring adults, friends and siblings. Dad's engulfing handshake and hug made me feel I'd graduated college, not just high school. Libby's father had flown in from some distant port and said, "These are the people you'll never forget. They knew you before you knew yourselves." Well-wishers dwindled and the receiving line folded in on itself. We hugged and kissed each other and promised to never forget.

But memory is involuntary so that we lose things we promised to remember and recall what we had tried to forget. Memory jogged by a song on the radio can cost us half an hour in real time and make us feel that, eventually, we will be more memory than forward motion.

I could not will myself to remember the last wrenching night in Zaire following graduation. There must have been a party, but I inquired of every sense and could not retrieve a single image, smell, touch, taste or sound.

I cannot remember the moment of departure from N'Djili Airport. Was anyone from school at the airport also leaving or saying goodbye? At least I had my sisters. Twelve-year-old Grace with her naturally curly dark hair already splayed in the wild locks she would wear all her life. Charity, her neck craned around, watching the arrival doors as if still wanting to bolt and stay behind in this country of our birth—hers and mine. There were Mom and Dad looking ahead, eager to see Hope again after two years of her homesick letters. We stopped a few days in Nairobi to tour a game reserve and marvel at how Africa was Earth's only continent with magnificent, free-roaming mammals—giraffes, antelope, zebra, cheetah, lions and elephants. From there, Mom would fly directly to her sister Amanda battling cancer in Switzerland. Dad would take his three youngest daughters to see the Great Sphinx and Pyramid of Giza as well as Valley of the Kings.

My foot must have lifted off tarmac, releasing me from the Congo basin. A silver wing flashed out a rounded window. Let's say, to prompt memory, that the Congo River and deep equatorial jungle dropped away, replaced by rippled desert dunes, our 747 shadow crossing mounded sand and landing in Cairo on the blue Mediterranean.

There Dad recorded in pictures a special tour with Charity, Grace and me to see the three tall pyramids of Giza and crawl through narrow mausoleum passageways, covered in tourist graffiti. The Great Sphinx extended lion paws; its giant man's head towered

Grace, me and Charity on camels at the Great Sphinx and Pyramid of Giza. (Ben Eidse photo)

over us. Dad bought us camel rides and we swayed side-to-side, not at all like horses.

From the Zurich airport we rushed to my aunt's hospital bed and sang for her in five languages, "God's Love Eternal." She teared up and smiled just for us. We spent time with our Uncle John and cousins Rob and Phil before heading back to the airport. There my parents bought me a gold Swiss watch for graduation, which I wore until it broke beyond repair.

At another airport—Charles DeGaul, Paris?—an American student sat with backpack and strummed guitar, strings cutting his fingertips. "Strumming my pain with his fingers, singing my life with his words, killing me softly with his song..."

Skies, constellations, galaxies of pain so that it was easier to be the guitar player than me deprived of Africa, emptied of a whole way of being. Like echoes of the refugee camp ten years before, I had stopped being me and could pick up the Roberta Flack tune midstrum, "telling my whole life with his words, killing me softly…"

Twenty years later during a reunion with Peanut and Libby at a campground on the Blue Ridge Parkway, Libby helped me recall. "June 6 was my birthday, just like it is tonight. I was seventeen. You made me a cake in the shape of a Primus bottle."

That meant that earlier my last afternoon in Zaire I had mixed a honey brown icing in the hostel kitchen—already released from the rigid rules of that place. I tried to recall the heft of that cake carried to the party, probably foil-wrapped for stealth and surprise.

There's a denying of last moments, last touches, last rites, until gradually out of blackness, slivers of memory return like a photo in developer. A snapshot appears. A wet, humid night around the AERWA pool. Friends on a stone bench set among jasmine bushes. Someone handed me a gift, a heavy Greek coin on a leather thong, cast with ruins of the Parthenon. Overhead, a veiled dawn dripped from fringed mimosa leaves.

EPILOGUE

Writing the I-as-eye-witness
By Faith Eidse

Today people ask me my name. Or where I'm from. Or who I am. I'm tongue-tied. I stammer. I can't answer. I'm not one thing from one place with one name. My name is "Faith" in English, *"Ufudielo"* in Chokwe, *"La Foi"* in French, *"Glaube"* in German.

Identity for me is amorphous. I grew up global. I was always trying to blend in, speak Chokwe like a Bantu, German like a peasant, English like a Canadian or American. I never truly belonged to the places I lived. I'm a "nationNIList." In the U.S., I'm an immigrant—though a hidden one. With my Dutch ancestry, I look white yet my memories are African-Canadian-American.

The gardener who planted an Eden on our mission told my little sister, Grace—while she ate his ripe red strawberries—how she'd lost her beautiful black color. She was thrown into a pot of boiling water at birth.

Our friends pinched our naked arms and gasped at how our skin blanched. We were "ghosts" but privileged. We often rode while they walked, flew while they stayed. Yet we ran to the river, hunted and played with them and closed the gaps between us.

In Canada, my parents' passport country, I am a visitor because I didn't settle down. For several years I attended Bible school and reported for the local newspaper but then kept traveling. Like Dad, I completed college and graduate degrees in the U.S. where he and Mom raised us in our early years. I fell in love, married an American physicist and raised multicultural sons who only wanted to leave their stable lives and travel. One studied in Montreal and Australia, the other in Indiana and Sweden.

If I have roots at all, these elastic tentacles dig shallow crevices here among tar pines in north Florida, there in the black dirt of the Manitoba breadbasket, elsewhere under bladed palms of a village in Congo. These shallow roots are vines that reach roughly around the world.

––––––––––––––

If we are rooted in anything, it is love and anguish. The year of the millennium, some of us dormmates sought mediation with the mission board in a quest for healing. We spoke not just for ourselves but for dormmates who were still experiencing difficulties. Out of that session, a healing commission was formed and other MKs surveyed. A delegate was sent to our dorm parent who apologized to us. The long shadow of my past began to diminish and I hoped healing would come for other MKs, too.

However decades later, we discovered others who had not been consulted in our process. Younger children, children from other missions. I asked the mediator and counselor if I were free to listen and speak of our experiences. Yes, they said, their process was complete. The counselor added that she would be happy to help anyone else if desired. She realized that for many MKs the healing process continues.

The dorm is no longer in operation. It has been leased as a dance studio and art gallery full of free movement, chic jewelry, flowing sculptures, vibrant batiks, paintings celebrating Congo's post-independence struggles and diverse musical instruments.

Strains echo still from the 1978 devotional held after parents, children and hostel parents met to discuss whether MKs could attend school dances. My sister Grace was the school social manager and she suggested the closing song, "I am the Lord of the Dance." Our former dormmate and then dorm parent, Ruth Keidel, struck up the piano cords and children and parents blended their voices. The final decision after years of regulation and punishment was a resounding yes. "Dance, dance wherever you may be…"

The dorm is now leased as an arts emporium and dance studio. (Laurie Bowers-Conolly Braun photo)

AFTERWORDS

by Leola Falk Becker

Faith, her sisters, and I played together as evacuees in 1964 and were grade school hostel roommates, sharing the small airplane flights back and forth to southwestern Congo. Our family visited the Eidse family at Kamayala during school vacations or vice versa at Kajiji. Later, we attended the same high school, church, and community socials—Faith in the hostel and I as a day student.

Ask any missionary child about their childhood, they will say, "It's the only childhood that I knew." We were taught to be positive, since we were blessed by God, and to be confident that God would take care of us. We accepted adult responsibilities as young children because we were, in many ways, raising ourselves. Traumas were pushed down because our significant adults were too busy dealing with larger problems than caring for our emotional needs. Our joyous play and laughter covered the searing grief of historical events, moves and the loss of family and friends.

We listened to the women talking on the Sunday evening picnic blankets with the tropical sunset over the river and did not imagine an existence without rebels fighting, our houses burning or fleeing for our lives. Ours was a childhood of nighttime gunfire, daytime tropical storms, and regimented living away from home. We could not imagine, as we played jacks in the empty refugee houses or later sweated in the hostel dorm room, that we would become adults and have a life in a different cultural world. This turmoil was our reality that hung in the hot air.

One wants to flee from trauma, to push it down, to hide, to forget. It is painful to search through our minds and body reactions seeking explanations and historical context. It takes guts to explore the dark spaces, to relive the events, to openly share the beauty and ugliness of our lives. However, we need to go through the past to understand and be free for the future. By acknowledging and re-counting the traumas, we free ourselves to live fully, and to prevent our hurtful legacy being handed down to our children and grand-children.

This book is the tale of Faith's struggle to define herself in a unique cultural milieu, at a specific time in world events, in a par-ticular family constellation, and a specific school and expat commu-nity between third and twelfth grades. It is the story of Faith's search for approval, acceptance, love and gender identity as she answers the question, "What does it mean to be me?" It is also a story of salva-tion, of a girl becoming, as Faith chronicles her growing acceptance of herself.

Although the stories are specific to her unique experi-ence, Faith's truths can help us process our own lives. Only in sharing, reflection, and putting incidents into context are we able to make sense of our child-hoods, to find our own healing so that we are free to choose our own futures.

Faith's roommates, Leola Falk Becker with Maid of Honor Jeanette Buller Slater at Leola's wedding, June 7, 1980.

ACKNOWLEDGEMENTS

So many dear friends and family helped and encouraged me, including my sisters, dormmates, schoolmates, writing group, members of Tallahassee Writers Association, M.R. Street (Turtle Cove Press), Suzan Kurdak and others. Beverly Shellrude Thompson and Dianne Darr Couts published an early, concise version of this work on MKSafetyNet.com after Ruth Van Reken opened my eyes with *Letters Never Sent.*

FSU professors encouraged me: Bob Shacochis cheered me on, the late Jerome Stern told me to "make a scene"—as did my professional editor Adrian Fogeline. Hunt Hawkins urged me to tell my story and gave me its postcolonial context and Jerrilyn McGregory encouraged folklore explorations of my various traditions. The story of the antelope child (Chapter 2) was recorded by anthropologist Rachel Irene Fretz who came to Zaire from Stanford University to study with Dad. It was excerpted here by permission.

My husband Philip Kuhns cared for our children, Anthony and Stefan, many nights and weekends while I wrote. My hostel roommate Leola Falk Becker, my sisters Grace and Charity and late poet friend, Barbara Hogan, line-edited and Hope helped me remember.

For the wealth of my growing-up years I thank my parents Ben and Helen Reimer Eidse and my sisters Hope, Charity and Grace. My hostel siblings and school friends may recognize themselves in these pages, though some names have been changed. Shirl, Carl, Linda, Marcia, Becky, Brenda, Gerald, Candy, Kathy, Gavin, Bill, Beth, Hans, Ragui, Vangie, Evelyn, Peanut, Libby, Pat, Hassina and so many others, thank you.

BIOGRAPHICAL SKETCH

Faith Eidse's memoir, *Deeper than African Soil*, won FSU's Kingsbury Award as well as the English Department's Ann Durham Outstanding Master's Thesis Award. Two chapters also won nonfiction firsts in the *Seven Hills Review* (2021, 2022).*

Her compilation, *Voices of the Apalachicola* (2006, University Press of Florida) won Florida's oral history of 2007. She co-edited several collections on growing up global, which were selected as Princeton textbooks: *Unrooted Childhoods: Memoirs of Growing Up Global* (2004, Nicholas Brealey Intercultural, now a Hachette Book Group title), which was syndicated in *The Times;* and *Writing Out of Limbo: International Childhoods, Global Nomads and Third Culture Kids* (2011, a bestseller for Cambridge Scholars Publishing LLC, UK). She also published her parents' oral history, *Light the World* (2012, Friesen Press) and a novel drawn from six years volunteering in women's prisons, *Healing Falls* (2018, Faitheyes Press, LLC).

Eidse taught writing for twenty years as adjunct professor at FSU, Barry and Keiser Universities.

*Portions of this memoir were previously published: Chapter 18, "Melted Hands," won first place nonfiction in *Seven Hills Review,* Vol. 26, 2021, and Chapter 6, "Missing Hands" won first place nonfiction in *Seven Hills Review,* Vol. 27, 2022; a version of Chapter 3 "River Run" was published in *Rhubarb,* Spring 2001, No. 7.

WORKS CITED

"1953 Atlantic Hurricane Season." Wikipedia. en.wikipedia.org/wiki/1953_Atlantic_hurricane_season

Anderson, Pat. *Treasure of Memories: Eidse Family.* Morris: Self. 1992.

Bertsche, James. *CIM/AIMM: A Story of Vision, Commitment and Grace.* Elkhart, IN. 1998.

———. "Kwilu Report: Rebellion within Rebellion." *Congo Missionary Messenger.* July-Sept. 1965. pp. 5-32.

———. "Of Gorillas and Grace." *Congo Missionary Messenger.* Oct.-Dec. 1965.

Buller, Peter. "Mukedi Evacuated." *Congo Missionary Messenger.* Jan.-March, 1964.

Close, M.D., William T. with Miatudila, M.D., M.P.H., Malonga. *Beyond the Storm: Treating the Powerless and Powerful in Mobutu's Congo/Zaire.* Marbleton: Meadowlark Springs Productions, L.L.C., 2007.

Corchado, Alfredo. July 5, 1995. "Drug Trade Corrupting Mexico's Once Sturdy Mennonites." Dallas Morning News. https://archives.seattletimes.com/archives/?date=19950705&slug=2129776

Eidse, Ben. "The Witness of the Church in Rebel Areas." *Congo Missionary Messenger.* July-Sept. 1965. pp. 5-32.

Egerton, Brooks. "HP minister accused of sexual molestation: Six women allege abuse on Africa mission in '60s." *The Dallas Morning News.* Page 1. 26 April 1999.

Falk, Leola. "The Relationship Between the Baptist Missionary Society and the Congo Free State." Associated Mennonite Biblical Seminaries. 18 December 1978.

Falk, Peter. Unpublished manuscript: Interviews with adults maimed as children and British Baptist letters archives. McMaster Divinity College, Canadian Baptist Archives. 1971. mcmasterdivinity.ca/canadian-baptist-archives/

Forbath, Peter. 1991. *The River Congo: The Discovery, Exploration, and Exploitation of the World's Most Dramatic River.* Houghton Mifflin.

French, Howard W. "Anatomy of an Autocracy: Mobutu's 32-year Reign." *New York Times.* 17 May 1997. archive.nytimes.com/ www.nytimes.com/library/world/africa/051797zaire-mobutu. html?scp=14&sq=32&st=cse

Friedman-Rudovsky, Jean. Jan. 27, 2023. "I Covered the Story that Inspired 'Women Talking.' Here's What I Wish More People Knew." TIME. https://time.com/6250526/women-talking-mennonite-bolivia-real-story

Fretz, Rachel Irene. *Storytelling Among the Chokwe of Zaire: Narrating Skill and Listener Responses.* Pp. 168-172. Ann Arbor: UMI Dissertation Services. 1987.

Goertzen, Ron. Dayspring Christian Ministries, 309 Road 10, Henderson, NE 68371. rongoertzen@hotmail.com

Hege, Ruth. *We Two Alone: Attack and Rescue in the Congo.* Greenville: Emerald House. 1997.

Hochschild, Adam. *King Leopold's Ghost.* Boston: Houghton Mifflin Company. 1998.

Kalb, Madeleine G. "The CIA and Lumumba." *New York Times Magazine.* 2 August 1981. www.nytimes.com/1981/08/02/magazine/the-cia-and-lumumba.html

Keidel, Levi. *Caught in the Crossfire.* Kitchener, Ontario: Herald Press. 1979.

Kelly, Sean. *America's Tyrant: The CIA and Mobutu of Zaire.* Washington, D.C.: The American University Press. 1993.

"Kinshasa Then and Now." "Leopoldville 1891 - Dr. Sims builds a Chapel." Kosubaawate.blogspot.com 4 May 2016. kosubaawate.blogspot.com/2016/05/leopoldville-1891-sims-chapel-built.html

"Mennonite." Britannica. www.britannica.com/topic/Mennonite#ref795029

"Münster." Britannica. www.britannica.com/place/Munster-Germany

O'Brien, Conor Cruise. *To Katanga and Back.* New York: Faber & Faber. 1915.

Pollock, David, and Ruth Van Reken. *Third Culture Kids: The Experience of Growing Up Among Worlds.* London: Nicholas Brealey Intercultural. 2001.

Rabéarivelo, Jean-Joseph. "Cactus." *International Quarterly: The Middle East and the Africas*, Vol. 1, number 3, p. 19.

Rambo, Beth. "Travelers." *Notes from a Traveling Childhood.* Ed. Karen Curnow McCluskey. Washington D.C.: Foreign Services Youth Foundation. 1994.

Roseveare, Helen in Justin Taylor. 2016. www.thegospelcoalition.org/blogs/justin-taylor/a-woman-of-whom-the-world-was-not-worthy-helen-roseveare-1925-2016/

Russell-Kraft, Stephanie. "Can Religion Give You PTSD? Meet the 'exvangelicals' seeking therapy for religious trauma." *The New Republic.* 23 March 2021. newrepublic.com/article/161772/can-religion-give-ptsd

Scheverien, J. "The Long-Term Impact of Boarding School." *Brighton Therapy Partnership.* 6 June 2016.

"Simba Revolution." Wikipedia. en.wikipedia.org/wiki/Simba_rebellion

Strash, John. December 6, 2012. "The Memoirs of John Strash, Jungle Pilot." Unpublished Autobiography, pp. 425-426.

Taylor, Justin. 2016. https://www.thegospelcoalition.org/blogs/justintaylor/a-woman-of-whom-the-world-was-not-worthy-helen-rosaveare-1925-2016/

Tari, Mel, and Cliff Dudley. *Like a Mighty Wind.* Creation House. 1971.

Tiessen, G., Schellenberg, C., Stautenburg, L. 1995. "The Peace Seekers: The Story of the Canadian Mennonites From the Reformation to the Present."

Turnbull, Mary Henk. Telephone interview. 1999.

Twain, Mark. *King Leopold's Soliloquy: A Defense of His Congo Rule.* Boston: The P.R. Warren Co. Second Edition. 1905. msuweb.montclair.edu/~furrg/i2l/kls.html

Wrong, Michela. *In the Footsteps of Mr. Kurtz: Living on the Brink of Disaster in Mobutu's Congo.* 2002.

Young, George A. "God Leads Us Along." In the Public Domain. 1903. library.timelesstruths.org/music/God_Leads_Us_Along/

Made in the USA
Las Vegas, NV
30 March 2023

69917007R00195